A Short History of Canada
for Americans

A Short History of

CANADA

for Americans

by

ALFRED LEROY BURT

THE UNIVERSITY OF MINNESOTA PRESS
Minneapolis

Copyright 1942 by the

UNIVERSITY OF MINNESOTA

Printed in the United States of America

HUMPHREY MILFORD, OXFORD UNIVERSITY PRESS, LONDON

PUBLISHED SIMULTANEOUSLY IN CANADA BY THE
EDUCATIONAL BOOK COMPANY OF TORONTO, LIMITED

To

MY WIFE

the most helpful critic I have known

Foreword

When the director of the University Press asked me to write this volume I said there was no need for it because an American edition of *The Romance of Canada*, which I wrote a few years ago, at the request of the Educational Book Company of Toronto, for use in Canadian schools, would suffice. But the Press, after a careful examination, reported that it would not do, and I had the uncomfortable experience of rereading my own book to see what was wrong with it. Then I discovered that the Press was right. I had not realized how much I had included that would interest readers in Canada but not outside, and how much I had omitted that could be taken for granted by Canadians but that others could not be expected to know. More than a decade of living in the United States and teaching in an American university made it easy to learn this lesson in relativity, which I have attempted to apply in the pages that follow. I must also confess that this attempt is better than it would have been without the assistance of daily intercourse with my own children, who have had the stimulating, if sometimes confusing, advantage of being educated on both sides of the line.

In rewriting the history of Canada for American readers, I have naturally drawn upon previous publications of mine, particularly *The Romance of Canada*. I have also seized the opportunity to bring this history up to date in scholarship as well as in time, for it is a living subject. Indeed there are few, if any, national histories that have been more revolutionized by research since I began to lecture upon it in a Canadian university some twenty-five years ago.

I cannot begin to acknowledge what I owe to other scholars in this field, for I should not know when to stop. But I cannot refrain from saying that I am most indebted to those with whom I have discussed almost every phase of Canadian history during the many summers I have spent in the Public Archives of Canada—members of the staff of that institution and visitors from almost all the Canadian universities and not a few Ameri-

A Short History of Canada

can ones. For the historical illustrations in this volume I have to thank the Public Archives of Canada, which supplied copies from its large collection of pictures, and Dr. J. F. Kenney, who has charge of this collection and greatly helped in making the selection here reproduced. For the photographs of present-day scenes I have to thank the National Film Board of the Dominion government and its chief photographer, Mr. E. M. Finn.

Permission to use the coat of arms of the Dominion of Canada on the title page and endsheet maps of this book was granted by E. H. Coleman, undersecretary of state of Canada. I am also under considerable obligation to two members of the staff of the Press—to Miss Jane McCarthy for drawing the maps and to Miss Mary Elinore Smith for her careful editorial work upon the text.

A. L. B.

February 1942

Contents

Illustrations

A Short History of Canada

xii

Illustrations

Gold-rush town, pencil drawing by an unknown artist

Mule team on the Cariboo Road

The Fathers of Confederation, 1867; from an original painting in the Parliament Buildings, Ottawa, which was destroyed by fire during the First World War

Louis Riel, contemporary crayon portrait

Sir James Douglas, from *Canada and Its Provinces*

Fort Garry, colored lithograph by A. S. Strong

Sir John A. Macdonald, 1886

Alexander Mackenzie

Sir Wilfred Laurier

Camp of the North West Mounted Police, September 1874; engraved from a sketch by an artist who accompanied the expedition and printed in *Canadian Illustrated News*, September 26, 1874

A "mountie" arresting an Indian, by John Innes

Winnipeg at the corner of Main and Portage in 1872

Ugly customers at Smart's store, Battleford; by Sydney Hall, 1881

The capture of Batoche, contemporary sketch by special artists on the staff of the *Canadian Pictorial and Illustrated War News*

BETWEEN PAGES 160 AND 161

Montreal yesterday and today: Beaver Hall Hill and the Hay Market early in the nineteenth century; panoramic view of the city from Mount Royal

Toronto's growth over a hundred years: the waterfront in 1834; sky view of the modern business center

Calgary, the growth of a prairie city: pencil sketch by Sydney Hall in 1881; central section of the city today

Vancouver, from wilderness to metropolis: sketch of the site by W. Willis in 1861; the city of today

A Short History of Canada

xiv

Illustrations

xv

A Short History of Canada

Maps

Cartoons

These cartoons, all drawn by J. W. Bengough during the 1870's and 1880's, appeared in Grip, a humorous weekly published by Bengough in Toronto.

A Short History of Canada
for Americans

CHAPTER I

Comparisons and Contrasts

Aᴍᴇʀɪᴄᴀɴ geographies have long shown maps of the United States in full color with a blank white space north of the Great Lakes and the forty-ninth parallel. Nearly as blank were the minds of some twelve hundred high school seniors in the United States when, not so long ago, their knowledge of Canada was tested. Their ignorance, said President Hauck of the University of Maine, who conducted the inquiry, was appalling. One of these students confessed, "I am terribly ignorant in regard to Canada, and all I think of is fish, snow, cold, ice." And another, "Canada is so close and yet so far away from me. I know less about it than almost any other place in the world." The plain fact is that most Americans have known little and cared less about their northern neighbor.

The average Canadian, on the other hand, has been fairly well informed about the United States and has realized that it has much in common with his own country by way of heritage and development. At the same time, he has been acutely conscious of his own country's separate identity and how it differs from the "great republic to the south." He has known that even though Canada is a member of the British Commonwealth of Nations she is likewise an American nation and very dependent on the United States. He has also been inclined to resent the indifference of the average American. But the mental attitude of which this indifference was only a part has now been rudely shattered; and Americans, wishing to know about and to understand Canada, are beginning to see that there is life and color between their northern boundary and the Arctic wastes.

The general similarity between the two countries is so striking that it is deceptive and tends to obscure fundamental differences. The area of Canada is slightly greater than that of the United States and has much the same proportions; but Canada is divided into only nine provinces instead of forty-eight states, and by far the greater part of the enormous area covered by the Dominion is and will remain a wilderness. Still the country could support many more people than it does. Its population is only about eleven and a half million, almost the same as that of Greater New York City.

The large majority of Canadians live within a hundred miles of the United States, along a sort of northern fringe attached to our country. Canada has length but not breadth. It is not a natural unit, or even nine natural units corresponding to the nine provinces; for geography has divided it into four quite separate sections. One comprises the three Maritime Provinces of Prince Edward Island, Nova Scotia, and New Brunswick, which are almost severed from the rest of the Dominion by the northward thrust of the Maine salient. These are the smallest provinces and the only ones that resemble most states of the Union in having their population spread over their entire area. The next region of unbroken settlement, in Quebec and Ontario, is commonly called Central Canada, not because it is geographically central but because the bulk of the Canadian population, about two thirds, is concentrated there, and it contains the principal seat of economic and political power.

There is no Middle West in Canada. Instead there is an enormous and largely uninhabited waste of rocks, lakes, rivers, and Christmas trees, across which no road save the railway ran before 1942. It has thus been impossible, without going through the United States, to motor from Central Canada to the next unit, the Prairie Provinces.

Manitoba, Saskatchewan, and Alberta make up this third geographical section of the Dominion, which is cut off from the fourth, British Columbia, by the formidable barrier of the Rocky Mountains. The mountainous axis of the continent becomes more rugged and compressed in Canada, and the passes here present more difficult engineering problems for highway construction than they do in the United States.

Thus separated and stretched out from ocean to ocean, the inhabited portions of the Dominion of Canada are like beads on the steel thread of its railways. Few countries in the world are so disjointed physically. "To find even a rough analogy in the U. S.," says a recent writer (*Fortune,* September 1938, page

113), "you would have to imagine a country composed of Maine, Ohio, Minnesota, and the Dakotas, Washington, and Alaska, situated as they now are and with nothing in between them but wilderness." Yet it would be a great mistake to suppose that Canada enjoys only a tenuous existence and has no strong common life.

The cultural resemblance between Canada and the United States is very marked, and this is not surprising. Are not the two peoples substantially the same, descended from the same British stock enriched by the addition of many strains from continental Europe? Do they not speak the same language? They even have a common slang, peculiar to North America. Their accents and dialects vary locally rather than nationally and are so much alike that Canadians traveling in other parts of the British Empire are usually taken for Americans. Neither in their work nor in their play is there any definite national distinction between them. The ordinary Canadian boy never thinks of baseball as an American game; it is his own. It is a national sport in these two countries, and in no others. In business and the professions Canadians and Americans have the same common pattern. Indeed their whole manner of living is the same, marking them off from people in other lands. There are greater differences of speech within either country than there are at any place across the border. The western Canadian is more akin to the western American than to the man from Ontario, just as the Bostonian seems foreign to the Middle Westerner.

Americans are likely to be misled by this appearance of identity and are surprised at the Canadian's consciousness of difference. While Canadians may normally feel more at home with Americans than with Englishmen or Australians or South Africans, they instinctively dislike to be taken for Americans and will offer the prompt correction, "I am a Canadian." The old American prejudice against England has had its counterpart in the Canadian prejudice against the United States. Though Canadians appreciate their great neighbor much better than do any of the peoples south of the Rio Grande, the fears that have made Latin Americans suspicious of the United States have also infected Canadians, and Canadians have always lived much nearer to the cause of these fears. Besides, Canadians have a lively national spirit and a national pride quite equal to that of the people of the United States. Would they be worth their salt otherwise?

The resemblance between the political and legal institutions of Canada and the United States is even more extensive than their rich common heritage from England, for both countries have added much from their experiences under similar conditions, and Canada has borrowed more than a little from her independent elder sister. All this makes mutual understanding easier, but here too there are important differences, familiar to Canadians if little known beyond their borders. Canada copied federalism from the United States, but she made some radical changes. As for the rest of the American Constitution, with its Bill of Rights, its checks and balances, and its separation of powers, the Canadians would have none of it. They are thoroughly convinced that the system they have imported from the mother country, with its flexibility, its fusion of powers, and its focusing of responsibility, is much superior. The Canadian provinces may look like states of the Union, but they have a different status and are governed in quite another way; and the nature of the national government places Ottawa between Washington and London. Other important governmental features spring from peculiar Canadian conditions.

When an American drives into Mexico or sails to Brazil, he is at once conscious of being in a very different country among strange people, and he has the same impression of foreignness when he goes into Quebec for the first time. The existence of French Canada is very strange to Americans, and stranger still is the constitutional position of the French in British North America. It must be remembered that it was first a French colony, and while other Europeans have come to English Canada and been assimilated there, the French, who number almost a third of the population, have remained a race* apart, proud of their long descent from families who settled New France three hundred years ago. They have grown apart from their cousins in France without acquiring many characteristics of their English-speaking neighbors. Few of them speak anything but

* The word *race* is here used in the popular sense with no intention of offending anthropologists, even professional ones.

Comparisons and Contrasts

their native tongue, which is not at all like the Parisian French of today or the French we try to learn in school and college. In pronunciation and idiom it is older and more provincial—very little changed from the speech of their forebears, most of whom came from Normandy in the seventeenth century. The vocabulary contains an occasional word of English origin instead of the modern French equivalent, because what it represents was introduced by the people who conquered their country—such as the word *potates* instead of *pommes de terre* for potatoes.

Religion too has played a powerful part in preserving the separate identity of the French in Canada. They are almost all devout Roman Catholics, and very few have turned Protestant. Of course in Canada there are English-speaking Roman Catholics in about the same proportion as in the United States. When these are added to the French, they constitute between 40 and 50 per cent of the whole population, practically double the ratio found in the United States. In Canada, however, the racial cleavage within the church is quite pronounced, and the average Protestant Canadian identifies Roman Catholicism with the French.

The country is thus divided not only by geography but also by race, language, and religion. These last have cut Central Canada in two, for all its seeming geographical unity. Ontario is English and Protestant; Quebec is controlled by the French Catholics. There is a very lively English minority in Quebec, and there are French minorities in the other eight provinces; only in British Columbia are they negligible.

French Canada and English Canada each form a nation within a nation. It is hard for Americans to grasp this fact, so foreign to all their ways of thinking, but this dual nationality must be recognized before one can begin to understand the country. It is extremely interesting, for there are few places in the world, and not another in this hemisphere, where such complete duality prevails. One of the greatest Canadian problems is the coordination of these two disparate peoples; and almost every public question in the Dominion must be viewed with a French eye and an English eye or it will be seen out of focus.

The dual nationality of the country is published on every Canadian postage stamp and on the paper currency issued by the government, for they are printed in both French and English. It is echoed in the Supreme Court and in the houses of Parliament, where according to the constitution of Canada French stands on a parity with English as an official language. The same is true of the courts and the legislature of Quebec, though not of the other provinces, and their liberty to be monolingual is an offense to many French Canadians. The common law of England has less currency in Canada than in the United States, for the civil law of Quebec, which includes more than a quarter of the Canadian population, is French and Roman, whereas Louisiana, with less than a sixtieth of the American people, is the only state of the Union that has not adopted the basic English law.

Race has also endowed religion with special rights unknown to Americans. In Quebec, for example, the Roman Catholic church is supported by the tithe, the payment of which is enforced by law; and in the greater part of Canada religious minorities, Protestant or Roman Catholic, are privileged by the constitution to organize and maintain tax-supported schools for their own children.

From what has been said of the physically disjointed character of the country and of the racial division that has pitted the western half of Central Canada against the eastern half, it will be obvious that the Dominion is more split up than the United States. Not even the Mason and Dixon's line cuts so deep as the boundary between Quebec and Ontario. There is consequently a greater tendency toward sectionalism in Canada, and when this is related to the governmental structure the contrast between the two countries becomes more pronounced. The Old South is not so isolated geographically as are the Maritime Provinces or the Prairie Provinces, and in all the Union no single state coincides with a sectional area as does each of the other provinces, Quebec, Ontario, and British Columbia. Yet for all its divisions Canada is more united today than it ever was in the past.

It is a strange country, but so also is the United States to foreigners. Canadians understand the United States better than do any other outsiders because they are much closer to it. From this very closeness spring two interesting reactions that may sur-

Comparisons and Contrasts

prise many Americans. One is that Canadians tend to be critical of their only neighbor. This is natural because they are a small nation beside a big one. The other reaction, which is most revealing, is that Canadians instinctively defend the United States against the criticism of all other nations. They are themselves wounded by an attack on their nearest relative, with whom they have grown up.

Unlike Canadians, Americans generally have not bothered to know their closest neighbor. If they have thought of Canada at all, it has seemed so like their own country that they took it for granted—until recently, when they were startled to realize that the United States might be committed to war through Canada. Now that both have become partners in a second World War, Americans feel a growing interest in what lies on the other side of their northern border. Because Canada is so near to them in body and in spirit, there is not another country so easy for them to know; and for the very same reason Americans can understand Canada better than can the people of any other country. It is to facilitate this understanding, since no one can really know another country without knowing how it came to be what it is, that this brief history is offered.

CHAPTER 2

The Establishment of New France

It was no accident that Canada was cradled in the St. Lawrence or that the founders of New France rejected the land that became New England. The explanation lies in the French conception of an empire in America, which was so different from any English notion that it is important to understand it right away. The French end was there in the beginning. The man who discovered Canada was sent forth by the French king in the hope that he would discover for France a navigable passage through North America to the waters of the Pacific, which Balboa had seen at Panama in 1513 and Magellan had reached seven years later through the strait named after him. This hope took generations to die, and meanwhile Frenchmen dreamed of the day when they might hold the world in fee by controlling the most direct route from Europe to the Orient.

Jacques Cartier discovered Canada in 1534 and 1535, when he went up the St. Lawrence as far as Montreal, but its permanent occupation by the French did not begin until more than two generations later. During the interval French fishermen frequented the Gulf of St. Lawrence in growing numbers and, landing to dry their catch, fell into commerce with the natives. Thus the fur trade was born, and around 1600 it had grown to such proportions that the French government was granting monopolies of the tempting traffic to merchants, if in return they undertook to pay for the colonization and exploration of the new land.

When the French examined the New England coast with an eye for settlement, they naturally turned their backs on this region. They found it inhabited by agricultural Indians, which meant that it was relatively poor fur country; and it opened no inviting door into the interior, for it was not traversed by any large river. What they wanted was to be found on the St. Lawrence. The French did form little establishments in Acadia, but

The Establishment of New France

their main effort was directed to the great river on which, in 1608, Samuel de Champlain built a post at Quebec to serve as a center for the fur trade, a base for the exploration of the interior, and a nucleus for settlement.

In addition to exploration and the fur trade, there was another initial motive behind French colonial activity on this continent that had nothing to do with locality. It was a religious motive, but the very opposite of the one that brought the first New Englanders across the Atlantic. These Englishmen came to save their own souls; the French came to save the souls of others, for the Roman Catholics were generations ahead of the Protestants in attempting to convert the benighted heathen. The Puritan immigrants, a wit once said, first fell on their knees and then on the aborigines, but the French embraced the Indians and sought to make them brothers, Christian and civilized. The maintenance of missionaries was a third condition attached to the trading monopoly. When the successive companies proved remiss in this regard, for they were organized to serve mammon rather than God, pious men and women in the mother country took up the good work enthusiastically. New England has lost its original Puritanism, but the religious fervor that inspired New France still lives.

Every Canadian today, English as well as French, knows Champlain, for he is the father of their country. Both races revere him, for he was a man above reproach. To this soldier, sailor, explorer, geographer, and author, whom merchants knew as a manager, the king as a loyal friend, and the church as a devout son, Canada owes more than to any other man. He dominated French colonial effort from the time he founded Quebec until he died there. More than once he saved the colony from being abandoned. All seemed lost in 1629 when he was obliged to surrender the little settlement to conquerors from England, and he himself was carried off to England as a prisoner of war. At the end of this, his twenty-fourth voyage across the Atlantic, he found he was a free man because peace had been signed, and at once he threw all his weight behind French diplomacy to force a recovery of New France.

The treaty of restitution was signed in 1632 and in the following year Champlain returned to the land he had made his own, bringing with him a hundred colonists to join the few he had advised to remain under the conquerors. In 1634 he welcomed forty more from France and established Three Rivers as another trading post and nucleus of settlement. At last his colony was taking root, but he did not live long to see it, for his body had been sadly worn by a life of frequent hardship and incessant toil. In the autumn of 1635 he fell ill, and on Christmas night he died. The spot where he was buried is still a matter of dispute, but Canadians have the satisfaction of knowing that his body was laid away somewhere in the heart of the colony that was his only child.

For almost a generation the governors who followed Champlain were ordinary men who could not begin to fill his shoes. This was a period of neglect when the government of France, distracted by foreign and domestic wars, seemed almost to have forgotten the existence of New France. But the church of France did not slumber, and through it came practically all the strength that New France received from the mother country during this time. Already one of the most glorious chapters in the history of Christian missions had begun in North America.

The principal heroes were the Jesuits, the greatest missionary society in the world. The black-robed priests aspired to convert and civilize the whole continent of red men, to establish the kingdom of heaven in the New World, and they set about their mighty task in a strategic manner. Though not neglecting the nearer but inferior nomadic Algonkins of the St. Lawrence and Ottawa valleys, they put forth their chief effort where it promised to be more effective—among the Hurons. These were a superior agricultural people who lived south of Georgian Bay, about fifty miles north of the present city of Toronto, and were beginning to serve the French trade as middlemen by drawing furs from a widening circle of surrounding tribes. By 1640 the Jesuits had definitely established themselves in this center, and the light was spreading.

Montreal, now the second largest French city in the world, was founded in 1642, a by-product of this missionary endeavor. Over in France the reports of the missionaries were published annually, and these *Jesuit Relations*, as they were called, were eagerly devoured by many readers and inspired a number of pious people to establish some of the best known religious foundations of Canada, such as the Hôtel Dieu of Quebec and the mother convent of the Ursulines in the same city.* The same inspiration brought together a group of men and women who formed a company to plant a hospital and a seminary of priests on the uninhabited island of Montreal. Some of the company remained behind to support the venture while others went out to execute it. To devout French Canadians this origin of the city is nothing if not divine.

While the hand of God was thus reaching out into the interior, the devil broke loose. The Iroquois confederacy, which occupied what is now the upper part of New York State, had long been the enemy of the Hurons, though they were Iroquoian too, and of the Algonkins, who inhabited the St. Lawrence and Ottawa valleys. As the Algonkins and the Hurons controlled the route to the West and the source of more furs, the French naturally sided with them. So long as this native war was fought with only native weapons neither side could make much impression upon the other, but firearms were now spreading among them, and the death struggle was approaching. The allies of the French might have won if the Dutch had not settled on the Hudson. This decided the issue in favor of the Iroquois, for it gave them a base from which they could not be cut off, whereas by raids down the Richelieu from Lake Champlain they could easily sever their enemies' line of supply. The paralyzed Hurons were destroyed with terrific slaughter. The end came in 1649, when the remnant of a once proud race was scattered like chaff before the wind and the captured missionaries were put to death with fiendish cruelty.

The French on the St. Lawrence also felt the scourge of the Iroquois. It was so bad by 1642 that the governor pled with those who had come to found Montreal to remain at Quebec, and he tried to plug the mouth of the Richelieu with a fort. This was the beginning of the town of Sorel, founded a few weeks before the heroes of Montreal reached their goal. Year by year the Indian terror grew until in 1660 it seemed about to engulf the colony. A swarm of blood-drunk demons was descend-

---

* Agnes Repplier's *Mère Marie, of the Ursulines* is a charming account of the first mother superior of this convent.

ing the Ottawa while another lay waiting below Montreal, and it looked as if the two were about to join for a clean sweep of the St. Lawrence. But the advancing host encountered a handful of young Frenchmen in an improvised fort at the foot of the Long Sault Rapid on the Ottawa. The story of how these men, led by Adam Dollard, sold their lives so dearly that the chastened savages slunk home without falling on the colony is one of the most glorious in Canadian annals. It is too long to tell here, but the reader may find it in one of the most thrilling chapters that Francis Parkman ever wrote, "The Heroes of the Long Sault" in his *Old Régime in Canada.*

Louis XIV, *le roi soleil,* took over the colony from the merchants in 1663 and determined to make it strong. Two years later a new set of officials, able men, arrived in Quebec accompanied by the first body of regular soldiers to be sent out from France; and a new day dawned on the St. Lawrence. This Carignan-Salières regiment of six hundred men is by far the most important military unit in Canadian history. It quickly cured the scourge that had been sapping the life of the colony. The Iroquois fled in panic when these troops invaded their country, and from their hiding places they saw their strongly fortified towns, with all their stocks of food, disappear in flames lit by the avenging French. Having learned a great lesson by the light of these fires, a large deputation of chiefs went down to Quebec to beg for peace. And this was only the beginning of what these soldiers did for Canada.

The colony now found its feet under the guidance of three outstanding men. One was Jean Talon, the first and greatest intendant of New France. The office he held, for which there is no English equivalent,* is explained by what was happening in France. There the monarchy was becoming more absolute and efficient by undermining the position of the semi-independent provincial governors, relics of the feudal nobility, in favor of career men who, with the title of intendant, were entrusted with much of the business of provincial administration. This development, having proved its value at home, was carried into the French possessions overseas, where, however, the governor retained more power than his namesake in France. The new

---

* The meaning of the name is suggested by our word *superintendent.*

official was immediately responsible for "justice, police, and finance," while the old official, as the personal representative of the king, had general supervision over the government of New France and was also military commander in chief. As might be expected, there were quarrels between these two functionaries, but there was little friction until after the first intendant had left the country.

Talon straightway saw that the colony's most pressing need, after protection, was more population, for it had barely reached 3,000. If he had had his way, the French would have greatly outnumbered the English in America, and that would have been quite possible because there were then about four Frenchmen for every Englishman in the world. But settlers would not come voluntarily; the only people who wanted to leave France were the Huguenots, and they were excluded from New France. Parkman's New England background made him think that these French Protestants might have built up New France if the government had allowed them to go there, but this is a very debatable question. As it was, colonists had to be found and sent out by the government, and all Talon's pleadings brought only a few hundred a year. The majority were women, to balance the usual surplus of men found in every new country, and there was a merry marriage market when the ships arrived. What the intendant could not get by ship he sought in the cradle, encouraging early marriages and large families by generous bounties. He also had penalties imposed on recalcitrant bachelors. If they were caught hunting, or fishing, or trading with the Indians, or going into the woods on any pretext whatever—activities that he denied them by law—they were turned over to the courts. From the time Talon arrived until he finally departed in 1672 the population doubled, and thenceforth there was hardly any immigration from France. From such a small number of families are the French Canadian people descended! That is why it is easy for many of them to tell offhand if a French surname is Canadian or not. Here it may also be of interest to note that a genealogical dictionary of all French Canadians from the first settlement until after the British conquest has been published in seven volumes by the Abbé Tanguay.

Talon was interested in more than numbers. Finding that

many of the Carignan-Salières regiment were willing to take their discharge in this country, he planted them as a military colony along the Richelieu to bar the gate through which the dreaded Iroquois used to come. The names of various officers of the unit—such as Chambly—are printed on the map of this region, for the places where they settled were called after them. The intendant also gave solidity to the growing settlements of the country by mingling experienced pioneers with newcomers, by seeing to it that each little community had skilled workmen who would be useful to their neighbors, by establishing a model farm near Quebec, by fostering domestic spinning and weaving, and in countless other ways. He was even responsible for the first temperance measure in Canada—the erection of a brewery to wean the inhabitants away from wicked brandy. Before he came the colony never produced enough food or clothing for its own needs and had to depend upon supplies sent out from France, but before he left, its much larger appetite was fully satisfied by local production and he was able to report, "I am now clothed from foot to head with home-made articles."

A very different man from the intendant was Bishop Laval, the father of the Canadian church. Born of one of the most illustrious noble families in France—his full name was François Xavier de Laval-Montmorency—and endowed with great natural ability, he had a brilliant worldly career before him until he renounced it to follow the Cross. When he first came out, in 1659, he found the colony in a miserable plight, and when he went home for a visit in 1662 he used all his powerful influence with the government to do something for Canada. Many think that he was chiefly responsible for the vital change that began in the following year, when the king took over the colony.

But it is not for this that his name stands out in Canadian history. Every Canadian knows him for the work he had already undertaken very soon after he first set foot in Quebec. Until his arrival the colonists had no clergy of their own apart from the missionaries. Laval resolved to establish a real Canadian church, for which he procured a royal decree in the spring of 1663 on the eve of his return to New France. He was of course the head of the new organization, but the heart and soul of it was the seminary that he founded in Quebec. It was a training college

The Establishment of New France

for young Canadians entering the priesthood, and it was much more; it was the home of the clergy. Laval would not allow them to be appointed to parishes permanently but insisted that they return every now and then to live in the seminary for a short while. There, in conversation, reading, and prayer, they rested and gained new life, which was of untold value when they went out to continue their labors; and, instead of being a number of individuals going their own several ways, they were knit together as one family. To support them, the decree just mentioned introduced the tithe, of which more will be said later. After he resigned his office in 1688 regular parishes were organized with their own priests, but the seminary was still their home.

Though other bishops succeeded Laval, none could ever replace him in the hearts of the people. For almost half a century, except when he occasionally visited France in the interests of the church, he resided in Canada; and he has left his mark upon the land. He was ever a champion of righteousness, and he feared no man. He fought both governor and intendant when he believed that they were wrong, particularly over the sale of brandy to the Indians, a traffic he vehemently denounced. As a private individual, especially during the long years after he gave up his episcopal charge to resume the status of a simple priest, he lived the life of a saint, and as such he is venerated to this day by several million descendants of those who knew him face to face and worshiped with him. Many English-speaking Protestants have also felt his spell, as readers of Willa Cather's *Shadows on the Rock* may testify.

The third great figure of this period was the central hero of Francis Parkman's epic history, Count Frontenac, dubbed "The Fighting Governor." At fifteen he entered the army, at twenty-three he was a colonel, and at twenty-six a brigadier general. Shortly afterward the coming of peace turned him into a courtier, but his noble birth was his only qualification for this career. His pride would not let him stoop to please, and it placed such a strain upon his lean purse that he lived above his means and fell into debt. In 1672 he seized the offer of the appointment as governor of New France, and then, though he was past fifty, he entered upon the most active and glorious years of his life. He loved pomp and power, and he knew how to use them; but he could brook no rival. The first to cross his path was François Perrot, the governor of Montreal, who claimed a certain independence in his local command and was a competitor in the fur trade. Frontenac crushed him. The poor fellow was arrested and sent to France, where he spent some little time in the Bastille before he returned to Montreal a much subdued man. No one else in the colony dared to challenge this high and mighty governor during his first three years. In 1675, however, a ship arrived bringing not only Bishop Laval, who had been in France for four years, but also a successor to Talon, whose office had been left vacant for three years.

At once the colony proved far too small to hold three such big men, but we must not cast upon Frontenac the whole blame for the rows that followed. In the absence of a successor to Talon the home government had allowed the governor to exercise also the authority of the intendant, and Frontenac naturally resented the new appointment, which clipped his wings. The two heads of the Canadian government, who were intended to be a sort of check upon each other, quarreled violently and openly and filled their correspondence home with all manner of mutual accusations. Nor was Frontenac wholly responsible for his quarrel with Laval. The governor belonged to the anti-Jesuit faction in France, whereas the bishop was a firm friend of the Jesuits; and the home government, jealous of ecclesiastical power in the colony, had instructed the governor to keep the church in its place. Naturally the bishop and the intendant worked together to keep the governor in his place. For seven years the strife raged until the home government could stand it no longer, and in 1682 both the governor and the intendant were replaced, while the bishop, who could not be removed in this way, remained and seemed to stand out as the victor. But after another seven years Frontenac returned in triumph because he had already demonstrated how indispensable he was to the colony.

Frontenac's great service to Canada was to give it security. When he first arrived in Quebec it was becoming obvious that the fiery lesson administered to the Iroquois just a few years before was losing its effect. These savages were growing insolent, and no one could tell how soon they might break the peace. But even if they kept it they were on a fair way to ruin the fur trade, the only paying business of New France and the main support of its government, for the Iroquois were spreading their influence over the tribes of the interior and drawing their furs to find a market on the Hudson instead of the St. Lawrence. Seeing the danger, Frontenac struck out boldly in the summer of 1673.

With the strongest force he could muster he ascended the St. Lawrence to Lake Ontario and there, at Cataraqui, where Kingston now stands, he met the Iroquois, who came in answer to his summons. Then followed many days of talking, feasting, and toiling. The toil was performed by Frontenac's men, who were building a strong fort under the very eyes of the Iroquois envoys and in the midst of the country that they had come to regard as their own. But the Iroquois did not object; there were too many armed Frenchmen, and the spell that Frontenac cast upon the savages was too powerful. Never has any white man displayed a greater genius for handling red men. He could play upon their natures as a master plays upon a violin. The Iroquois quickly made up their minds that this man, the "great Onontio,"* as they fondly and reverently called him, would be a kind and loving father to them if they were good but a terrible avenger if they were bad.

When his guests went home and the governor departed, the whole face of things had changed. Fort Frontenac, firmly built and strongly garrisoned, stood at the foot of Lake Ontario to keep the stream of furs flowing down the St. Lawrence and to serve as an advance post for further French expansion into the interior. It was also a reminder and a threat; it reminded the Iroquois that the eyes of the great governor were upon them, and it threatened them with the thunder of his wrath if they should dare to provoke it. As long as Frontenac remained in Quebec, they would be no problem.

That he alone could hold them in awe became more and more apparent after his recall in 1682. First one and then another governor came, but neither could hold the Iroquois in check. By the end of seven years Frontenac's work was undone; the wild savages were slaughtering the red allies of the French around the Upper Lakes, Fort Frontenac was blown up and abandoned, and

* An Indian corruption of the name of a previous governor—Montmagny.

scores of Frenchmen on the St. Lawrence were massacred. To make matters worse, war had broken out between France and England. New France was in peril, and old France, engaged in war at home, felt unable to send military aid. But Frontenac was an army in himself, and in the fall of 1689 he returned to save the colony.

Thenceforth the history of New France is more or less overshadowed by the great struggle for empire that ended with the British conquest, and because it is well to treat this subject as a whole in another chapter we may turn aside to glance at the daily life of the Canadian people after the colony became firmly established.

CHAPTER 3

Life in New France

Two centuries and more ago a traveler sailing up the St. Lawrence might easily have imagined that he was sliding along the broad street of the longest village in the world. Though roads were built or being built along the banks, and were more and more used, the river was the one great highway of the country, in summer and winter alike; and across this broad highway two rows of houses faced each other. They began some miles below the little town of Quebec and continued, with here and there a church and a mill, to the wilderness just above the even smaller town of Montreal. At Three Rivers there was a little cluster of houses and at Sorel a less noticeable one. Running into the great highway at an acute angle from the south was another liquid street, the Richelieu River, also with houses on either side. In the early years there were gaps in the lines of houses, but the growth of population gradually filled these gaps and caused settlement to creep up other tributaries. Before the end of the French régime it forced some people to take up land in the rear of the first settlers, but even then there were few places where farms were more than two or three deep.

Everybody wanted to live beside the water, and there was no reason why they should not. Each family cultivated only a few acres near the river and neglected the rest of their long, narrow farm, which stretched back for a mile or more. Labor would have been wasted on this land, not because it was poorer, for it was not, but because there was no market for anything it might have been made to produce. France, a rich agricultural country, was easily capable of feeding not only herself but also her colonies. The only market for supplies in New France was to be found in the towns of Quebec and Montreal, and their demand was relatively small, so each family grew little more than was necessary to feed and clothe themselves. Economically they were almost entirely self-sufficient.

A Short History of Canada

A small field of wheat provided enough flour, ground in the neighboring mill, for all the bread the family could eat in a year; and from a little patch of corn came meal in plenty for the many cakes that were consumed in a twelvemonth. Sometimes too oats, rye, and barley were grown, and there was always a garden near the house. Potatoes, as already mentioned, were uncommon before the British conquest. Beans and peas were the favorite vegetables. There was always a pot of pea soup on the fire, and this is still such an established custom that impolite English Canadians sometimes refer to French Canadians as "pea soupers." Almost every family had at least one fruit tree, and the children did not have far to tramp to gather an abundance of wild berries in season. Every farm had cattle and poultry, the woods abounded in game, and the fishing was excellent. Tea, coffee, wines, and spirits were drunk in the towns by the few who could afford such luxuries, but the habitant did not miss them. His household was never short of milk or of home-brewed ale. He also grew and cured many pounds of tobacco, for he and his sons smoked incessantly and even the women frequently indulged in the filthy but delightful habit.

As the habitants were better fed, so also were they much better clad than their cousins in France. Their clothing was all homemade from materials that cost them nothing but a little labor—wool, fur, and leather. Every farm had some sheep, and every cottage had both a spinning wheel and a hand loom. From the forest came furs, which only the richest in Europe could buy but even the poorest in Canada could and did wear. Of home-tanned leather there was an equal abundance, stout oxhides from the farm and soft skins from the forest, which various members of the family made into heavy boots and light moccasins. The house was built of logs or stone. Every spring it was freshly whitewashed, as it is still, so that in summer it stood out in gleaming contrast to the green hills behind and in winter seemed almost a part of the snow that lay all around. The front door opened into a good-sized living room with a huge fireplace. The kitchen, with another fireplace for cooking, was on one side, and on the other was a bedroom. There was usually a small army of beds in the low garret upstairs, which covered the whole space of the house and had little windows poking out of the

Life in New France

roof. Almost every stick of furniture, from the ever-present cradle to the cupboards for dishes and pots, was made by the men of the family, who were also handy at making kitchen utensils. Candles were rare, but they were not often needed. In that northern latitude the summer days are much longer than farther south, and in winter big logs in the fireplace threw out a vigorous light. A storeroom was stuck onto the back of the house, and hard by stood a log stable and barn. Not far off was a root house, half bulging out of the ground and half buried in it. There was also an outdoor oven built of stone, and it was seldom cold for more than two or three days, for a dozen or more children could soon devour an enormous batch of bread.

Since there was no need for careful farming methods, the land was tilled carelessly, the cattle were small and scrawny, and the sheep were poor. The horses, however, were better cared for, because they were kept almost entirely for pleasure. Though these were luxuries, every habitant had one or two good steeds. He thus anticipated the twentieth-century American farmer with his "flivver." In harvest time men, women, and children toiled together in the field, but during the rest of the year life was not very strenuous. As often as not, the habitant might go to bed resolved, when he awoke, to yoke a span of oxen and make them do some ploughing with his homemade, iron-shod wooden plough, only to forget all about it next morning and go off hunting instead.

Here we touch upon one of the most interesting and important features of life in New France, a feature that calls for careful examination because it explains so much. The society and the institutions of France were fundamentally different from those of England, and therefore some writers have imagined that the same differences were reproduced in the New World when the sons of these two countries crossed the Atlantic. But the contrast between the English colonies and New France appears to have been much less marked than has been commonly supposed, and this is natural because the conditions of life in North America were a powerful molding influence upon both societies and tended to make them more alike.

Some English and American historians have criticized France for introducing the feudal system into Canada, though anything else would have been about as strange as if the English had thrown their system of land tenure overboard when they were crossing the Atlantic. Feudalism was as natural to the French as was their own tongue. But the feudalism of New France was not like that of the mother country. The royal authority pruned it when the shoot was planted in North America, for the parent system had degenerated and produced many abuses. This operation, however, does not explain the undoubted fact that the Canadian habitant, though holding his land of a seignior, was in a very different position from the average peasant in France. It was physically impossible for anything like the feudalism of France to exist in this colony. The competition of the Old World was turned upside down in the New World. Here where land was plentiful and people scarce, the competition was among seigniors for tenants, and not among peasants for the land of seigniors, as it was in France. This inversion emptied feudalism of its substance.

American conditions of life emancipated the French peasants who crossed the Atlantic. With liberty forever beckoning through the trees and up the waters flowing past their doors, how could they be ridden by feudal lords? If any man found life in the colony too cramping, no power on earth, not even his wife, could hold him from running away into the woods to live a wilder life of freedom with his friends the Indians. Indeed, from the earliest years of French settlement on this continent such flights occurred. The men who escaped in this manner were known as *coureurs de bois*. A few of them became real explorers, many engaged in the fur trade, and others became nothing more than white savages.

Frederick Jackson Turner, who revolutionized our concept of American history by his studies of the frontier, long ago drew attention to the fact that the same type appeared on the fringe of English settlement. But no English colonial government ever worried as did that of New France over its men who slipped beyond the pale of civilization. This fact raises a suspicion that the proportion of French who thus escaped was greater than that of the English, perhaps indicating that life in New France was less free than life in the English colonies. This conclusion, however, does not necessarily follow, for there were several other conditions that may account for the difference in proportion, if it actually existed.

As we have already seen, the general attitude of the French toward the Indians was much friendlier than that of the English; and this is not surprising, for wherever Frenchmen have gone in other parts of the world they have mingled more freely in native society than have the English. There was also the influence of geography, which lured the French inland while it discouraged the English from penetrating into the interior. Then, too, the harvest of furs within reach of any English colony was not to be compared with what could be gathered from Canada. But even if the relative numbers of *coureurs de bois* and of English savages was the same, French officials had greater cause for concern, because the monopoly that characterized the French traffic was forcing these illicit Canadian traders to carry their furs to the English, thereby reducing the profits of the monopoly upon which the government in Quebec depended for its revenue. Moreover the population of the colony was so small that any loss of men was serious.

French official worries were expressed in a series of royal decrees to extinguish this daring breed of men who seemed to be sapping the life of Canada. The severest penalties were prescribed, heavy fines, confiscation, the lash, and death, but they were all of no avail; the outlaws would not return to be punished. Equally futile was the policy of granting them a general pardon. The drain continued, preventing the colony from growing as fast as it might otherwise have done. But the important point to note is that this loss in numbers brought a great gain in spirit. As Turner so often observed, the West repaid with interest what it drew from the East. In return for the men whom the wilderness stole from New France, it gave back a priceless boon—the spirit of liberty.

The mere fact that the Canadian could depart enabled him to remain in freedom. He could not be tied to the soil. He could get, and we have seen that he did get, much more land than he could ever use; and he got it at a trifling rent, such was the disparity between supply and demand. His tenure resembled that of most English colonists more than that of French peasants, except in outward form; and even in this there was less difference than is often supposed, for we sometimes forget that the majority of the English colonies were settled on the semimanorial system still prevalent in their mother country. The feudal dues that the habitant paid in kind, in money, and in labor were trifling compared with what peasants in France had to pay, and all together should be compared with the obligations of quit-rents and leaseholds in the English colonies. Indeed the land that most English colonists got cost them as much; and the habitant's possession of his farm was just as secure, unless he thought so little of it that he abandoned it, in which case the law provided for the substitution of another tenant.

The annual feudal dues were paid on St. Martin's Day, which came early in November when the harvest was all in and threshed with a flail much like that used in Biblical times. On this day the habitant and his family drove to the house of the seignior to make the payment and to have a good time with their neighbors. The rent was small, a fat fowl and a bushel of wheat for every couple of hundred feet of frontage, and a few coppers scraped together somehow—in all no more than fifty cents an acre would be to a modern farmer. In addition the habitant had to work for his seignior, but never more than six days in the year and usually only three, one for ploughing, one for seeding, and one at harvest time. On these occasions the seignior had to provide him not only with the necessary tools but also with food, and the habitant usually had a good appetite.

No other feudal obligation imposed any burden upon these Canadians. Nature saw to that. The seignior had a legal right to collect what is called a mutation fine on every transfer of a holding otherwise than by direct inheritance. It amounted to one twelfth of the estimated value, one third of which might be deducted for prompt payment. This looks serious but in practice it was not, for the seignior seldom got a chance to collect it in a country where parents were so prolific and the competition of virgin land was so strong. Of the local monopolies possessed by feudal lords in France to the injury of the peasants, only two were ever claimed in Canada, and here they amounted to nothing. One was practically frozen out. It was the right to have the only bake oven in the community and of course to charge for its use. The other was that of the mill, which occasioned more grief to the seigniors than to the habitants, if we may judge by the complaints it produced. They came mostly from the seigniors, whom the law required to build and operate the mills substantially at cost, under pain of forfeiting by nonexercise a right that might become profitable to their heirs. This official interference may seem arbitrary, but the government was merely doing what conditions in New France required.

Equally interesting is what happened to the feudal lord's right to administer justice among his tenants. It was one of the greatest grievances of peasants in France, where it was jealously guarded as a source of revenue. In New France, on the other hand, the population was so thin that the right had no fiscal value, and therefore it survived only in so far as it was a convenience to all concerned. Anyone could appeal to a royal court, where justice was speedy, cheap, and sound, and yet there were few appeals from the seigniorial courts. Even less burdensome was the right of the seignior to have his tenants gather before his house every May Day and there erect a maypole around which they danced in his honor. This was to them more a pleasure than a duty—an annual spring picnic for which he, and not they, provided the refreshments.

Privilege sickened and died in the vigorous atmosphere of the New World, in New France as well as in the English colonies. New France was no place for the noblesse of old France, who were preserved in the glass case of their hereditary caste. They could not soil their lily-white hands by touching any gainful occupation, nor could they degrade themselves by even the slightest social commerce with their inferiors. The difference between society in the mother country and in the colony was as wide as the ocean between them. In New France, habitants frequently became seigniors, which peasants could never do in old France; and this made little or no change in their manner of living, for many other Canadian seigniors, including some of the few titled ones, had to live and work like habitants. It was not uncommon for the lord of a manor, his lady, and his daughters to toil together in the fields. Such was the leveling influence of frontier life.

The inferiority complex of the modern psychologist did not at all infect the Canadian habitant. He was a superior being, and he knew it. According to the Jesuit Charlevoix, a contemporary historian who lived for several years in Canada, "he breathed from his birth the air of liberty" and showed it in his bearing; and according to the literary noble La Hontan, another contemporary who visited the country, he lived in greater comfort than an infinity of gentlemen in France. He was not a coarse and boorish rustic like the peasant at home, said Hocquart, who was intendant in the later years of the French régime, but a well-dressed fellow with good manners. The very name by which he was called reflects his loftier spirit! Technically he was a *censitaire* or *roturier,* like peasants in France, but his scorn for such labels of servility led to the substitution, even in official correspondence, of the classless appellation of habitant.

He was a typical farmer of the North American frontier, where nature made men free and equal by enabling all to become economically independent. A man who thus stood erect on his own feet and could look the whole world in the face was not likely to be a hewer of wood and a drawer of water for his church, no matter how much he might be devoted to it, and there can be no question of his devotion. Every Sunday, unless he happened to be away off in the woods, he went to church with all his family; and throughout his life the best and wisest friend he ever had was the curé. Yet the habitant was no slave of the clergy, as a glance at the history of the tithe will show.

When this ancient institution was introduced into the new country by the royal decree of 1663, which ordered the payment to the church of one thirteenth of all the fruits of human labor as well as those of the soil, with one accord the people refused to pay. In Three Rivers they would not allow the decree to be read or posted, and from a village near Quebec they chased out the priest who came to serve them. The decree raised such a storm that Bishop Laval had to bow before it. Commencing with the parishioners of Quebec, who had contributed to the building of their church, he exempted them from the first year's payment. Then he reduced their obligation to one twentieth for the next six years and soon extended this concession to the rest of the colony. Still the general opposition was menacing, and he continued his retreat. He issued a circular explaining that the words of the royal decree did not mean what they plainly said;

what was to be taxed was not all the fruits of human labor as well as of the soil, but only the produce of that labor that was applied to tilling the soil. In old France the clergy might collect wood, hay, fish, eggs, fleece, and livestock; but they could not do so in New France. The bishop also announced that the lower rate, instead of holding for only six years, was to last through his lifetime. As the people were not yet appeased, he put off all payment until the vessels of 1665 arrived, so that the popular objections might be laid before the king. But payment did not begin in 1665, or for another two years. Finally, after consultation with some of the leading residents of the country, the government in Quebec issued an ordinance in the fall of 1667 establishing the tithe at a still lower rate and with a further exemption. Nothing was to be paid from newly cultivated land until five years after it was broken, and only one twenty-sixth was to be taken from any land. So at last, four years after the first demand, the burden was scaled down to suit the people and they shouldered it. Light as it was, however, it occasioned many local disputes with the clergy right down to the end of the French régime and afterward, as the first British governor of Canada testified. It is therefore not surprising that all clerical attempts to raise the rate and broaden the base of the tithe were defeated.

The freedom that permeated Canadian society also baffled the royal autocracy. One illustration of this has already been noticed —the many futile decrees to keep the people from wandering in the woods. The weight of the government fell heavily on the masses at home, but the population of this colony would not bear it. Impossible in New France was the arbitrary imposition of forced labor by the state that bent the backs and crushed the spirits of French peasants. Here the service was required for the benefit of those who performed it, chiefly in building and repairing their own roads. This was essentially the same, even in the provision for commutation, as the statute labor that American farmers have contributed to their own communities.

The taxes that ground the common people so mercilessly in France were unknown in New France. In fact the habitants paid no taxes at all. Their economy was so self-sufficient that they needed to pay no customs duties, and they were never subjected to a direct levy. In 1704 the king proposed the establishment in

Canada of the *capitation* or the *taille,* two of the worst direct taxes in France, to help defray the expenses of the Canadian administration, and thenceforth the home government repeatedly urged it on governors and intendants. The officials in Quebec, however, knowing full well how stubbornly the habitants were opposed to any imposition, were always afraid to undertake it. Thus did the obstinacy of the Canadians triumph over the royal will. They were a frontier people, like the Americans of whom Turner wrote, and they had their own independent life. Government meant relatively little to them. In so far as it touched them it had to accommodate itself to them; otherwise it could not command obedience.

In various ways throughout the French régime, governor and intendant sought this accommodation, and they found it most completely in the militia captain of every parish. He was never a seignior and except in the towns was always a habitant. Originally little more than a musketry instructor, he quickly grew to be the general factotum of the government. He was its mouth, its eyes, its ears, and its hands. Every Sunday after Mass the congregation gathered outside the church door to hear him read and see him post all public notices before tongues broke loose in an exchange of the neighborhood gossip. It was the militia captain's duty also, like that of the curé, to see that the commands he uttered on Sunday were observed on weekdays, and in this he seems to have been quite effectual because he was something more than the legal agent of autocracy. Practically he was the elected representative of the people. The seignior usually recommended him to the governor as the habitant who was the fittest for this employment, or in other words the natural leader of the community. The governor then ordered the appointment to be proposed to the parish, which was done at the regular Sunday assembly, and he gave or withheld the commission according to whether the people of the parish approved or rejected the nominee. Can our more formal and artificial elections produce as true a representation?

Here was real democracy, faithfully conforming to the familiar North American type. In contrast to that of the Old World, which developed out of a mass struggle to gain the freedom that existing conditions of life denied, the democracy of this continent has existed because the individual would not surrender the freedom that the conditions of life conferred upon him— the freedom of the frontier. This fresh and invigorating breeze from the West blew through New France as well as through the English colonies.

To resume the picture of French colonial life with which this chapter began, we may turn for a moment to the people of Acadia. To a still greater degree than the Canadians the Acadians were left to themselves, for their part of New France was half forgotten by the home government. The feudal system there, even compared with that in Canada, was a mere shadow. The Acadians scarcely knew what a government was, and what little they had of it was almost entirely supplied by their beloved priests. The French population of Acadia numbered only 1,700 when their country was ceded to Britain in 1713. The Canadians were then ten times as numerous, the difference being accounted for by the much greater immigration to Canada, small as that was. Only a few score families had come to Acadia from France, and these mostly in the twenty-five years after the restoration of 1633.

Instead of clearing the forest, as the Canadians did, the Acadians settled on low-lying land where the growth of trees had been prevented by the tide. They transformed the salt marshes into rich meadows by building dikes where the sea was wont to enter, and on occasion they let the high tide flood the land to restore its wasted fertility. Such methods were not new to these people, for they came from the west coast of France where their ancestors had done the same thing for many generations. The Acadians were indeed a different people from the Canadians, most of whose ancestors came from the north of France, particularly Normandy; and even to this day they remain distinct, though only people who are familiar with the French language can note the difference in speech.

In conclusion, to follow up the hint in Hocquart's reference, something should also be said of the social life of the Canadians. Then, as now, the French inhabitants of Canada were noted for their good manners, their social ease, and their never-failing liveliness. They have been called ignorant because few of them could read; but literacy was not very common on the frontiers of the English colonies, and this French colony was wholly on the frontier until after the British conquest. The Canadians were not bowed down by toil, and they understood one of the greatest secrets in the world, a secret relatively few English-speaking people have shared with them: They knew how to enjoy life. They did not struggle for things beyond their reach. They loved the soil, they loved their church, they loved their children, they loved good company and a merry time; and all these they had in plenty.

They found society even with their animals. To their oxen pulling the plough they talked familiarly, and they addressed their horses with voluble affection. These were never ridden but always driven. The summer vehicle was the *calèche,* with its seat poised high in the air over a single pair of wheels. When the snow came, the *calèche* gave way to the *carriole,* with its solid wooden runners, low seat, and high back. Of course this sleigh was well provided with fur robes. For all their fondness for their horses, the Canadians often drove them like Jehu, and on their way home from church they frequently matched the speed of their animals, the smooth, hard surface of the frozen river making an ideal racecourse. Skating was another favorite pastime, and in the winter the valley rang with joyful shouts.

Indoors likewise the winter months were filled with good cheer. A large family made quick work of the chores in and around the house, and then there was little to do but have a good time. There was an almost endless round of festivity, as neighbors visited back and forth, and the rafters of many a cottage must have shaken over the merry gathering below. Almost every parish had at least one fiddler, who seemed to be forever called upon to inspire a dance, and the older folk often joined the younger in tripping away the hours. Cards were another thief of time, and frequently the game was as boisterous as the dancing. Many an evening also slipped by with marvelous rapidity while one or two or three people related stories that made the listeners' hair stand on end or their sides shake with laughter, tales of men turned into wolves or of fish that talked, for the French of Canada have always been capital storytellers.

Even richer than their folklore was the great body of their folk songs. In recent years thousands of them have been collected and

CHAMPLAIN'S "HABITATION" BUILT IN 1608 AT THE FOOT OF CAPE DIAMOND,
QUEBEC; THIS IS THE BEGINNING OF CANADA (CH. 2).

SHIPS FROM THE MOTHER COUNTRY ARRIVE IN NEW FRANCE (CH. 2).

ARRIVAL OF THE URSULINE SISTERS IN QUEBEC (CH. 2).

MÈRE MARIE, FIRST MOTHER SUPE-
RIOR OF THE URSULINES (CH. 2).

FRANÇOIS DE LAVAL, FIRST BISHOP
OF QUEBEC (CH. 2).

JEAN TALON, FIRST INTENDANT, VISITS A SETTLER'S HOME (CH. 2).

THE HABITANT'S OUTDOOR OVEN BAKED BREAD FOR HIS FAMILY (CH. 3).

RETURNING FROM MIDNIGHT MASS (CH. 3).

Life in New France

studied. Many were brought from France, where they have been traced back for centuries, and many were made from time to time out here. The best known, though not the best, "Alouette," has such a contagiously rollicking tune that it has become immensely popular with impromptu choruses in English Canada. When the members of Parliament have finished the business of the session and are waiting for the final ceremonies, they invariably sing this song, led, of course, by one of the French members. The music and the words of the first stanza of "Alouette" are printed below.

2. Je t'y plumerai le bec . . .   3. Je t'y plumerai les yeux . . .
   Et le bec, et la tête . . .   Et les yeux, et le bec, et la tête . . .
   4. (etc.) le bec, le cou, les ailes, le dos, les pattes, la queue

Whenever two or three Canadians were gathered together—at home, in the fields, in the woods, or on the river—they were sure to burst into song. They sang when they met in one another's houses; they sang as they guided the plough or wielded the axe; and in the canoe their paddles kept time with the song that sped them along. No children of the earth ever had a gayer or more wholesome existence.

33

CHAPTER 4

The French Empire in America
Its Rise and Fall

F RENCH place names appear scattered all over the map of the United States between the Allegheny Mountains and the Rockies.* These names, such as Detroit, St. Louis, Vincennes, and Louisiana, are a reminder that the French Empire once covered the greater part of this continent. A Canadian child who had recently moved to the United States once came home from school after a lesson on this early period of American history saying, "That's *Canadian* history!" It is true that the early histories of the two countries overlap, but what is common to both is not equally appreciated by both. The story of this French Empire, which extended over such a large territory and lasted for several generations, scarcely figures in American history, whereas it looms large in Canadian history. This is quite natural, for it is not only a proud heritage of French Canadians but it is much more. Just as the patriotism of American immigrants and their children has made them conscious heirs of the past glories of the United States, so has love of country made English Canadians equal sharers in this heritage of the French Canadians. And because they possess it in common it is a living force drawing and holding them together, a most valuable asset in a country with a dual nationality. But the history of this empire, its rise and its fall, has more than a Canadian significance, for we see in it the struggle between the French and the English for the possession of the greater portion of this continent, the French assuming leadership and holding it for a long time before they finally lost out to the English.

Discovery is the beginning of possession, and the real discovery of North America, which Columbus only began, was largely

* With the exception of the Texan territory, which was not annexed until 1845.

34

The French Empire in America

the work of Frenchmen rather than of Englishmen, though the latter greatly outnumbered the former in the New World from the earliest days of settlement. Why the French should thus have taken the lead is partly explained by geography, as suggested in the last chapter. Back of the narrow Atlantic seaboard runs the line of the Allegheny Mountains that hemmed the English colonists in. No such barrier stood between the French in the St. Lawrence Valley and the heart of the continent. Rivers and lakes were then the only highroads running through America. An immense system of these highroads converged at the point where Montreal now stands and indeed is the original reason for the growth of that city. Almost any European people who settled on the St. Lawrence would have been tempted to push up the waters that flowed past their very doors.

Further reasons may be found in the motives behind the founding of New France. No English colony was established with an idea that it would control a water passage through the continent to the Orient, or with any thought of discovering such a passage. On the other hand, from Champlain's time down to the British conquest of Canada, Frenchmen hoped to find a way to the sea beyond, and this hope lured them deeper and deeper into the continent. Nor was any English colony planted with the intention of paying for it out of the profits of the fur trade, as was the French colony on the St. Lawrence. This traffic, never more than an incidental feature of English colonization, was fundamental to French colonization, and it led naturally to exploration. Moreover, the very nature of the fur trade prevented its stabilization. As the nearer regions were trapped out, the French were drawn farther and farther into the interior in search of furs. The missionary impulse, which the English lacked, also drove the French inland, and though there was some conflict between the search for souls and the search for skins, the missionary motive operated in conjunction with the commercial motive as well as with the desire for exploration. There was thus inherent in New France a triple force of expansion, and this in time was strengthened by a patriotic urge to extend the glory of the mother country, an urge that was much less marked in the English colonies.

The principal road to the West was not the upper St. Law-

35

rence but the Ottawa, a more direct route and one less infested by Iroquois. From the Ottawa it ran up the Mattawa, across to Lake Nipissing, and thence down the French River to Georgian Bay. (See map, Canada by the Proclamation of 1763, in Chapter 5.) For several centuries this was the great highway to the interior. That is what it was to the Indian before the white man came, and that is what it was from Champlain's day right down to the third decade of the nineteenth century.

The first step in the westward movement of the French was the establishment of the Jesuit missions among the Hurons between Lake Simcoe and Georgian Bay. The second followed as the result of the destruction of these missions and the expulsion of the surviving Hurons to the region around Sault Sainte Marie. Neither party could endure the separation, for each had become dependent on trade with the other. They reached out to restore the contact, a few red men venturing down the Ottawa and a few French traders venturing up. Hitherto the exchange of furs had taken place on the St. Lawrence, the Hurons bringing down what they gathered in the West, but now it became apparent that the French could get more by going after them. At the same time the missionaries reached out after their scattered flock and found that an eager welcome awaited them in the West.

So it happened that when the chastisement of the Iroquois made travel safe along the Ottawa, traders and missionaries appeared in growing numbers in the vicinity of Sault Sainte Marie, so named after the Holy Virgin because it began as a mission station. The Jesuits, who founded it, were more than preachers of the gospel; they were scientists and explorers and made full reports upon the country. In 1671 they produced the first real map of Lake Superior and the northern parts of Michigan and Huron. Meanwhile, as soon as the upper St. Lawrence also became safe for travel, other missionaries, the Sulpicians, appeared on Lake Ontario. Their order had recently acquired the whole island of Montreal from the company that established settlement there, and incidentally the Seminary of St. Sulpice is still the greatest landowner in and around Montreal.

The new government in Quebec also pushed this western expansion. Talon, whose interest was not confined to the lower St. Lawrence, wanted to extend French influence over the inte-

The French Empire in America

rior, and to this end he used every means he could find—missionaries, fur traders, and adventurers. One of them was Louis Jolliet, after whom the city of Joliet in Illinois was named. Born in Quebec and educated by the Jesuits, he early resolved to be a priest and at twenty-one distinguished himself as a public debater in philosophy. Shortly afterward he abandoned his holy calling, but not his good character, to become a fur trader, merchant, and explorer. His most famous expedition was in company with Père, or Father, Marquette, who little dreamed that he would one day give his name to an American railway. This devout Jesuit, who had a remarkable gift for learning Indian languages and a burning zeal to preach the gospel to new tribes, had already spent several years on the Upper Lakes when Jolliet brought him orders for the two of them to discover in the heart of the continent a great river of which reports had come in. From Michilimackinac the young Canadian trader and the Jesuit Père Marquette together made their way out to the Mississippi and down the river as far as the mouth of the Arkansas. They had gone far enough to dispel the hope that some people had held—that this great river within reach of the Great Lakes flowed into the Pacific—and to identify it with the river the Spaniards had found emptying into the Gulf of Mexico.

While the French were thus reaching out to establish their far-flung fur-trading empire, they encountered two challenges in the interior of America. Neither of them came from the English colonies. One was the work of the Iroquois, who, as already explained, were extending their control over the tribes around the Great Lakes, drawing the furs of the interior down to the Hudson instead of the St. Lawrence. In other words, the Iroquois were building an empire of their own, likewise based on the fur trade, and the lines of this red empire cut right across those of the French. As we have seen, Frontenac boldly met this challenge in the summer of 1673, when he summoned the Iroquois to Cataraqui and there built a fort bearing his own name.

In following up this strategic blow, the imperialist governor used the most famous of all the French explorers in North America—La Salle, the man he had sent to summon the restless Iroquois. This young scion of a noble French house, on coming to Canada to seek his fortune, had got a seigniory at the head of the rapids just above Montreal, the modern Lachine. This name, the French word for China, was given to it in derision shortly after he sold it to buy a trading outfit to support him while exploring the western waters; for it was said he was trying to find the way to China. With Talon's blessing he had discovered the Ohio; but his name will ever be associated with the Mississippi, though Jolliet and Marquette had beat him to the discovery of the father of waters.

Frontenac found in La Salle a man after his own heart, for both were empire builders, and together they planned to appropriate the whole stretch of the continent from the Great Lakes to the Gulf of Mexico. According to the basic French conception, the exploration of this vast territory would lead the fur trade on and be paid for by it, and the posts established to support the trade would grow into colonies.

With Fort Frontenac as his base and the governor as his political protector and silent business partner, La Salle set out to execute this grandiose design. He built vessels on Lake Ontario, established a post at Niagara, built another vessel above it, and set up various posts beyond. But when he got to the Illinois, where he planned to construct a vessel for the navigation of the Mississippi, some mysterious fate swallowed the ship that had brought him to Lake Michigan and that he had sent back laden with furs to satisfy his creditors and pay for the gear of the Mississippi craft. This was the first of many terrific blows that descended upon La Salle. His property in Canada was seized by his creditors, his own men betrayed him, his goods were stolen, and Indians destroyed some of his forts. He was partly the author of his own tragedy, for he was not a good businessman. His trading on the Great Lakes cut into the field of jealous rivals in Canada, his failure to command loyalty suggests a defect in his character as a leader, and the depredations of the red men look like the work of the Iroquois, whose economic empire he would have destroyed. Yet nothing save death could stop him. With fifty men in half a dozen canoes he explored the Mississippi to its mouth, and there, in April 1682, he formally took possession of the whole country for his king, after whom he named it Louisiana.

Returning to Canada, La Salle found his patron gone and an

enemy ruling in his stead. Thereupon the unconquerable explorer went to France, where he persuaded the king to send him with a company of colonists to occupy the mouth of the Mississippi. They sailed in 1684, but by some strange mischance missed the mouth of the river and landed on a desolate part of the coast beyond. Two years later, his colony having been reduced to great straits, he set out overland with half his people to get aid from Canada. Lost on the way, he was murdered by some of his followers, and only seven of the leaderless party survived to tell the gruesome tale. Those who had been left behind perished at the hands of Indians. Though La Salle's great scheme thus ended in death and destruction, he had established a French claim to the broad valley of the Mississippi and had pointed the way for others of his race to follow.

Meanwhile French imperial designs based on the St. Lawrence faced a challenge in the North with the establishment of the Hudson's Bay Company, for which two Canadian *coureurs de bois* were chiefly responsible, Radisson and Groseilliers. These two bold fellows, who were among the few who ventured west before the first French soldiers arrived to bridle the Iroquois, conceived the idea that a fortune in furs awaited those who would go to Hudson Bay for it. Though for half a century this great inland sea had been known and various explorers had visited its shores, none of them had established commercial contact with the Indians there. But these young men knew from their experience in dealing with the natives how to do it, if they could only get there.

Running away from Quebec, where they were frowned on as illicit traders, they found their way to England. There they persuaded a number of wealthy and influential men to fit out an expedition that sailed for the Bay in 1668 and returned the following year with such a rich cargo of furs that the famous company was formed and chartered by the king in 1670. By this charter, which was to stand for two centuries, the king gave the company a monopoly of the trade, the ownership of the land, and the right of government in all the territory drained by the rivers emptying into Hudson Bay and Hudson Strait. How enormous this area was—about the size of Europe—neither he nor anyone else knew; and generations were to pass before the company, which still exists, tried to establish its rule over the vast domain of which it thus became the titular lord. For a long time the men of the company had no thought of pushing inland. Why should they? Into the forts that they built at the mouths of the rivers the red men poured with their furs.

Though hundreds of miles away, the French on the St. Lawrence were alarmed. The English in the North were so much nearer the source of the furs that for all practical purposes they had got in behind the French. For some years the French nibbled at the root of the danger. Talon sent spies to watch these English and if possible to strike a blow at them in the rear. Traders from Canada, using their superior knowledge of how to handle the natives, pushed farther north than they had yet gone and got many an Indian pack that the English would otherwise have bought. Radisson and Groseilliers were persuaded to desert back to their own people, but the company carried on without them, even though they were its founders. Then a Canadian company was formed, and in 1682 it sent the two adventurers around by sea to Hudson Bay, but when they returned with what they had gained by plundering the English and trading with the Indians, Frontenac's successor treated them even worse than he did La Salle. He confiscated their furs and ordered them to report to the home government for attacking the English, with whom the French were then officially at peace. Thus the Canadian company was ruined.

Another governor soon arrived, however, and he struck boldly at the English in the North. A military expedition of a hundred men started up the Ottawa in 1686 and after three months' toiling over streams and portages this force burst like a whirlwind upon the English, capturing the three forts they had erected on James Bay. The only one left in the North was at the mouth of the Nelson; this would have fallen too if the fiery visitors had been able to reach it, but it was as far away again as the distance they had already come. If such things could happen while England and France were still at peace, it is not difficult to imagine what happened when they went to war, as they did shortly afterward.

Meanwhile there was another growing conflict between the English and the French on the Atlantic seaboard over Acadia,

a conflict that began before the expanding French Empire encountered the Iroquois' challenge around the Great Lakes or
the English trading company's challenge in the North and a
conflict in which English colonists did actually challenge the
French. The first blow in the fight over Acadia was struck in
1613.

The governor of Virginia, incensed to hear that the French
had intruded upon land which he maintained belonged to England, determined to expel them. For this purpose he dispatched
an expedition under the freebooting sea captain Samuel Argall,
who had just abducted Pocahontas and held her as a hostage for
her father Powhatan's English prisoners. Argall uprooted a settlement the Jesuits were planting on Mount Desert and destroyed the buildings at Port Royal on the Nova Scotian Annapolis Basin, thereby making homeless the few Acadians of that
day. The founding of New England in 1620 under the Scottish
king of England, James I, suggested that as James VI of his
northern realm he should see to the creation of a New Scotland
beside New England, and in the following year, when one of his
Scottish courtiers urged it, the king granted him the country to
develop as a colony. The name then given to it, Nova Scotia, or
New Scotland, has been carefully preserved in the Latin of the
original charter and has never been vulgarized by retranslation,
a reminder that Scots have long been famous for their superior
education. Though Nova Scotia thus existed on paper from
1621, no Scots established themselves there until 1629, when
some settled at Port Royal and others on Cape Breton, while the
English captured the colony on the St. Lawrence, as we have seen
in the second chapter. But the Scots did not remain longer than
the English. Three years later, by the treaty that restored Quebec to France, these British were withdrawn from Acadia. In
1654 an expedition fitted out by Oliver Cromwell seized the
colony again, but thirteen years afterward it was given back.

These comings and goings were the beginning of the confused
history of Acadia. More trouble was in store for this land because
of its geographical position. Lying at the main entrance to the
Gulf of St. Lawrence, it controlled the front door of Canada;
and overlooking the seaboard to the south, it commanded the
communication between the English colonies and their mother

country. Therefore neither the French nor the English wished to see the other there, and this overlapping of interests made it the scene of repeated clashes in time of war.

The fate of the French Empire in America was not decided in America. Under Louis XIV France was by far the greatest power on earth. With the human and material resources this absolute monarch had at his disposal, he might have firmly established French dominion over most of the New World. But he had other ambitions. His desire to dominate the Old World involved him in European wars that more and more absorbed his attention and the resources of his country. The effect upon Canada was serious. The stream of immigrants ceased; scarcely any soldiers were sent out to protect the colony; and every effort at western expansion was discouraged by the authorities at home because it would mean an added expense and a drain upon the all too scanty population on the St. Lawrence. All this stands in marked contrast to the new day that had dawned in 1665 with the coming of a new set of officials and the Carignan-Salières regiment; and, as Louis XIV's long series of wars started in 1672, we may say that the twilight of French power in America began about the time that Frontenac, the great fighting governor, first set foot in Canada—though he seemed to be ushering in a more glorious day.

The great turning point of Louis XIV's fortunes came in the English Revolution of 1688. Before this event he was more than a match for any combination of his foes, and England was more or less under his thumb, as her rulers were his cousins, first Charles II and then James II. But when the English people drove out their half-French king they took in his stead William of Orange who, as head of the Dutch republic, had already become Louis XIV's archenemy. By changing monarchs, England changed sides in Europe, thereby swinging the balance of power against France and commencing a series of Anglo-French wars that lasted for a century and a quarter.

In this long, intermittent struggle, which has been called the modern Hundred Years' War, the British Empire devoured the French Empire. For this outcome, which involved the fate of Canada, Louis XIV was by no means wholly responsible. His successors likewise blundered, wasting on European battlefields

The French Empire in America

the men and the money that might have been used to build up the French Empire on the sea and in lands beyond. But because the English also blundered, the French Empire in America did not fall for more than seventy years after the English Revolution of 1688.

King William's War, the first phase of the long struggle, lasted until 1697, and though it saw considerable fighting in America, it settled nothing here. It was the outbreak of this war that sent Frontenac back to New France in 1689, and his return acted like magic upon the French and their Indian allies. It filled them with new confidence and vigor, despite the hostility of the Iroquois who were much more dangerous now that they were supported by the English as allies. Being a good commander, the governor did not wait to be attacked. He would strike first, and strike hard, and against the English rather than the Iroquois. This was good strategy, for the English were backing the Iroquois, not the other way around. In the depth of winter three war parties of French and Indians sped south on their snowshoes, and silently they approached outlying settlements of New York and New England. Then, dealing death and destruction, they burst upon the unsuspecting English, whose descendants to this day remember with a shudder the savage slaughter at Schenectady, Salmon Falls, and at Fort Loyal, where the city of Portland, Maine, now stands.

Meanwhile Frontenac sent a deputation to the Iroquois, whom he hoped to win through the return of some chiefs kidnaped by his predecessor. But the Iroquois, like wild beasts that had tasted blood, would not obey the voice of their old master, and he prepared to meet their renewed challenge. He had already sent soldiers to reinforce the garrison in a fort that had been built some years before at Michilimackinac, and the appearance of this new strength in their midst rallied the surrounding tribes, who were wavering in their friendship for the French and showing signs of going over to the Iroquois. Thereupon five hundred or more braves set out from the Upper Lakes for Montreal, their canoes filled with furs and their hearts with war. When they arrived the governor met them in a grand council and worked them up to a wild climax. Despite his seventy years, he seized a tomahawk, and brandishing it aloft he led in the war dance and

43

the war song. When they departed for their distant homes he knew, and others knew, that he had repelled a serious menace to the French power in the West.

In this same year, 1690, New York and New England struck back, for they were stung by the attacks from the north and they realized that these attacks had raised French prestige among the Iroquois. A conference at Albany planned two expeditions, one over Lake Champlain to take Montreal and the other by sea to capture Quebec. Of the former, no more than a few bold raiders reached their destination, and that only with their eyes as they gazed across the broad expanse of the St. Lawrence. They were unable to cross the river and were soon driven back.

The maritime expedition did not sail from Boston until its leader, Sir William Phips, a hardy New England adventurer, had succeeded in another enterprise already undertaken by Massachusetts. He captured, plundered, and abandoned Port Royal, whence French cruisers had been preying on the commerce of Massachusetts, and destroyed an Acadian settlement at the head of the Bay of Fundy. The much larger force that he conducted up the St. Lawrence did not reach its goal until the middle of October, when it was much too late in the season for any chance of success. Phips had to take Quebec at once or the winter would catch him and his fleet for the French. When he summoned the place to surrender, the only answer he got was from the mouths of cannon. Thanks to Frontenac, who had foreseen this attack on his capital, Quebec was now well fortified and garrisoned. After a week of useless bombardment Phips turned tail and disappeared down the river.

Having put forth their greatest effort in this year and being no more able than the French to secure aid from their mother country, the English colonists continued the war chiefly by hounding on the Iroquois against the French. Again these red demons swarmed on the Ottawa, damming back the stream of furs, and again they infested the outlying settlements, claiming many a victim. To these days belongs the heroic tale, so graphically told by Parkman, of Madeleine of Verchères. The scene was a village on the south shore of the St. Lawrence about twenty miles below Montreal, established by Verchères, an old officer of the Carignan-Salières regiment, and named after him.

The French Empire in America

For protection he had built a little fort, and now while he was serving with the garrison of Quebec his fourteen-year-old daughter, Madeleine, assumed command of the fort when it was attacked by some two score Iroquois. Though she had a garrison of only three men and two boys, she held the savages at bay for a whole week until help came.

The Iroquois power was growing. Though it was less able to destroy the colony than in the days of Dollard, it threatened to cut the French off from the West. Like the Hurons half a century before, the Indians who lived around the Great Lakes were less and less able to put up a good fight because the trade that supplied them with arms and ammunition was more and more interrupted. There was only one thing that could preserve to the French their empire over the interior, defeat of the Iroquois, and in the summer of 1696, thirty years after their first chastisement, these red gangsters suffered another and a worse one. Sending seven hundred men up to rebuild the demolished Fort Frontenac, the governor followed with twenty-two hundred more and a number of cannon. Crossing to the south side of Lake Ontario, this army ascended the Oswego River and made for the heart of the Iroquois country. The red men who had been so ferocious fled in terror of the approaching host. Again they saw their towns and food destroyed, again they groveled, and never again did they recover all the power they had once enjoyed. Frontenac smote them too effectively.

On Hudson Bay the official declaration of war meant merely the continuance of hostilities that had already broken out. Posts were captured and recaptured in bewildering succession. The French quickly found that they could not succeed against the English in the North unless they also conducted operations by sea, and for this purpose they got a few naval vessels from France. Upon those northern waters also appeared a most remarkable man, a military as well as a naval officer, of whom Parkman said, "No Canadian, under French rule, stands in a more conspicuous or more deserved eminence." He was Pierre Le Moyne, Sieur d'Iberville, the most famous of the leaders in the raids on New York and New England, a French hero in the contest over the possession of Newfoundland, the founder of Louisiana, and the dominant figure in the strife on Hudson Bay. There the amphibious exploits of this ubiquitous commander outshone all others. His most daring achievement was in 1697 when with a single vessel, because ice had separated him from his consorts, he engaged three English ships, sank one, captured another, and drove off the third. Then the fort at the mouth of the Nelson, for which this battle was fought, fell to the French for the third time. The war ended with the English almost, but not quite, driven from the North. Peace found them in possession of only one fort.

During the five years' interval before the next war, the French improved their imperial position in America. Now that Iroquois imperialism was finally crushed they met no challenge in consolidating their hold over the continent from the shores of Hudson Bay to the mouth of the Mississippi. There in 1699 d'Iberville founded Louisiana, and there some years later another Canadian, his own brother Bienville, founded New Orleans. In 1701 Cadillac, another old officer of the Carignan-Salières regiment, built at Detroit the first fort on the strategic strait between the upper and the lower Great Lakes. Soon afterward a settlement grew up around this key place of the fur trade, which has since become the center of the automobile industry. All the while the English colonies went their several ways without any concern for what was happening beyond the mountains that were their western horizon. Not until after the next war was over did they develop an interest in this great interior region.

Queen Anne's War, which began in 1702, resembled King William's War. Both of these American wars were touched off in Europe, but in the New World they were little affairs compared with the conflicts waged between England and France in the Old World; and both followed much the same pattern, except that the Iroquois were no longer a factor and the inglorious attempt to take Quebec was the work of a naval expedition from the mother country. There were the same ghastly raids of French and Indians from Canada, and they left bloody memories, particularly in Wells and Deerfield, Massachusetts. Again New Englanders plundered and conquered in Acadia, which was easier than Canada for them to strike. Twice in 1707 they tried to seize that "nest of pirates," Port Royal. Three years later, on obtaining aid from England, they succeeded, but this

The French Empire in America

time they did not abandon it. Again there were desultory hostilities in and around Newfoundland and on Hudson Bay. All this fighting was inconclusive, but over in Europe the coalition against Louis XIV inflicted such decisive defeats upon his armies that he was forced to sue for peace. Because England was the head of the victorious coalition and because her great military genius, John Churchill, first Duke of Marlborough, was chiefly responsible for bringing Louis XIV to his knees, England was able to write into the Treaty of Utrecht, which ended the war in 1713, some terms that altered the imperial situation in America. France surrendered Hudson Bay, Newfoundland, and Acadia.

Then ensued the one long period of peace between Britain and France during the whole century and a quarter when they were chronic foes. This peace lasted for nearly a generation, from 1713 to 1744, and like the two previous wars was the result of Old World conditions that need not be noted here. Meanwhile, however, the situation was changing in the New World, where the French tried to recover and strengthen their position, thereby rousing the British to the necessity for counter measures.

The Treaty of Utrecht did not decide the fate of Acadia, because it omitted any definition of Acadian boundaries and because it allowed France to keep the island of Cape Breton. The omission gave rise to a nice dispute, the French asserting that the ceded colony included only the Nova Scotian peninsula and the British that it also covered the present Province of New Brunswick and the state of Maine. The British were not only unable to make good their claim to this larger territory but were also in growing danger of losing the smaller one they had gained. Its only population was French, and France was preparing to recover it. This she could hope to do because she retained Cape Breton. There Louisbourg was now established, with public buildings finer than those of Boston and, what was of much greater importance, with fortifications stronger than any other place in America. From such a vantage point France might regain what she had yielded in this region. Moreover, Louisbourg was a much bigger and better Port Royal, a potential check upon maritime New England, and it gave a new security to Canada, for it guarded the entrance to the St. Lawrence.

The French were busy also on the natural highway that leads

47

straight from New York into the heart of old Canada, up the Hudson, along Lake Champlain, and down the Richelieu. Over this route, which railways and motor roads follow today, the English had tried to invade Canada in Frontenac's day, and they might try it again. The French first blocked their end of it by building a stone fort at Chambly, on the rapids of the Richelieu just below Lake Champlain. The British wanted to do likewise by occupying and fortifying the narrows at the southern end of this lake, but bickerings between the separate colonies prevented them, and, to quote a writer of the day, "while they were quarrelling for the bone, the French ran away with it." This was in 1731, when an expedition from Canada appeared at Crown Point and erected another stone fort which might stop a hostile English force from passing down the lake and from which the French could strike a blow at the back of either New York or New England. At once the people of these colonies united in denouncing this wicked invasion of British territory, but they would not unite to rid themselves of the danger.

In the nearer West, similar things were happening. Both French and British turned their eyes to Niagara, the key to the Upper Lakes, and sent agents among the neighboring Iroquois, who were still a power to be reckoned with. The French sought permission to build a fort there, for La Salle's post had long since been abandoned, and a later one at this point had suffered the same fate. The British, on the other hand, merely tried to persuade the red men to prevent the French from reoccupying the place. The French succeeded, and in 1720 their fort arose. As it interrupted the trade between the western tribes and Albany, the governor of New York determined to make a countermove by building a fort at Oswego. This he did in 1727, and as the western Indians preferred British goods and prices, they passed Niagara by and brought their furs to Oswego. Then it was the turn of the French in Canada to be alarmed. They wanted to send an army of two thousand men to take Oswego, but the home government would not agree to any such warlike measure. Thereupon they tried to tempt the Iroquois to destroy it, but the Iroquois were too shrewd.

Farther afield the French were reinforcing their imperial position without disturbing the peaceful dreams of the English. In

The French Empire in America

1718 Bienville founded New Orleans, and about this time permanent French settlements gathered around trading posts and Jesuit mission houses in the Illinois country, at Kaskaskia, Cahokia, and Fort Chartres—links in the chain between the St. Lawrence and the Gulf of Mexico.

In the North the French were turning the tables on the English in the only way that remained, and they were doing it rather effectively. Pushing farther overland, they tapped the Hudson's Bay Company's trade at its source, first in what is now northern Ontario and then, from 1731 on, penetrating beyond Lake Superior into the basin of Lake Winnipeg. This more distant operation was the work of one man, La Vérendrye, and his sons.

A native of Three Rivers, La Vérendrye had entered the French army and fought on European battlefields until the peace of Utrecht blocked his military ambition. Then he returned to his native land, entered the fur trade, and after a few years found himself in charge of several posts on the north side of Lake Superior. There he was visited by Indians who came from the West, and from them learned that their country was temptingly rich in furs. These visitors also gave him such a twisted notion of its geography that he thought it might be easy to find the way to the western sea. He seems to have got the idea that Lake Winnipeg, instead of stretching north and south and being drained into Hudson Bay, stretched east and west and was drained by a river flowing into the Pacific. Thereupon he persuaded the government in Quebec to give him a monopoly of the traffic in peltries beyond Lake Superior in the hope that he would use the profits to discover a practicable route to the ocean of the setting sun. Here we see, toward the end of the French régime, the original combination of furs, discovery, and empire—the vision of Champlain and La Salle. From Grand Portage, now in Minnesota, La Vérendrye and his sons worked up the chain of rivers and lakes along which the present international border runs, planting trading establishments on Rainy Lake and Lake of the Woods. Pushing beyond, they built posts on Lake Winnipeg, on the Red River which empties into it, on the Assiniboine, a tributary of the Red, and on the Saskatchewan. Although they did not find the way to the western sea, they achieved the other object that had drawn them into the Northwest. They stole the

49

trade of the English company while its men slumbered in their posts on the bay.

When Britain and France again went to war in 1744, once more releasing hostilities in America, the fighting did not extend to this far-flung province of the French Empire added by La Vérendrye nor did it touch the Mississippi Valley. It was confined to the East. There the British colonists had plans for attacking Canada and for protecting themselves, but they carried out none of them because they were divided by quarrels. The consequence was that the French, aided by their Indian friends, again descended with fire and slaughter upon the northern parts of New York and New England. But in another place the British colonists won a surprising victory.

In the summer of 1744 twenty-five Boston vessels were captured by privateers from Louisbourg. This was too much for the New Englanders. Massachusetts made up its mind to seize this fortress, strong as it might be, and proceeded to do so even though the other colonies lent little assistance. A force of about thirty-five hundred men was collected, and as they alone could not accomplish this amphibian task the British government sent a squadron of the Royal Navy to help the expedition, which sailed from Boston in the spring of 1745.

The siege of Louisbourg that took place then was not like other sieges. Rather it suggests musical comedy. Fortune was all on the side of the Massachusetts men, and they needed every bit of it to take such a stronghold. They were a motley crew of clerks, farmers, and fishermen, with little training or discipline and with only a merchant, William Pepperell, to lead them. A few good storms or vigorous sorties might have broken up this amateur army, but Heaven smiled in perfect weather and the French did not venture outside their walls. The attackers were improperly equipped. Though they brought a supply of big cannon balls, they had nothing but faith with which to fire them —until the French, by abandoning an outlying battery without spiking the guns, gave them exactly what they needed. Shortly afterward the men from Boston would have had to give up the siege for lack of supplies and ammunition, had not a French warship, heavily laden with these necessities, arrived and been promptly captured by the British squadron. In the middle of

The French Empire in America

June Louisbourg fell, having been sadly neglected by its own government.

This war lasted only four years, and it seemed to make no real change in America because at the end of it Britain restored Louisbourg to France in return for conquests won by the French in Europe and in India. But in some important respects the situation was not the same. The war made the French in Canada realize that they must do much more than they had yet done if they were to retain their hold upon this continent. It also taught the British in America that they would never be safe until New France was conquered. Therefore the peace negotiated in the Old World did not put peace into the hearts of the two peoples in the New World. Very soon a bigger war was bound to break out, this time in America. Nor could the peace restore what was at the bottom of the sea. In two great battles off the coast of Spain, the British had well-nigh destroyed the French navy. This destruction of the French sea power was, as we shall see, worth a hundred Louisbourgs.

More and more the French and the British in America resembled two dogs restrained from fighting by leashes held by their masters, and at last the leashes broke. Serious fighting began in America in 1755, a year before war was declared in Europe. It began in the West, in the center, and in the East.

The great crisis of empire was at hand, as a glance at the clash in the West shows. The population of the British colonies, long confined to the strip of land between the Alleghenies and the Atlantic, had increased until it was on the point of bursting over the mountains. The French were bound to lose their control over the interior if they did not block the British advance by a line of forts linking Canada with Louisiana. Could they do it, or would the British break through? As usual, the internal quarrels of the British colonists allowed the French to get ahead. French forts began to rise, the main one being Fort Duquesne at the forks of the Ohio, where the city of Pittsburgh now stands. Seeing the danger of being forever cooped up on the narrow seaboard, the British struck. Early in the summer of 1755, an army of American militia and British regulars under General Braddock was approaching Fort Duquesne when suddenly the woods around them became alive with foes. The red coats of Braddock's men made wonderful targets for the French and the Indians, who were as difficult to hit as the shadows of the forest. Five horses were slain under the brave general before he fell mortally wounded, and the shattered remnant of his army fled in panic.

EUROPEAN EMPIRES ON THE EVE OF THE SEVEN YEARS' WAR, 1755.

On the central highway from New York to Montreal blood was likewise flowing freely while Britain and France were still at peace. The British colonists, regarding Crown Point as a sort of spear aimed at their backs, decided to seize it; but the government in Quebec, having learned of their plan through military papers found in Braddock's baggage, sent an army south from Lake Champlain. The two forces met at the southern end of Lake George, where the British defeated the French and cap-

The French Empire in America

tured their commander. On this battleground, the British built Fort William Henry, while the French retired to Ticonderoga, where they erected another fort—to double bar the gate to the North.

In the East the storm had been more obviously gathering since the conclusion of the last war. To offset the loss of Louisbourg, the British government established Halifax in 1749. In the following year a British fort appeared on the isthmus of Chignecto to watch the French, and the French replied by planting another to watch this. We have seen that the French authorities, though they had given up Nova Scotia, had not abandoned hope of recovering it, and now to make its reconquest easy they stirred up the Indians and the Acadians to keep them French in heart. They did it through the red men's missionaries and the white men's priests. Louisbourg was the chief seat of this influence, and Beauséjour, the new French fort on the isthmus, was not far behind. If Louisbourg had been only an ordinary inland fort, the British might have seized both places, but Louisbourg was a real fortress, now much better held, and therefore they attacked only Beauséjour. Even this was too difficult for the little garrison of Nova Scotia, but in the summer of 1755 a large force of New Englanders came and did the job quickly.

As the New Englanders had to return home soon, their presence seemed to offer a good opportunity to deal firmly with the Acadian population. If these people were allowed to remain where they were and to continue in their existing frame of mind, they might betray Nova Scotia to the French. Either they must become loyal British subjects or else they must be removed. This was the judgment of the British authorities on the spot, half of them New Englanders, and they acted at once before the home government could prevent them. They summoned the people to take the oath of allegiance, and when this was refused they herded most of them into ships that carried them away and scattered them through the British colonies down the coast. Over six thousand men, women, and children were thus deported. It was a great tragedy, made familiar to Americans by Longfellow's *Evangeline*. Its readers should realize, however, that *Evangeline* is much better poetry than history, for it gives a quite misleading impression of what happened.

When Britain went to war with France in 1756, one might think that the French Empire in America would fall immediately. The British population on this side of the Atlantic exceeded 1,000,000, while the French numbered little more than 60,000. But this war in America, unlike its predecessors, was fought largely with regulars sent from across the sea, and France, with a population still two or three times that of Britain, could raise much larger armies. It was British sea power, however, that decided the issue. It prevented the French from sending as many troops as they needed in America, and it enabled Britain to throw her armies across the ocean when and where she willed.

Nevertheless four years passed before British arms drove French power out of America; and at first the war went against the British, the French capturing Oswego and Fort William Henry. This delay and these reverses are easily explained. As of old, the French on this continent had a unified command, while the British colonies still quarreled among themselves. Moreover, Britain had weak men at the head of her government. But the tide began to turn when William Pitt, later Lord Chatham, came into power.

Pitt possessed to a remarkable degree the qualities of a great man. He was a wonderful organizer; at a glance he could see what was to be done and how to do it. He gave enough orders to secure the best cooperation but not enough to cramp the initiative of those under him. He had an uncanny judgment of human nature. He could pick the right men for the work to be performed, and he would, if necessary, promote them over the heads of their seniors. He did this with Wolfe, and some jealous rivals then told the king that this young general was mad. The king, knowing what had happened, replied that he wished Wolfe would bite some of his other generals. Another secret of Pitt's power was his ability to inspire men, great and small. He stirred the people of Britain to a high pitch of patriotism, and he roused the American colonies to join in a wholehearted effort to destroy French power on this continent.

The British defeats were continued into 1758, when one of the old generals failed to take Ticonderoga. It was a case of bravery without brains, and it cost about two thousand men. But elsewhere this year saw important victories won by new

The French Empire in America

British leaders. In two places they cut the vital cord of the French Empire in the interior—by capturing Fort Frontenac with all the vessels the French had constructed on Lake Ontario and by taking Fort Duquesne, which was renamed Pittsburgh in honor of the great statesman.

In the same year the British cleared the way for an advance up the St. Lawrence by taking Louisbourg for a second and last time. The siege of 1758, unlike that of 1745, was a serious affair from beginning to end. A strong naval division and a large army of regulars, part of which was led by Wolfe, undertook the task in a businesslike manner. They were so well prepared that they had to use only one third of the powder they brought. Their powerful guns blasted a hole in the walls, and the attackers were about to storm the place when the French surrendered to prevent needless slaughter. Two years later, when the war was drawing to a close, the British government ordered the destruction of the mighty fortress, which was useless to Britain but might be of great value to an enemy, and it became the heap of picturesque ruins that it remains to this day.

Early in June 1759, twenty-two men-of-war under Admiral Saunders sailed from Halifax with an army of nine thousand regulars under General Wolfe to take Quebec. To the amazement of the French, who believed that no vessel could thread the dangerous channel of the river without a skilled Canadian pilot, the whole fleet went up without a mishap, and by the end of the month was anchored in front of Canada's citadel.

But it was one thing to reach Quebec and another to take it. Though the British guns blazed away at the French walls, they did little more than make some splinters fly. It was obviously impossible to take the place by attacking from the river, and it seemed almost as difficult to attack it by land. The problem was to get a footing on top of the riverbank, which rises precipitously for two hundred feet or more—over three hundred right beside Quebec. A handful of troops on the heights could easily destroy an army landing below. As the summer wore on, the British were as far from their goal as on the day they sighted it. With the arrival of September the time was approaching when the fleet would have to depart, for the British government could not afford to let the winter lock it up there.

A Short History of Canada

At last, we do not know exactly how, Wolfe learned that just above Quebec there was an improperly guarded spot where a winding path led down to a little bay, ever since known as Wolfe's Cove. There he decided to land his army, and he laid his plans with such masterly skill that everything went like clockwork. After nightfall he got his first brigade into small boats some miles upstream, and at a little past two in the morning they began to drift down with the ebbing tide. At about four o'clock these men jumped ashore. Stealthily climbing the cliff they rushed the guard on top. At the first shot the French officer in command leaped from his bed and ran for his life. Then there was some nice work below. Having discharged their men, the boats withdrew between the intervals of the approaching second brigade, which had followed at a distance, and crossed to the opposite shore. There they took on board the waiting third brigade and, returning with it, repeated the dovetail operation to land these soldiers on the heels of the second brigade. Daylight had now come, and as Wolfe's army drew up on the Plains of Abraham the French general, Montcalm, saw that he had to dislodge it to save the town, and he mustered an equal number of soldiers for the task. The battle was quickly joined, and in less than two hours, on the morning of September 13, 1759, the superior discipline of the British decided the day. Wolfe lay dead upon the field, and Montcalm, mortally wounded, was carried into Quebec to die. Five days afterward Quebec surrendered.

A year later this British army and two others, which descended the St. Lawrence from Lake Ontario and the Richelieu from Lake Champlain, closed in on Montreal. There the last French governor of Canada surrendered the whole colony without making any attempt at resistance, which would have been hopeless. The war was over in America. But it was still being fought elsewhere, and peace was not concluded in Europe until 1763 when, by the Treaty of Paris, New France was formally ceded to Britain.

CHAPTER 5

Liberty to be Themselves

IN THE Upper Town of Quebec, overlooking the river, stands a monument for which it would be difficult to find a parallel in any other country in the world. On one side is engraved the name of Wolfe and on the other that of Montcalm. One pile of stone erected to honor these two opposing generals who fell fighting against each other! But the incongruity is apparent only to strangers. In Canada Wolfe and Montcalm are both Canadian heroes, though neither was a Canadian. Their single monument is a perpetual reminder that the country has a dual nationality, and both French Canadians and English Canadians, as a gesture of mutual good will, subscribed the money to pay for it over a hundred years ago.

It was not on the St. Lawrence, however, that the duality made its first appearance, but in Nova Scotia. Though Britain acquired Nova Scotia half a century before she got Canada, the colony down by the sea long remained French in character, with no English-speaking people in it except the little garrison. The first effort to give it an English population came in 1749, when twenty-five hundred colonists were sent out to found the settlement of Halifax. Shortly afterward New Englanders began to arrive from older colonies to the south, and it was not long before they became the backbone of the English population— thanks to the deportation of the Acadians in 1755. This tragic event effected a permanent revolution in the character of the colony. On the eve of their removal, the Acadian inhabitants were about twice as numerous as these English newcomers; but never again did the French outnumber the English in this part of the country, even though most of the uprooted sons and daughters of Acadia wandered back to their old homes in the next few years. The English population grew greatly after the final capture of Louisbourg in 1758, for that victory removed the danger that France might reconquer the land, a danger that had discouraged many New Englanders from settling there. Almost at once, though the war was not yet over, they began to flock in, and this immigration movement continued after the war until it was stopped by the outbreak of the American Revolution. Nova Scotia thus became a real English colony before France ceded the rest of Acadia by the peace treaty of 1763.

Nova Scotia now got something it had never had—an authoritatively defined boundary—and this is important because twenty years later it was adopted as the eastern boundary of the United States. It was set forth in the fall of 1763, when the St. Croix River and a line straight north from its source to the boundary of the Province of Quebec was described as the western limit of the jurisdiction conferred upon the governor of Nova Scotia.

Within ten years of its establishment Halifax, the chief town of the colony, had a population of about two thousand.* It became a flourishing community, for in addition to being the market town of the surrounding agricultural settlement, which did not amount to much, it was a thriving fishing port, it had a considerable garrison, and it was a station of the Atlantic fleet. A lot of money was flowing into the pockets of its townspeople. Since Halifax was a military and a naval town, the British government spent large sums there, and there also the soldiers and the sailors spent their pay—as soldiers and sailors are wont to do! Much of its busy trade was in rum from the West Indies. So great was the traffic in this article that a settler from Boston remarked that the business of one half of the town was to sell it and of the other half to drink it! The first tax to be imposed in Nova Scotia was an excise upon liquor, and many other laws were passed to check the local consumption of this inspiring liquid.

These laws were enacted by an assembly elected by the people, just as in all the other English colonies. The creation of this assembly, it is interesting to observe, was not the result of any popular demand. It was forced upon the governor by repeated orders from the home government, which regarded an assembly as an essential feature of the administration of any colony. The institution, however, was certainly not representative in character. Although the Acadians were now a minority, they formed

* It had shrunk to less than fifteen hundred by 1755.

a considerable part of the population of the colony, for in addition to those who returned after the expulsion there were quite a few who had not been deported. But these people continued to live off by themselves, and they had absolutely no part in the assembly. They were Roman Catholics, and the penal laws of the mother country then excluded all people of that religion from holding office and even from exercising the franchise. The government of Nova Scotia was organized and carried on almost as if the Acadians did not exist. This was possible because they were now a minority.

Though the French might be thus ignored in Nova Scotia, it was utterly impossible to ignore them in Canada after its surrender. There they numbered over 60,000, and they remained practically the whole population of the country. Excepting those who came in the conquering army, only a few hundred English-speaking people entered the country, settling in the towns of Quebec and Montreal. These were mostly army hangers-on or droppers-off—merchants who had accompanied and served the army as sutlers, and discharged soldiers who followed their old taste by settling down as innkeepers.

For almost four years after the conquest Canada was governed by the leaders of the victorious army. They were holding the colony temporarily until France formally ceded it by treaty in 1763, and then they had to continue their administration for another year and a half until a regular or civil government could be set up. Because the army chiefs were in control during this period, which lasted until August 1764, the period is known as the military régime; and for reasons that will now appear this interim government was of great importance.

As a matter of fact the administration of the colony, though now directed by British army officers, was more Canadian in character than it had been during the French régime. It was conducted almost entirely through the natural leaders of the people, the militia captains who in addition to their old duties were given the powers of local magistrates. In this capacity they were required to apply the old laws, and though disputes too difficult for them to decide were brought before courts of British officers, these courts also adhered to the old laws and used the language of the country. Even their records were kept in French.

From beginning to end the military régime was a happy time

for the Canadians. They were heartily sick of war, and at last they could enjoy the blessings of peace. They also made the delightful discovery that the British, whom they had feared as terrible creatures, were really excellent fellows. Immediately after the fighting ceased, the British soldiers—they were not called "tommies" until the Boer War—befriended the habitants, even assisting the men in their fields and their daughters in their kitchens; and the officers proved to be kindly rulers. They did their best to make the people contented and happy. They saw to it that almost everything the army required of the population was justly paid for in cash, and they interfered as little as possible in the daily life of the country.

The explanation of the attitude of the British conquerors is simple. Their victory was so complete that it banished from their minds the fear that might have been the father of cruelty. The result was that both officers and men, living in daily contact with the Canadians, saw how these poor people had suffered during the war, and they pitied them. The officers were also following an established legal principle that the laws of a conquered country remain in force until they are specifically altered by the government of the conquering country. Moreover, they wished to preserve the full value of their conquest. They knew that a populated country is richer than an empty one, and they feared that at least some of the people would depart, as the capitulation and the treaty gave them a perfect right to do, if they did not like the new régime.

The importance of these four years can hardly be overestimated. They planted in French Canadian hearts the very trust in the justice of British rule that has ever since kept the country from being pulled asunder by its dual nationality. These years were also a turning point in the history of Britain's empire. Hitherto, generally speaking, it had been an empire of English colonies. Though foreign settlements, such as Dutch New York and French Acadia, had been added by conquest, they too had become English in character, for their population had been small and English-speaking immigrants had come in large numbers from the mother country or from other colonies. The French of Canada were the first considerable body of foreigners to be included in the empire, and they were the first to taste

Liberty to be Themselves

that larger liberty that has distinguished the British Empire and has contributed to its success—the liberty to be themselves. In short, the conquest of Canada marks the beginning of the change from what had been an *English* empire into the *British* Empire. Unfortunately, however, this fine beginning of British rule in Canada was well-nigh ruined by what followed.

On the signature of peace in February 1763, officials in London turned to consider what should be done with the possessions thus acquired, which in addition to Grenada, Florida, and the rest of Acadia, included the whole of New France as far as the Mississippi. While they were doing this the Indian problem in the interior rapidly became so urgent that they decided to deal with it at the same time and as quickly as possible. The upshot was the royal proclamation of October 1763, which is well known in American history because it established the so-called proclamation line that limited the western expansion of colonial settlements.

It used to be supposed that the object of this delimitation was to cramp the old colonies, but now it is known to have been part of an honest effort to solve this Indian problem, which actually exploded in the bloody Pontiac's Conspiracy before the proclamation appeared. The object was to ensure the independence of the red man rather than to bring about the dependence of the white. By preserving the hunting grounds of the savages from the intrusion of settlers, Britain hoped to destroy the causes of Indian unrest and thereby save herself and her colonies a deal of trouble. So a great native reserve was established, covering the heart of the continent; but there was no intention of cramping the old colonies, for the proclamation also made provision for the future acquisition of portions of the reserved land for the gradual extension of white settlement when this became both desirable and safe.

The proclamation also changed the name and greatly reduced the size of Canada. It was now officially called the Province of Quebec (though unofficially it was still called Canada) and extended over much the same area as the modern province of this name.

Two stretches of the boundary defined in 1763 have affected Canadian-American relations for all time. The international boundary that runs along the highlands above New England to the forty-fifth parallel and along it to the St. Lawrence has its origin in this proclamation, which made this line the southern boundary of Canada, for an interesting reason. The authorities in London were consciously cutting off unoccupied Canadian territory to the south in order to preserve it from French settlement—by annexing it to Nova Scotia and New England. The other stretch that was to have great significance commenced at the point where the forty-fifth parallel cuts the St. Lawrence and runs in a straight line to the corner of Lake Nipissing. How this came to govern Canadian-American relations is better explained in the next chapter. Here what we should note is that it cut Canada off from her natural and historical hinterland because, as we have just seen, this was to be made into a great Indian reserve.

How was this new and strange colony to be governed? The plan adopted in London was quite simple. It followed the traditional pattern: A governor and a council were appointed, and the governor was directed to call an assembly. Nothing was done to change the laws affecting Roman Catholics, with the result that governor, councilors, assemblymen, and all other officials had to be Protestants. In other words, the vast majority of the population were to have no share whatever in the government of the country. Moreover, the law courts were to apply to the French in Canada new and strange laws—the laws of England.

The whole scheme has been condemned as grossly unjust, but it is easy to explain the apparent stupidity of the home government. Officials in London did not understand the situation in Canada because it was so utterly foreign to them, so unlike anything they had ever faced before. Two other excuses may also be found for them. One was their expectation that a large English-speaking population from the south would pour into Canada, giving it a character more like that of the old colonies, and this expectation was not unreasonable in light of the fact that Nova Scotia was then being settled by New Englanders.

The other excuse was the hope that the Canadians might be persuaded to see the true light of religion and turn Protestant. Strange as this may seem today, it was not so very strange then. In Europe, Roman Catholic governments were beginning to

BOUNDARIES OF CANADA ACCORDING TO THE PROCLAMATION OF 1763.

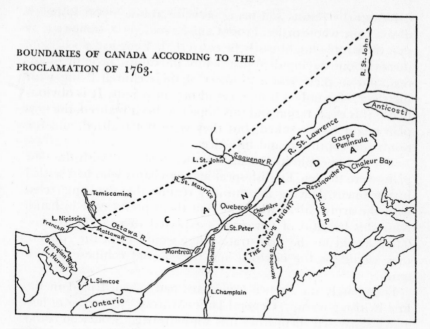

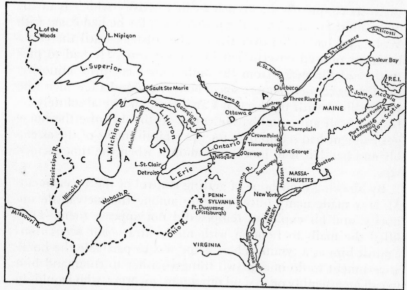

BOUNDARIES OF CANADA ACCORDING TO THE QUEBEC ACT, 1774.

63

drive out the Jesuits and bring pressure to bear upon Rome to dissolve the whole order. From Canada, moreover, came reports that the people might easily be converted. They had no bishop, their last one having died just before the capitulation of Montreal, and so there was a prospect of their church dying with the clergy, for only a bishop could ordain priests. It is obvious that if this expectation and this hope had been realized, the new plan might have worked; but they were not realized, and the result was confusion and injustice.

The only people in Canada who were pleased with the new plans were the few English-speaking merchants who had settled in the towns. During the military régime they had quarreled with the army chiefs, who had kept them pretty well in hand. Now this handful of newcomers expected to rule the colony. They would be the magistrates, they would form the council, they would be the electors, and they would compose the assembly.

Fortunately the French Canadians had a firm friend in the first British governor, General James Murray. No barrier of language separated them from this warm-hearted Scot, who could swear as eloquently in French as in English—which is saying quite a lot! He also knew the people well, for he had come with Wolfe and had ruled over the Quebec district until the establishment of civil government in August 1764. He had to pick justices of the peace from the ambitious mercantile minority; but for his council, a more select body, he found a few men who sympathized with the French Canadians, and he absolutely refused to call an assembly. He could do this because the home government had set no date for the establishment of the assembly and had left it to him to summon it when the time seemed ripe.

By blocking their hope of getting control of the government, Murray made many bitter enemies among the mercantile minority, and his explosive temper did not appease them. They filled the mails to London with most extravagant accusations against him as a tyrant. Their game was to persuade the home government to do one of two things—either to command him to call an assembly or to send out a new governor who would do it. Within two years they had Murray recalled, but they gained nothing by this. Though Murray's successor was of a very different type, a cold and calculating Anglo-Irishman, he was equally opposed to an assembly, which would have given a few hundred English the right to legislate for sixty or seventy thousand French. The new ruler was Colonel Guy Carleton, who became Sir Guy Carleton in 1776 and Lord Dorchester ten years later.

In spite of all Murray and Carleton could do, the government of the colony was a failure. A number of the merchants who had become justices of the peace so abused their magisterial authority that Carleton and the council had to pass an ordinance that took away much of their power and gave it to the judges. The attempt to substitute English law for French law broke down except in one particular. The new criminal law worked satisfactorily, but it was impossible to get rid of the French civil law. The people knew no other, and as their habits were molded by the law under which they and their ancestors had always lived, they continued to follow its regulations in arranging all their affairs. The courts decided disputes over property sometimes according to French law and sometimes according to English law, until at last nobody knew what law ought to be applied. This was very serious, because cases would often be settled in opposite ways according as one law or the other was applied. Furthermore, the absence of an assembly forced the council to undertake the responsibility of legislating for the colony, though it had no legal authority to do so, and left the government of the country without a revenue. The council did not dare to assume the taxing power, and to secure money to carry on the administration the governor had to draw bills on the British treasury. But, worst of all, the French Canadians were excluded from any share in the government.

The policy adopted for Canada in 1763 was utterly impracticable because it took for granted that this old French colony could be made over into a new English one. Imagine an English colony being remade into a French one under similar conditions! On the other hand, the problem of government presented by the cession of Canada was one of the most difficult in the history of the British Empire. As early as 1766 London began to see that there was something seriously wrong in Canada and to work toward a new and more satisfactory policy. For years British officials wrestled with the problem, and the more they wrestled the more they were forced to recognize how difficult and complicated it was. An entirely new approach was necessary, and this was largely provided by one man.

Carleton, practical, hard-headed, realistic, was not long in Quebec before he began to write home explaining what was wrong and what should be done to put things right. His main point was that, as far as one could then see, Canada would never attract English-speaking immigrants and would always remain French in character. He was right, for the Canada to which he referred is the modern Province of Quebec. Convinced that the country was destined to remain French, he urged that it should be given a government to fit this character, a government that would include the real leaders of the people. Only thus could the French Canadians be made loyal subjects of Britain. Otherwise they would yearn after their old mother country and seize the first opportunity to deliver Canada back to France. That such an opportunity might come at any time was clear. Britain and France were still chronic foes, and any year might see them at war again. Nor was this the only cloud on the horizon, for the storm was already brewing that was soon to burst in the American Revolution.

The boundary that took away from Canada the vast interior that had been dependent upon it also wrought confusion and injustice because the plans for the great Indian reserve had gone awry. Though the proclamation of 1763 forbade white settlements in this territory, it encouraged traders to go there, because they would serve the interests of the red men, the colonists, and the mother country. Obviously some kind of government was needed to control the dealings of the traders with one another and with the Indians. Plans for such a government were drawn up in London, but they broke down in America over the question of who would pay for this administration. In London it was supposed that the colonies, as the chief beneficiaries, would pay for it; but the colonies soon disclosed a constitutional objection to paying any taxes, and it was clearly unjust to throw the burden upon taxpayers at home. Then London threw up its hands and left the colonies to work out some method for the proper regulation of this traffic in the interior, and they too failed. The result was that the interior, being left without a government, threatened to become a haven for outlaws.

The fur trade too was in a fair way to being either ruined by lawless competition or stolen by French and Spanish traders who were working up the Mississippi Valley. Canada was chiefly affected and greatly concerned, because most of the trade of this region was conducted from Montreal, as in the days before the conquest. The control of the business had largely passed into the hands of newly arrived British merchants, but the rank and file of those employed in the trade—all the *voyageurs* and most of the traders—were still French Canadians. Therefore French and English, who thus had one interest in common, joined in crying out for the reannexation of this territory to Canada, to which it belonged historically, geographically, economically, and, one might almost say, even ethnically.

At last the home government, after the accumulation of voluminous reports and advices of all kinds, sought to repair the great mistakes that had been made, and its solution for the colony's ills was embodied in the Quebec Act of 1774. This new constitution of Canada was born as the American Revolution was breaking. That there was a connection between the two events cannot be denied, but it must be remembered that for several years the new constitution had been gradually taking shape; and a careful examination of the process strongly suggests that, until it was almost completed, the molding of this constitution was influenced more by the apprehension of another French war and by concern for the feelings and interests of the people of Canada than by fear of a colonial rebellion.

The first article of the Quebec Act extended the boundary of Canada to include the territory that had been cut off in the West —the country north of the Ohio. This change automatically gave a government to a land that had none yet needed one badly, at the same time that it benefited the fur trade by making wise regulation possible. The definition of this new boundary was carefully worded to avoid giving any offense to the old colonies. The line was specifically carried around the northwest corner of Pennsylvania, and to remove any doubt concerning the effect upon that or any other colony a special clause was inserted, though even to this day many Americans have overlooked it in their denunciations of the act. It stipulated "that nothing herein contained, relative to the Boundary of the Province of Quebec, shall in anywise affect the Boundaries of any other Colony." The old colonies' claims to the interior were thus preserved *in toto*.

In the second place, the act gave the colony something it needed but did not have, a legislature. The promise of an elected assembly was formally canceled, but the council was enlarged to make it more representative, and it was given proper authority to pass laws for the country. Though some people still condemn this rejection of an assembly, there were strong reasons against creating such an institution at that time. The small English minority had clamored for one, but they did not want it unless they could control it—an intolerable condition. As for the French Canadians, they neither understood nor desired an assembly; it was an English institution, something entirely foreign to them. Even if they had wanted one, they were not to be entrusted with it, for they were newly conquered subjects whose loyalty to Britain was doubtful in the event of another French war. Though an assembly was thus out of the question, the British government was anxious to give the French Canadians a legislature that would satisfy them. Therefore the new council was to be composed of men of both nationalities, men who would understand the country and the needs of its people. This of course meant opening the council to Roman Catholics.

The act did more for Roman Catholics in Canada than admit them to the council. What had excluded them from this body and from every other public office were the oaths that English laws required of all officeholders before they could assume their functions, these oaths having been purposely worded to prevent any Roman Catholic from taking them. The Quebec Act specifically exempted all Roman Catholics in Canada from having to take any of these oaths, requiring instead a new oath of office so framed that it would not offend Roman Catholic consciences. Such a change was only just and necessary, and it is rather interesting to observe that Roman Catholics thus gained political emancipation in Canada more than half a century before they got it in Britain.

Another thing the act did for the people of this religion in the colony concerned the material foundation of their church.

Liberty to be Themselves

There had been some disquieting doubts about the legal status of the tithe. Was the old law that imposed this payment still in force, or had it lapsed with the cession of the country to a Protestant sovereign? The act swept away these doubts by confirming the old law but, out of regard for the Protestant minority, declared that the Roman Catholic clergy could collect the tithe only from their own people.

The most difficult problem with which the Quebec Act dealt was that of the legal system. For some years it had been apparent that the old laws would have to be restored to some extent, but there had been considerable difference of opinion among the legal advisers of the government, both in London and in Quebec, over how far this restoration should go. The minimum that had to be allowed to the French Canadians was their old law governing real property and inheritance, because that touched them all in a vital way. The uncertainty of the law in these particulars had jeopardized all their individual and family property rights. What the act did was to prescribe English criminal law and French civil law subject to amendment by legislation in Quebec by the governor and council. As the English criminal law had caused little trouble, its continuance raised no serious question. But the return to the old civil law of Canada was not so simple a matter, even though the French formed the great bulk of the population. An unqualified adoption of the old civil law would mean that the little English minority would lose the right of habeas corpus, that they would no longer have jury trials for civil suits, though they would retain them for criminal cases, and that they might no longer have their commercial transactions governed by the laws to which they were accustomed. These things meant nothing to the French Canadians but were most precious to the English-speaking merchants in the colony, and the British government had no intention of allowing them to suffer such an injustice. But how could they be saved from it? The government in London might have attempted to solve the problem by modifying the restored law in the act itself, but this had the disadvantage that it might give the English too little or the French too much, and then the error would have to be corrected by another act of Parliament. The method that was chosen seemed simpler, more practical, and more expeditious. Power was given to the men on the spot to work out a satisfactory solution. That is why the law now established was made subject to amendment by legislation in Quebec, and the governor was formally instructed to advise his council to amend the law so that the minority might continue to enjoy the right of habeas corpus, trial by jury for civil cases, and the operation of their own commercial laws.

One other point remained to be settled in Britain. How was the government of the colony to get a revenue? According to what was recognized as a fundamental constitutional principle in the British Empire, only an elected legislature had the power of imposing taxes; and as the legislature of the colony was not to be elected, the only way left was to have the British Parliament do this important business for Canada. So another measure was passed, the Quebec Revenue Act, which levied customs duties and required tavern-keepers to secure licenses for which they had to pay fees.

Having regard for the exasperatingly complex and novel problem of government that the conquest of Canada had thrust upon Britain, we find it difficult to see what better solution could have been attempted than that embodied in the Quebec Act. Though the French population of Canada could never become English, they might develop into true and loyal subjects if Britain won their hearts by guaranteeing them their religion, their laws, their customs, and their nationality, and by giving them a government that would protect their interests—by freely according to them the liberty to be themselves. This was the hope that inspired the Quebec Act.

Unfortunately the man who applied the act, Governor Carleton himself, more than half defeated its purpose. The Quebec Act won the profound gratitude of the clergy and the seigniors, but that was all. Though in later years the French Canadian people came to consider it the Magna Charta of their liberties, they regarded it very differently then. They became suspicious when they learned the nature of the new government, for the council, as it was now composed, did not represent them at all. To form the French part of the council, Carleton chose only seigniors, because he had sadly mistaken notions about the nature of Canadian society. He never understood how American conditions had emancipated the habitants. He imagined that they were like the peasants of old France, held down by their seigniors. He could not help seeing that they had an independent spirit, but he thought that it was of recent growth, that they had taken advantage of British rule to assert themselves. He had a rigidly aristocratic disposition, and this was not weakened by his wife, an English noblewoman who had lived in the gay French court. He believed that the habitants could, and should, be put in their place again. Of course the seigniors encouraged his illusion and rejoiced at the prospect of becoming what they had never been—the real lords of the land. The result was natural: A great uneasiness spread among the people.

To the community of English-speaking merchants, the act should have brought no injustice. Though it disappointed some by denying an assembly, this was no real grievance because, as we have seen, the only kind of assembly they wanted was one controlled by themselves, and they had no right to any such power over the French Canadian population. The English minority, however, had a great and just grievance because Carleton chose to disobey his instructions. He did not propose the amendments that would have protected them when the old laws were revived. The British government's intention in this regard he kept a close secret. His reason seems to have been a fear that the French Canadians would be offended by any concession to this small group of newcomers. The consequence was that these native-born British subjects not only lost the right of habeas corpus, jury trials for civil suits, and their commercial law but were led to believe that the British government had intended to rob them of all these things, their British birthright. No other people in America, save the inhabitants of Boston, had then as great a reason for reviling the government of the mother country.

Thus it happened that the Quebec Act, instead of spreading satisfaction on the shores of the St. Lawrence, spread something that smelled very like sedition, and this at the very time that the American Revolution was about to break out and threaten a new conquest of Canada.

CHAPTER 6

Canada and the American Revolution

THE British conquest of Canada precipitated the American Revolution. The fall of the French Empire on this continent had a tremendous psychological effect upon the thirteen colonies, for it banished the fear that had held them loyal to their mother country. Though growing to maturity, they had continued to cling to her as long as the great power of France threatened them. Now that this menace was gone, the conscious need for dependence on Britain was gone too. The outcome of the war thus gave them a new spirit of independence that prepared them for the revolution. Then they were pushed toward revolution by the attempt to tax them, another result of the war that had piled an enormous burden of debt on the mother country. The colonies were on the verge of revolt when they were roused by yet another stimulus that sprang from the conquest of Canada —the Quebec Act.

British officials, as we have seen, had had to wrestle with the problem of governing Canada many years before they worked out this solution, and it is not in the least surprising that the whole business was beyond the comprehension of the people in the old colonies. Made sensitive by their own mounting quarrel with the government in London, they naturally interpreted the act as a dastardly blow aimed at them through Canada. By extending the Canadian boundary down the Ohio, was not Britain trying to keep them from expanding westward, just as France had sought to do? By reestablishing Roman Catholicism, which they abominated as the religion of tyranny, and by denying popular government, the very article of their political faith, was not Britain undertaking to forge in Canada a weapon with which to strike them in the back? What other explanation could these startling changes have? Americans could see none. Thus the Quebec Act innocently revived the terrors of bygone days when France threatened them in flank and rear. Now Britain seemed to have stepped into France's shoes, and she was more dangerous because her control of the sea would enable her to strike in front as well. Many Americans at once feared that their cause would be hopeless unless they could prevent Britain from using this French and Roman Catholic colony against them. This is why they invaded Canada in 1775.

The American invasion of Canada might never have occurred, and the Revolution itself might have been nipped in the bud, if the government in London had actually harbored the wicked design attributed to it in the old colonies. Early in 1767 Carleton had urged a plan that would have given British military power a strangle hold on America. With a masterly eye for strategy, he proposed the erection of strong fortifications at New York and Quebec and, to tie these bases together, the restoration and effective garrisoning of the old forts that had guarded the communication between them. When the home government turned a deaf ear to this advice, Carleton began to plead for permission to raise one or two French Canadian regiments for the regular army. If he was thinking of using them against the old colonies, he did not say so in his dispatches home. The only motive he gave was to please the French Canadians, whom France had employed and Britain was neglecting. His repeated prayers went unanswered until after the news of Lexington and Concord reached England. In the fall of 1774, when he was confident that the Quebec Act would win the hearts of French Canada, he felt so little need for soldiers in the colony that he sent away half his small garrison in response to an appeal from Gage, who found himself too weak to cope with the resistance roused by the so-called Intolerable Acts in Boston. As a result when the Revolution began there were less than eight hundred effective soldiers in the whole of Canada, and they were scattered in detachments all the way from Quebec to Michilimackinac.

The door of Canada was wide open for the Revolutionaries to enter, and there were more reasons for this condition than the negligible number of troops in the country. The English-speaking minority were really an American community settled in the heart of Canada. They naturally sympathized with the American cause, and Carleton had hardened their hearts against the mother country by concealing the home government's desire to give them justice. As for the French Canadians, Britain had won the loyalty of the seigniors and the clergy but not of the masses, as we have already observed. They were in a mood to welcome deliverers.

Before appealing to arms, the Revolutionaries tried to neutralize the dreaded Canadians by using propaganda. In October 1774 the Continental Congress addressed them in a long letter, proclaiming their rights as British subjects to government by their own elected representatives, to trial by jury, to habeas corpus, to free tenures, and to liberty of the press. It pointed out how the mother country had violated these fundamental principles by imposing a government composed of tools of the governor, who in turn was the tool of the government in London. It invited them to join in an eternal brotherhood of liberty and, as a first step, advised them to form a provincial congress that would send delegates to the next Continental Congress in May; and it solemnly warned them that they would be treated as foes if they would not be friends. The utter ineptitude of this appeal, of which the unlettered habitants could grasp only the last blunt point, reveals the wide gulf that separated the American Revolutionaries from the French Canadian population and presages the failure of the Revolution to include Canada.

But if the gospel of the Revolution according to Philadelphia could not move the French inhabitants of the St. Lawrence, there were among the English-speaking minority some eager missionaries who knew these people and translated the gospel to suit their taste. Now they were reminded that they had taken an oath not to fight against the English, which of course included their American brethren. They were told that the Bostonians were "as numerous as the stars" and would lay their country waste if they ventured to appear in arms against them. No less effective with a race that had been sickened by perennial wars was the assertion that Britain meant to draft them off to fight her battles under distant skies. These were only some of the wild rumors that, raising untold hopes and fears, went flying through the land during the winter and spring of 1774–75. They were so effective that messages began to pour southward, announcing that the people of Canada were all friendly and would even join in revolt against the mother country.

Canada and the American Revolution

Carleton heard fleeting echoes of what was going on, for here and there a priest laid hands on an incriminating document and reported his find to Quebec. One letter written by the governor at this time betrays a fairly clear consciousness that the ground was slipping from under his feet, and yet he did nothing. He thought of calling out the militia but shrank from doing it. He said it would "give an appearance of truth to the language of our sons of sedition." He seems to have been like a man in a trance until he was startled into action in May 1775.

On the very day after Carleton heard from Gage that hostilities had begun in Massachusetts, another messenger brought news that alarmed him more. Ticonderoga on Lake Champlain had fallen to Ethan Allen's thunderous summons, "In the name of the great Jehovah and the Continental Congress!" The insurgents had immediately seized Crown Point and then had made a momentary appearance at St. Johns on the Richelieu, where they completed their control of Lake Champlain by capturing the one remaining vessel on its waters. The Green Mountain boys had cleared the path for the invasion of Canada.

The governor rushed up to Montreal to direct operations for the protection of the colony. St. Johns, at the northern end of navigation over Lake Champlain, was the bottleneck through which the invaders would pour, and he tried to cork it tightly. He had all summer for the work because the American forces on the lake, being small in number, hastily assembled, poorly organized, and at first disowned by the Continental Congress, were not prepared to deal another effective blow for several months. By the end of the summer he had built and garrisoned a fort at the strategic point. As his available troops were very few, Carleton sought to draw upon the man power of the colony, but he could not draw very much. Though the clergy preached patriotism, the French Canadians as a whole refused to stir. Nor were most of the English much better. He could have turned the tables on the Americans if he had let loose the Iroquois tribes, who now offered to perform this service. Some of his friends, whose loyalty was strongly tinged with vengeance, were insistent that he should frighten "the rebels" with this red nightmare, but, to his eternal honor, he would not yield to this temptation.

Carleton could muster only a few hundred regulars and a few

75

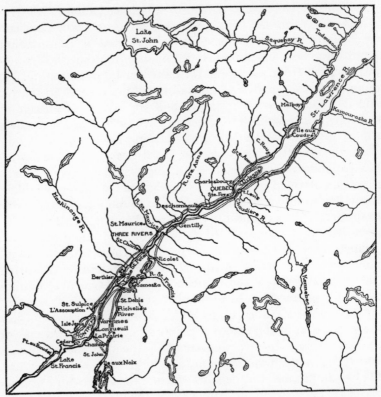

CANADA AT THE TIME OF THE AMERICAN INVASION, 1775.

score militia to hold St. Johns, the back door of Canada. Meanwhile a Revolutionary force several times this number gathered on the lake; for the Congress in Philadelphia, reversing its earlier attitude, declared for the invasion of Canada and its conquest if possible. This decision was partly the result of the battle of Bunker Hill and partly the effect of public opinion in the colonies within reach of Canada. They feared what Britain might do if she were allowed to concentrate her strength there, and they hoped to be able to take the country quickly, knowing that it had only a handful of troops and a disaffected population.

In the middle of September 1775 General Montgomery's army swarmed round the little fort, and some of his men passed beyond to occupy the country as far as the shore opposite Montreal, while others pushed on to the mouth of the Richelieu. The habitants living within the triangle formed by the two rivers treated the invaders like visitors, and several hundred of them turned out as their companions in arms to fight for American liberty— whatever they may have thought this term meant. For nearly seven weeks the further advance of the American host was held up by the little garrison of St. Johns. Then its fall laid the colony wide open to the invaders. They nearly took Carleton prisoner at Sorel as he was hurrying down to Quebec, the only strong place he had left. The victorious army, which now occupied Montreal and all the adjoining country, had as yet no intention of pursuing him. It was actually beginning to break up and go home, because its men had been enlisted for only a few months and they had "done their do." Canada was no longer a sword of Damocles.

Then came word that forced new plans upon Montgomery. Weeks before, Benedict Arnold had started out with about thirteen hundred men on a mad adventure. By going up the Kennebec and down the Chaudière he hoped to surprise Quebec while the governor and all his forces were busy on the Richelieu, but the way was so wild that when the insurgent leader reached his goal he had lost half his men and the other half were in a most bedraggled condition. As soon as Montgomery heard how Arnold had appeared before Quebec, he decided that he was in honor bound to go down and join in the siege of the colony's capital, and he called upon his men to reenlist until spring. He managed to keep only eight hundred, more than half of whom he had to leave as garrisons in the part of the country that he had conquered.

The siege of Quebec began early in December 1775, with the odds decidedly against the Americans. They numbered scarcely a thousand and they were all amateurs, except their general. The garrison was composed almost entirely of amateurs too, Carleton having lost most of his regulars in St. Johns; but the defenders of Quebec were more numerous, and the governor was only one of a group of professional officers who commanded them. The American guns were too few and too light to make any impression on the walls, where more and heavier pieces were mounted. There was no chance of taking the place by blockade, for it had enough supplies to last until spring, when the besiegers' term of service would expire and a British fleet would arrive.

Realizing the futility of bombardment or blockade, Montgomery and his officers decided they would have to take Quebec by a surprise assault under cover of darkness and, if possible, of a snowstorm. They tried it in the early hours of December 31, 1775, when they attacked the Lower Town at both ends and ran into two traps. Arnold, who led the attack on the north side of the town, was not caught, because at the very outset he was wounded and carried back. But more than a hundred of the assailants, including Montgomery, were slain, and some four hundred and thirty were carried as prisoners into the place they had hoped to capture.

They had attempted the impossible. Even if they had taken the Lower Town, they would have been in little, if any, better position to take the Upper Town, which was the real fortress. It has been a British fashion to praise Carleton for saving Canada by saving Quebec on this occasion; but if he had lost Quebec he would have deserved to be courtmartialed. And Quebec would have been soon recovered, for the armament that Britain sent in the spring was calculated to blow out any American garrison. The astonishing thing about the siege is that it was not broken by this terrible repulse. The besieging force had lost half its number and the survivors were attacked by smallpox. Carleton could have swept them away by a vigorous sortie but for some unknown reason he did not try to do so, and there they remained, clinging to their hopeless task, partly out of bravado and partly out of fear of what would happen to them if they withdrew.

In little better plight was the small army occupying the upper part of the colony, where General Wooster was in command. He is reported to have prohibited midnight Mass on Christmas Eve, an insane thing to do in a Roman Catholic country, and he was almost panicstricken by the news of the disaster under the walls of Quebec. When it reached Philadelphia, this news electrified the Continental Congress, but it could not electrify the people because they did not yet have a government and were not yet a nation. However, the congressional resolve to retrieve the disaster and complete the conquest of Canada started a stream of

Canada and the American Revolution

reinforcements flowing north, and congressional commissioners, led by Benjamin Franklin, went up to Montreal to regulate the occupation.

The Revolutionary conquest of Canada was impossible. For all the increase in their numbers, the invaders were not a real army. They were fatally short of guns, ammunition, supplies, and discipline; and smallpox swept through their ranks, many men inoculating themselves to escape duty or to gain immunity. The colonial forces in Canada became a churning mass of confusion. The congressional commissioners threw up their hands and made for home. The French Canadians, who had been so friendly in the beginning, grew more and more hostile to the Americans in their midst. The latter were obviously incapable of bringing the salvation they had promised to the habitants. The exhaustion of American money and supplies also let the burden of the invasion fall on the backs of the people, who were forced to give their goods and their services for nothing. More important still was another influence suggested by the report about Wooster. The invaders were Protestants, and rather bigoted ones, in a Roman Catholic land.

Still more decisive was what Carleton and the home government had done. When St. Johns was beseiged, the governor had written to London again urging his old idea of cutting the American colonies in two. In this dispatch he pointed out that there was no better base for operations than the St. Lawrence and that a completely equipped army of ten or twelve thousand men sent to Canada in the spring "might greatly change the face of things on this continent." This appeal, being followed by word of the fall of St. Johns and the march on Quebec, persuaded the ministry to do exactly what the governor desired.

Here we come upon a crucial turning point in the course of the Revolution, a turning point that has escaped the attention of most Americans because they have been little concerned with what happened north of the border. Though the invasion of Canada was bound to fail, it started a train of events that probably saved the Revolution from being crushed before it gathered much headway. In the first place it diverted Britain's main military effort for 1776 from striking straight at the seat of the war and turned it off to the periphery of the struggle. What would have happened if the powerful armament sent from Britain in the spring of this year had sailed into Boston harbor instead of up the St. Lawrence? But even when it reached Quebec it might still have been used most effectively against the incipient Revolution, as the government in London expected it to be, and it is interesting to see why it was not. To do this we have to examine Carleton's strange behavior during the next few weeks. It is almost incomprehensible.

The besiegers ran away from Quebec "as if the Devil was after them," to quote the words of an eyewitness, when they caught sight of two vessels sailing up the river on May 6, 1776, although they had no idea of what was really coming. They thought they were fleeing from a much smaller reinforcement sent from Halifax, and they were thrown into such wild confusion that they fled for many miles without being pursued at all. Recovering from their panic and strengthened by the arrival of a considerable body of troops coming up from the south, they halted their retreat at Sorel and turned back to capture Three Rivers, blissfully unaware of the fact that Carleton was concentrating his new army there. The result was that they walked right into a perfect trap, which caught some and should have caught all. Most of them escaped when Carleton recalled the contingent that blocked the only way out. Even then the governor had all the Americans in the country still at his mercy. They had not yet discovered how overwhelming was his strength—three score vessels and ten thousand regulars—and they were loath to abandon Sorel.

The whole disorganized body of the invaders was soon in a bigger trap from which not one of them should have escaped. Carleton ordered Burgoyne, who had come with the fleet, to follow but not to press the Americans up the Richelieu while he himself sailed up the St. Lawrence to the vicinity of Montreal with the main body and then marched the fifteen miles to St. Johns to catch them in the rear. He was just below Montreal on the afternoon of Saturday, June 15, and he could easily have reached his objective on Sunday while the retreating Americans were still many miles below. But he sat still while they scrambled on. Late Monday evening they tumbled into St. Johns. On Tuesday, their boats having just come up from the south, they embarked. As the last of them drew out of range, Burgoyne's men dashed into St. Johns. Carleton and his army did not arrive until the next morning, Wednesday!

If Carleton had sprung his trap according to plan, he could have done much more than capture the whole body of the invaders. He could have seized their shipping, and this would have given him what cost him the rest of the campaigning season to procure by building—the command of Lake Champlain and the immediate means of moving his army over it. Then he could have struck straight down the Hudson to New York, according to his original idea and the home government's intention, for the conditions that were to entangle Burgoyne in the following year had not yet developed. Such a cut right down through the middle of the colonies, coming on top of the loss of their northern army, might have made short work of the Revolution. Carleton's amazing delay in reaching St. Johns led to Burgoyne's surrender at Saratoga; this precipitated France into the war; and French sea power tipped the scales against Britain. American independence owes so much to Carleton that he has long deserved a monument in Washington!

There is something very puzzling in this British general who thus refrained from applying his own commanding strategy when at his own request he was fully equipped to carry it out. Apparently the statesman in him had suddenly overruled the soldier. This is suggested by his generous treatment of the prisoners he had taken and by various passages in his letters of that time. He was only one of many prominent Britons who pitied the "rebels" and thought they were "deluded subjects" led astray by designing demagogues. He said he wanted to prove that "the way of mercy is not yet shut," and to give "such testimonies . . . of the humanity and forbearance with which His Majesty's just resentment toward his revolted subjects is tempered as may serve effectually to counteract the dangerous designs of those desperate people whose fatal ascendency over them has already conducted them to the brink of ruin." As the Declaration of Independence was still in the future, he may well have imagined that in letting them all go he was holding his hand from pushing them over the brink. He may also have thought that the blow that he held back could be delivered with telling effect at a later date should his humanitarian calculations prove vain. Neither he nor anyone else could foresee that the military opportunity he threw away was then forever lost.

Another interesting thing that has been discovered by digging into the Canadian archives that touch upon the American Revolution is how complete has been the misconception of Burgoyne's campaign in 1777. It used to be said, and it is sometimes repeated today, that Burgoyne was reaching out to effect a junction with Sir William Howe, who was to have marched north from New York for this purpose and would have done so had not the secretary of state in London forgotten to send him the necessary orders. Now we know that before Burgoyne left Montreal Carleton gave him a letter from Howe saying that he expected to be down in Pennsylvania and therefore could not help him, and that neither Burgoyne nor Carleton seems to have had any misgivings. The idea of Burgoyne's conducting only half a campaign sprang from his capitulation at Saratoga and had no official existence prior to that event.

The consequent entry of France into the war naturally revived the project of conquering Canada. What the Americans had not been able to do by themselves they might be able to accomplish with the aid of their ally. France had more soldiers than Britain, a fleet that qualified her command of the sea, and the ability to exert a tremendous pull upon the people of Canada, who were bound to her by ties of race, language, and creed. In the fall of 1778, the Continental Congress adopted an elaborate plan, which had originated with Lafayette, for conquering Canada the following spring. American forces from various points were to advance on Detroit, Niagara, Oswego, and Montreal, while a French army was to sail up the St. Lawrence to capture Quebec.

Already the foundations of British rule in the North were shaken by the news that France had declared war on Britain. The tidings flew from village to village, awakening old memories and stirring new hopes in Canadian hearts. They leaped at the call of the blood. A few days after the congressional decision was reached, the French admiral in American waters, D'Estaing, published an address in which he appealed to them, saying, "Vous êtes nés français, vous n'avez pu cesser de l'être"; and mysterious hands soon posted this proclamation on church doors throughout Canada. The two classes upon whom Carleton had relied to confirm the masses in their new allegiance were themselves being drawn back to their old allegiance. Sedition was seething on the shores of the St. Lawrence, and the days of Canada as a British colony seemed numbered.

Why did this colony survive as part of the British Empire? There were both American and French reasons. General Washington condemned the scheme before the French government could pass any judgment upon it. He wrote a letter to the Continental Congress heaping up all kinds of material objections, from the impossibility of providing the troops with supplies to the difficulty of coordinating armies operating from widely separated bases and the necessity of first clearing the old colonies of British forces. His real reason he explained privately to the president of the Congress. Would French troops surrender the key of Canada once they had secure possession of it? France, reestablished on the St. Lawrence, and Spain, her ally controlling the mouth of the Mississippi, could throttle the United States. Congress shelved the plan early in January 1779.

But the American desire for Canada was not so easily killed, and Washington changed his mind about the designs of France. In the spring of 1780 and again in 1781, after the surrender of the British army at Yorktown, he revived the idea of a northern campaign. Then the French vetoed it, the first time on the ground that the proper objective was the British headquarters in New York and the second time with the excuse that they had joined the Americans to help them win independence, not conquests. But behind these words lay a deeper reason. The French government calculated that Canada in the hands of Britain would keep the Americans dependent on France, just as, when in the hands of France, it had kept them dependent on Britain. Neither of the allies wished the other to get this colony. Each preferred Britain to keep it. Thus it happened that the alliance that made Canada almost fatally vulnerable was politically, though not physically, incapable of striking the combined blow that might have torn it from the British Empire.

The interaction between Nova Scotia and the American Revolution is a very different story. Nova Scotia did not attract American hostility as did Canada, because the Revolutionaries saw no danger there. Indeed, they hoped that it would join them of its own free will. Three quarters of the population of Nova Scotia were New Englanders who had gone there in the previous twenty years, and their natural sympathies were with the land of their birth. Only a fraction of the other quarter, the English and the Scots, could be expected to show any active loyalty to Britain during the war, for the remainder were Acadians, Germans, and Irish. There was actually such an official distrust of the popular temper of the province that the assembly that had been elected in 1770 was not dissolved until 1785—a colonial "long parliament." Why, then, was Nova Scotia not drawn into the Revolution?

Some have suggested that the material interests of this province, and particularly of its capital, tended to hold it in the empire. What were these interests? One was the annual parliamentary grant that was required to balance the budget of the colony. Another was the local expenditure of British money on military and naval establishments, which was considerable and might be multiplied by the war. Also, according to some, Nova Scotia could hope to supplant New England in the fisheries and the valuable West Indian trade, from both of which the people of the old colonies were now excluded by parliamentary enactment. Halifax would grow fat on the war, and its mercantile community was so identified with the official class that together they formed a fairly solid body that dominated the town and commonly controlled the assembly, where they were overrepresented and where attendance was difficult for the country members.

This combination, however, cannot explain why Nova Scotia remained aloof from the Revolution. Other colonies had been receiving extensive financial aid from the mother country, yet they revolted. Nova Scotia had been, and still was, little interested in trade with the plantation islands, which she could not begin to furnish with supplies. As for the fisheries, so many men from Massachusetts were now evading the legal prohibition by taking up residence in Nova Scotia that British officials were afraid of the political contamination they were bringing. But what of Halifax? The capital was the only real town, but it was a small place and the petty oligarchy that ran it had very little influence over the rest of the province. This was inevitable because the population of Nova Scotia lived in more or less isolated communities scattered around the long, indented coast with scarcely any land communication between them. Halifax could not hold them in the empire, but the very factor that prevented Halifax from holding these dispersed settlements within the British fold also prevented them from leaving it. It was the sea. Who controlled it?

A glance at the only overt attempt to draw Nova Scotia into the Revolution brings out the point clearly. Not all the New Englanders who had migrated to the Northeast had settled on the Nova Scotian peninsula. Some were on the north side of the Bay of Fundy, and some on what is now the coast of Maine. There lay Machias, only a few miles from the St. Croix boundary, which was as yet unidentified, and from Machias came a proposal, submitted to Washington in the late summer of 1775, to dispatch an expedition of a thousand men who would rouse the Revolutionaries and subdue the Tories of Nova Scotia. The shrewd general commended the spirit of the promoters but politely condemned their scheme because any force that invaded Nova Scotia would be cut off by sea. Neither he nor the Continental Congress nor the legislature of Massachusetts would send such an expedition, though the appeal was renewed and reinforced by a growing cry for deliverance from Americans in Nova Scotia.

But Jonathan Eddy, one of the New Englanders who had settled in Cumberland County by the isthmus, was not to be denied. In the fall of 1776 he set out from Machias to take Fort Cumberland, which he knew well. Though he started with only twenty recruits, he counted on gathering others by the way and on rallying most of the population, his own neighbors, when he arrived. At the head of the Bay of Fundy, he landed with seventy-two men, and then he was joined by about a hundred New Englanders and Acadians, but not all these local insurgents ever appeared in arms at the same time. The people of the vicinity had little heart for an attempt to take a fort held by two hundred regulars. Eddy sent back to Boston for guns and men, but the only reinforcement that appeared was for the garrison—two companies of marines accompanied by a man-of-war. A night attack destroyed the camp of the besiegers and blew them away in the greatest disorder. Some sixty inhabitants, too compromised to remain, followed Eddy on his flight back to Machias. The cry for deliverance continued, but there was no further answer save words.

The dispersion of the Nova Scotian population in small settlements isolated from one another rendered them powerless in these days that tried their souls, but even if they had been living in close mutual contact they would still have been powerless. Though New Englanders were the bulk of the population, they were too few to try conclusions with the British garrison, which could be augmented when and as necessary, by sea; and they were too inaccessible to the old colonies for any Revolutionary army to rescue them. Like their Acadian predecessors in this land they were unwilling prisoners of British power and they likewise pleaded for permission to remain neutral.

Before the end of the war, the Continental Congress prepared a constitution that provided for the inclusion of Canada, but not of Nova Scotia, in the new independent union. This may seem curious in light of the fact that Nova Scotia, which was thus rejected, had a New England population while Canada, which was still desired, was completely foreign in character. But the reason for this distinction is clear. No protecting arm of the sea separated the United States from Canada, and for almost another generation Americans continued to live in fear of a British attack from the north, whereas Nova Scotia had never seemed a menace to them and was obviously beyond their reach.

In the peace negotiations in Paris during 1782 one of the greatest difficulties arose over the definition of the boundary between the United States and British North America. There was little trouble over the two parts of the line of which we have already noted the origins, for they were the previous boundaries of Nova Scotia and of Canada as far as the St. Lawrence. The hard problem was to determine where the boundary should run from this point westward. We are so familiar with the line that runs along the St. Lawrence, through the Great Lakes, and up to the northwest corner of the Lake of the Woods that it seems as natural at the watercourses it follows. But it was not natural then, and it calls for some explanation.

Canada and the American Revolution

By agreeing to this stretch of the boundary, Britain gave the United States a huge territory. In all the country north of the Ohio American forces had gained no foothold except in the southwest corner, and that only temporarily under George Rogers Clark, who had been obliged to withdraw. The Revolutionary War closed with Britain still in actual or virtual military control of the whole of the "Old Northwest" of the United States. It belonged to Canada historically, geographically, and economically, as we observed in the last chapter; and most of it continued to be economically dependent on Canada until the end of the War of 1812. Moreover Britain had signed a treaty with the Indians in 1768, following the policy of 1763, guaranteeing this as a native reserve. Why did she promise to give it up?

Britain might not have been so generous in 1783 if she had not cut off the whole of Canada's natural hinterland in 1763. It was the severance of this hinterland in 1763 that necessitated its reannexation to Canada in 1774 as the only way to provide a government for the interior. By this time, however, the growing quarrel between the old colonies and the government in London had reached such a pitch that they interpreted the reannexation as an attempt to coop them up on the Atlantic seaboard. This interpretation created a strong American determination never to make peace as long as the boundary laid down in the Quebec Act was allowed to stand. It would have to be withdrawn to the limit prescribed by the royal proclamation of 1763—the line from the St. Lawrence to Lake Nipissing. This was the decision of the Continental Congress and the demand of the American peace commissioners.

What prevented the United States from obtaining all of what is now the older part of Ontario with the exception of a narrow strip along the Ottawa River was a sudden turn in the fortunes of war in the Old World. The British government was on the point of yielding to the American demand when London heard that Gibraltar had not fallen, as was feared, before a mighty attack of combined French and Spanish forces. At once the British price of peace went up.

The American commissioners then saw they would have to compromise. They offered to continue the international boundary along the forty-fifth parallel to the Mississippi or, if the British preferred (as they did), the river and lake line that we have today. The British accepted it, though it cut through their fur trade, because it was mutually understood that this was to be no ordinary boundary; there was to have been a generous provision for reciprocity so that the British might still possess this trade and even enjoy a sort of commercial empire over the interior. Political developments in England, however, blocked the conclusion of this supplementary agreement.

If the American Revolution took land from Canada, it gave Canada something of far greater value. It gave people, and they were some of the finest in the old colonies. We must not forget that the Revolution was in its nature a civil war in which those who strove for independence subdued or drove out those who opposed breaking away from the empire.

Many Canadians believe that their country received most of the colonial Loyalists, whereas actually it received only a minority. Those who could afford to do so went to live in England. Many returned to their old homes or found new ones in the United States. Some retired to other British possessions, notably the West Indies. The rest settled in what remained of British North America, where the government supplied them with land and provisions to commence life anew. There they exerted a tremendous influence. They had as little love for the United States as Americans had for Britain, and from their settlement sprang that anti-American prejudice that has been the Canadian counterpart of the anti-British prejudice of Americans. But this is only one way in which they left their stamp upon Canadian history. Their very arrival in their new homes wrought fundamental changes.

To Nova Scotia, which still included New Brunswick, went some thirty thousand. They went in 1783 as fast as ships could be found to transport them, and their arrival increased the population threefold. The old Nova Scotia thus experienced a second revolution in its character. It had been French until the expulsion of the Acadians; then it became English, or rather American; and now it became overwhelmingly British.

About nine thousand Loyalists settled on the St. John River, forming the nucleus of the Province of New Brunswick. Nearly as many gathered in the township of Shelburne in the southwest

Canada and the American Revolution

corner of Nova Scotia, while others were planted at Halifax, Fort Cumberland, Annapolis, Digby, and other places. Between two and three thousand took up land in Cape Breton. Some six hundred joined the English-speaking population of about a thousand already living on the Island of St. John, later christened Prince Edward Island in honor of Queen Victoria's father. As might be expected, these various settlements did not retain all who first gathered there. Shelburne, for example, became a ghost town, its people scattering as they found more and better land elsewhere.

For the most part these newcomers were civilian refugees who had been gathered in New York under the protection of the retiring British army. A large number of them were city-bred folk, and not a few of them belonged to what had been the upper class in the old colonies, principally New England. Here were family heads who had been judges, doctors, lawyers, or business leaders. They had lost all their property, but they retained their spirit and their education. It has been said that a list of these Loyalists reads very like an honor roll of Harvard graduates. In later days it was often remarked, as it still is, that the Maritime Provinces have produced much more than their numerical proportion of the leading men in Canada. Of the eleven prime ministers of the Dominion one was born in England, two in Scotland, two in Quebec, two in Ontario, and *four* in the Maritime Provinces. These four include Sir Robert Borden, who led Canada through the last war, and Mr. R. B. Bennett, who has since retired to England and entered the House of Lords as Viscount Bennett. A surprisingly large number of university presidents have also come from the Maritime Provinces. Whether the explanation is their fish diet, as other Canadians often jokingly assert, or their descent from the selected and educated Loyalist stock, we shall not undertake to decide.

Great were the trials these people faced in the early years. They had heard such glowing tales of Nova Scotia that it seemed like the Land of Promise—until they came to live in it. Then it seemed very far from heaven. Their old enemies in the new United States, hearing of their difficulties, chuckled over them and nicknamed the province Nova Scarcity. The trouble was not so much with the land as with the people. Men who had earned a comfortable living in professions or business were not fitted for the rough pioneer task of making farms out of forests, and yet they had to do it to provide food and clothing for their families. Likewise women who had found life easy with the aid of servants were out of place in the backwoods where they had to toil like beasts of burden. The grinding struggle was too great for some Loyalists; it killed them or drove them away. But it could not subdue the large majority. They clung to the land, they conquered their difficulties, and they made the Maritime Provinces.

The Loyalists who laid the foundations of Upper Canada, or Ontario, were of a very different type. They included a few families who soon moved up from the Maritime Provinces, but with this small exception they were almost all backwoods farmers from the interior of the old colonies, chiefly New York. They had lost little property and they had acquired little formal education. Instead of going as a body after the war was over, most of the men had drifted up to Canada by devious routes throughout the hostilities. They went to get a chance to fight, and consequently they were organized in military units that conducted countless raids against the back settlements of the old colonies. Some of their families accompanied them on their first journey through the wilderness, some were rescued in subsequent raids, and some were fetched after the fighting had ceased. These Loyalists were also much less numerous than those of the Maritime Provinces. Less than six thousand—men, women, and children —formed the Loyalist settlements of Upper Canada.

The father of these settlements was the courtly General (later Sir) Frederick Haldimand, Carleton's successor as governor. One of the French Swiss who joined the British army in the middle of the eighteenth century, he had risen to the top of the service by his own merit in an age when political and family connection greatly influenced promotion. He has left upon the history of this period in North America a greater mark than most people know, for he was an industrious collector of all the documents he could lay his hands on. There are two hundred and thirty-two folio volumes of Haldimand manuscripts in the British Museum, and there we find, among many other things, the fullest information concerning the Loyalists who founded Ontario.

These people were to have been placed in Lower Canada. Lord North directed Haldimand to put them on the south side of the St. Lawrence in what have since been known as the Eastern Townships. But the governor objected. He pointed out that they would there be such close neighbors to their old enemies that they might stir up new trouble across the border. Also, he said, this land should be reserved for the French Canadians, who would naturally expand into it and, because of their racial difference, would raise a more effective barrier. His arguments persuaded the home government to agree to the settlement farther west. Only a thousand Loyalists remained in Lower Canada, where he had already found room for them, half around Sorel and the other half on the bays of Gaspé and Chaleur.

The great year of the settlement in Upper Canada was 1784. At least five sixths of the Loyalists were established in a line of townships along the upper St. Lawrence and the adjoining Bay of Quinte. The remainder, except a mere handful who settled across the river from Detroit, were planted at Niagara, the only place where some of them had already begun to cultivate the soil.

The Loyalists in Upper Canada had a much happier early history than those in the Maritime Provinces. Their whole life had been devoted to opening new country, and here they were doing it again but under more favorable circumstances. When Carleton, now Lord Dorchester, visited them in 1788, most of them declared that they were better off and happier than they had been before the Revolution, thanks to the liberal land grants and other generous assistance received from the government.

Still another and more important difference arose from this difference in type that distinguished the founders of Upper Canada from the Loyalists who settled on the Atlantic seaboard. The latter at once became and long remained the dominant element of the population there. The migration from the United States to the Maritime Provinces stopped with the last shipload of refugees from New York. But the Loyalists of Upper Canada soon ceased to be its whole population, and in a few years they even became a minority. Having improved their lot by settling there, they naturally invited friends and relatives whom they had left behind, frontiersmen like themselves, to come and do the same.

They did, and then they repeated the process. It went on and on, increasing with the years until the outbreak of the War of 1812. The Upper Canadian Loyalists were thus only the vanguard of a great army of American immigrants who went to get land. The government welcomed them because they were willing to live under the British flag and were the very kind of people who were needed to develop the country.

The settlement of the Loyalists in what was left of British North America led to its further division. In 1784, to accommodate those who were living north of the Bay of Fundy, New Brunswick was cut off from Nova Scotia and made a separate colony with its own governor, council, and assembly. In the same year Cape Breton was also separated, but it had a much smaller population and was not given an assembly. Since the Island of St. John, as Prince Edward Island was called until the end of the century, had already been erected into another colony in 1769, what had been Nova Scotia was thus split into four parts, only one of which retained the old name. This division of British North America was soon carried one step further—in Canada—but meanwhile there was a move in the opposite direction.

The loss of the richest and most populous part of Britain's colonial empire inspired her political leaders to attempt to draw together what was left of the American wreck. To this end, lieutenant governors were substituted for governors, and the colonies were placed under one governor-in-chief. This change, by the way, foreshadows a condition in the Dominion of today. There is no governor in all Canada. Each province has only a lieutenant governor and the Dominion has a governor general. The man selected to consolidate British North America was Carleton. In 1786 he was raised to the peerage as Lord Dorchester and sent out to Quebec, which was to be his principal residence. But the idea of the government in London could not be carried out for another eighty years. Distance worked against it. Because the only communication between his capital and the Maritime Provinces was by sea or by foot, it was impossible for Lord Dorchester to exercise his authority over those colonies. On top of this disappointment came another that completed the ruin of the high hopes with which he sailed from England. Canada itself was divided.

Canada and the American Revolution

The coming of the Loyalists unsettled the Quebec Act by destroying its foundation. At last, a quarter of a century after the conquest, a rapidly growing English-speaking population appeared beside the French, and the colony needed a new constitution to fit its new character. But officials in London could not see what should be done, because there was a difference of opinion in the old Province of Quebec. As in earlier days, the mercantile minority cried out for an assembly and now they got many French Canadians to join them. On the other hand, the seigniorial class cried out against an assembly, and they too gathered a large following. Few people in either group seem to have had a clear notion of what they were doing. Then there were the Loyalists living west of the Ottawa. They wanted a separate government for their part of the country; but those living east of the Ottawa, English as well as French, denounced such a demand. The much-perplexed home government asked Dorchester for guidance, but he too was puzzled.

The home government was finally brought to a decision by the problem of finance. The proceeds of the Quebec Revenue Act had fallen far short of what the colony needed, and the mother country was having to pay the difference. The colony needed more revenue, but Parliament could not repeat what it had done in 1774 because, after the unfortunate experience with the American colonies, it had passed an act in 1778 declaring that it would never again tax a colony. The only way left to provide what was needed was to have the people of the colony tax themselves through their elected representatives. An assembly would have to be established.

This conclusion forced the adoption of another plan that had already been considered, the division of the old Province of Quebec into two separate colonies, since one assembly for the whole was plainly impossible. The country was too large, and there was too great a difference between the older French Canadian society on the lower St. Lawrence and the new Loyalist settlements above. So in 1791 an imperial order in council divided the country into Lower and Upper Canada, and earlier in the same year Parliament passed the Constitutional Act, which provided each with a government after the traditional English colonial pattern.

CHAPTER 7

Bad Neighbors: The War of 1812

THOUGH the United States and Canada have set an example for the rest of the world by living side by side in peace and growing friendship for more than a century, for many years after the recognition of American independence they were bad neighbors. We are all familiar with the tragic fact that the most serious damage war inflicts is the suspicion and hate it leaves in people's minds and hearts. The American Revolutionary War was no exception. As soon as Britain and the United States signed the peace treaty, both violated it. Each side entered upon this unhappy course quite independently and then tried to cast the blame upon the other. The result was a nasty quarrel that in 1794 nearly involved British North America in war with the United States.

The British complaints were over debts and Loyalists. According to the treaty, British creditors were to meet with no legal obstacle to the recovery of their debts in the United States; Congress was to recommend to the various state legislatures that they restore property taken from the Loyalists, who were to be free to return and to remain unmolested for a twelvemonth while they endeavored to recover what they had lost, and there were to be no further prosecutions or confiscations arising out of anyone's participation in the war. But London merchants were unable to collect American debts, and except in South Carolina, where considerable justice was done, the "traitors" still suffered.

The difficulty lay in the fact that the United States had not yet established any real national government. The state legislatures were sovereign, and they had not signed the treaty. Nor had they given to Congress any authority to undertake obligations that might bind them. The men who signed the treaty for the United States—John Adams, Benjamin Franklin, and John Jay—were merely the agents of Congress and were therefore unable to give, though they might receive; and during the negotia-

94

tions they carefully explained to the British that, while they might make promises, they could not guarantee that these would be kept. As a matter of fact these promises were for the most part carried out. With great difficulty better-thinking Americans made the legal changes necessary for the collection of British debts, but to put these changes into effect required several years, and meanwhile the British were naturally irritated. Congress kept its word in sending recommendations in favor of the Loyalists, and, strictly speaking, the failure of the states to respond by restoring the seized lands and other goods was no breach of the treaty.

But the treaty was broken by the continued seizure of Loyalists' property and by the mistreatment of Loyalists when they returned to get what they had lost. Not a few were tarred and feathered, and many were again glad to escape with their lives. As we have seen, Congress had no power to protect these Loyalists, but no knowledge of its helplessness could keep British blood from boiling angrily over tales of persecuted Loyalists; and it should not be forgotten that the great majority of the English-speaking population of British North America on the morrow of the Revolution was composed of these exiles from the United States.

The British violation of the treaty has been much better known in the United States, just as the American violation has been better remembered in Canada. Because the war had ended with British forces still occupying American territory, the treaty bound Britain to evacuate this territory "with all convenient speed." She quickly withdrew her forces from New York, but she made not the slightest move to recall her garrisons in the interior at the upper, or western, posts, the chief of which were Oswego, Niagara, Detroit, and Michilimackinac. Because these posts were the keys to the country south of the international line drawn through the Great Lakes, Britain thus retained control of an enormous area that she had just signed away. Why?

British writers have justified the holding of these places as a reprisal for the American treatment of debts and Loyalists, while Americans have insisted that it was simply an attempt to hold this territory because of its valuable fur trade. We now know that both were wrong and that the prime cause was fear of the

Indians, who really owned the land between the Great Lakes and the Ohio. Britain had actually forgotten her red allies and protégés in the negotiation of the boundary, until it was too late. The Indians naturally accused her of betraying them by promising to give their territory to their enemies, the Americans, and they threatened to massacre not only the Americans who tried to enter it but also the British who were there. Only twenty years had passed since Pontiac's revolt, and it seemed there might be another bath of blood in the interior.

To avoid this catastrophe Governor Haldimand persuaded the home government that the garrisons should not be removed and suggested that the Loyalists might be pleaded as an excuse. Being careful to keep clear of the forts held by British soldiers, American forces invaded the territory that was theirs by treaty, but they were defeated with great slaughter by the redskins. Only the weakness of the American government and the strength of some of its leaders prevented an attempt to seize the western posts by force, which would certainly have renewed the war with Britain. Though every British official who had anything to do with the nasty situation strove his utmost to persuade the Indians to make peace with the United States, the Americans naturally blamed the British for this continuance of the native war in the West. The mere presence of the British garrisons, intended to keep the Indians quiet, encouraged them to resist every American advance. And where did these red men get the arms and ammunition for their bloody work? From British traders in these posts on American soil!

Instead of improving, the situation grew steadily worse, and Britain found new reasons for clinging to the keys of the West. Here it is necessary to recall a half-forgotten chapter in American history. These years were the so-called critical period of the young Republic, when its whole future was darkly clouded. The loose union born of war began to dissolve on the advent of peace. The thirteen colonies, having thrown off the yoke of one superior power, were reluctant to place their necks under another, even one of their own making. The country had only a shadow of a government, and that faded away in the fall of 1788, when the Continental Congress expired of inanition. For nearly six months there was not even a shadow of a government, and when the constitution, ratified by only nine of the thirteen states, gave birth to the government of the United States in 1789, there were grave doubts about the life of the new infant. Meanwhile the obvious indications that the United States might soon fall apart conjured up before British eyes a tempting vision. It was the possibility of building an empire in the heart of the continent to make up for what had been lost on the seaboard. Time alone could tell whether this could be realized, and, so far as we know, the British government considered no positive move on the confused American chessboard. However, the advantage of playing a waiting game could hardly be missed in London. A premature surrender of Britain's strategic position on the Great Lakes, based on the retention of the posts, might throw away the opportunity of winning an enormous prize.

While Britain was still waiting to see what might happen in the interior of America, France unconsciously came to the rescue of the United States when she declared war on Britain early in 1793. Then Britain found her hands so full in Europe that she wanted to get free of possible difficulties in the New World. At the same time the growing danger of war with the British over the Indian territory moved President Washington to send John Jay, who had been one of the negotiators of the peace treaty and was now the first Chief Justice of the United States, on a special mission to London to settle outstanding Anglo-American differences. The result was Jay's Treaty of 1794 by which Britain promised to evacuate the posts in 1796 in return for an American promise not to interfere with the Canadian fur trade in this American territory. As the conclusion of the treaty coincided with the Battle of Fallen Timbers in which Anthony Wayne at last crushed the Indian confederacy in the West and persuaded the tribes to accept the sovereignty of the United States, the heavy cloud that the Revolutionary War had left hanging over Canadian-American relations was largely dissipated.

Of even greater historical importance was a remarkable innovation conceived by Jay himself—and it was a happy circumstance that it occurred so early in the history of the United States. By providing for the arbitration of various outstanding disputes, including that over the collection of debts mentioned above and the one that had arisen over the identification of the St. Croix

River boundary, Jay's Treaty inaugurated the modern use of the judicial process in international affairs. Nowhere else has this practice been so useful as in the regulation of Canadian-American relations, but though here it has proven to be indispensable it could not prevent the outbreak of war in 1812.

The United States was caught between Britain and France, who were then engaged in the mightiest struggle the modern world had yet seen. Napoleon was trying to bring the whole of the Old World under his sway, and only Britain, protected by her sea power, seemed to stand in the way. Unable to invade the island kingdom, he tried to reduce it by his continental system, by shutting the European continent to British goods and British vessels—a sort of inverted blockade. He decreed that any vessel touching British shores would be regarded as a hostile craft. Britain replied by orders in council which declared that she would treat as an enemy any ship that sought to enter a port controlled by Napoleon without first going to Britain. All this meant that neutral vessels could not approach a European port without being liable to seizure, either outside by the Royal Navy or inside by Napoleon's officials. There were many seizures of American ships and cargoes by both sides; and the United States, the only important neutral left, had thus ample justification for declaring war on both France and Britain. But though such an action was unthinkable, on the other hand, national honor demanded action to defend American rights. For some time the government in Washington tried to escape the dilemma by playing one power off against the other, but ended in being tricked into the false belief that Napoleon had revoked his decrees and that Britain remained the sole offender.

The other great issue in the Anglo-American quarrel was impressment, for which there was no counterpart in Franco-American relations. Britain's sea power, the only thing that stood between her and downfall, was threatened by a drain upon its very lifeblood—the desertion of British sailors to the American mercantile marine. Therefore she insisted upon searching American ships on the high seas and removing fugitive British seamen from them, which often meant the kidnaping of American sailors, who were then commonly indistinguishable from British sailors in dress and speech. This impressment of men sailing under the Stars and Stripes was the British counterpart of the unrestricted submarine campaign launched by the Germans a century later, in that it touched American lives.

Contrary to an old tradition in the United States, British tampering with American Indians was not a cause of the war. It is true that there was growing trouble with the western tribes, but this was of American origin, and an examination of the Canadian archives reveals that British officials used what influence they had gained from their trade connections to keep the Indians from breaking the peace established in 1794.

Though the United States went to war in defense of its maritime rights, it is a notorious fact that the maritime interests of the country—concentrated in New England—were almost solidly opposed to the war, and this apparent contradiction calls for some explanation. The opposition of the maritime interests is quite understandable. New England would soon be strangled economically unless her ships were free to ply the sea. She was therefore willing to submit to the conditions imposed by Britain, the mistress of the seas. It seemed to the South, whence came most of the voting strength that carried the resolution for war, that New England would sacrifice the national honor for a mess of pottage; and national honor had to be upheld. Moreover the South, being engaged in the production of staples that were chiefly consumed on the continent of Europe, was the one section of the country that was vitally dependent on access to the markets controlled by Napoleon. It was not a commercial region, but its very life was tied up with commerce. Here was another reason for championing the maritime interests in their own despite.

It has often been asserted that the war was unnecessary and that it might have been averted had there been an Atlantic cable in those days, because Congress voted for war not knowing that Britain had just repealed the orders in council. But as a matter of fact the repeal was not effective. It was loaded with conditions that the American government could not accept; and Britain refused to budge on the impressment issue. Indeed there is now little doubt that the war would have come long before it did if the United States had been better prepared for it.

The war itself was one of the strangest that was ever waged, and stranger still have been the accounts of it in the school texts of Canada and the United States. There have been sensible revisions of late, but forty years ago in Toronto some Canadian boys had a lively altercation with American visitors of their own age, each group crying, "We licked you in 1812!"—so different were the versions they had been taught.

Few Canadians realize, though few Americans ever forget, that the War of 1812 was oceanic as well as continental. The nature of the war at sea was simple. No battle between fleets was possible because the United States Navy was then negligible and the Royal Navy was invincible. So each side sought to reduce the other by crippling its commerce in the only way it could, the Americans by raiding and the British by blockade. But all the prizes gathered by American raiders made little impression on the British mercantile marine, and though Americans remember with just pride that their government's frigates took a handful of British war vessels in single-ship engagements, these victories had no military value because the consequent reduction of the power of the Royal Navy was infinitesimal. It should also be remembered that there was some profitable British privateering too, from a natural quarter, Nova Scotia. To the Nova Scotians, fighting in this war meant sailing under letters of marque; and relatively they were as successful as the Americans.

The decisive factor in the naval war was the blockade of the American coast, with the exception of one part to be noted presently. This blockade stifled the maritime activity of the United States and thereby crippled the power of the American government to continue the war on land. It was doing this very effectively even before the fall of Napoleon released a powerful army of British veterans for use in North America. Then, too, we must not overlook the point that as a last resort British sea power could have been used to make the United States disgorge even a considerable land conquest. Here was an ultimate guarantee, which was not called upon because it was not needed, that British North America would survive the war.

It was not on the sea but on land that the war was a strange affair. The American military objective was as plain as a pikestaff. The only way in which the United States could hope to wring from Britain a recognition of the American rights she had

The War of 1812

violated was to strike her where she was vulnerable, to conquer as much as possible of her adjoining colonies while her hands were tied in the Old World.

It seems to us now that the United States could have overrun most of these colonies easily. They had less than five thousand regulars in scattered garrisons, and the mother country could not be expected to send any aid while she was engaged in her life-and-death struggle with the European monster. All together these colonies had a population of scarcely 500,000 as against 7,750,000 in the United States. Of this 500,000 the majority were French, who had been sullenly neutral during the War of Independence and were now openly resenting the rule of their British masters, and the minority included a large proportion of Americans, who formed the bulk of the Upper Canadian population. Moreover, British North America was a long, thin line of settlement that was not even continuous, and it stretched for more than a thousand miles along an indefensible border.

There was only one thing that matched this wonderful opportunity for American conquest, and that was the way the forces of the United States muffed it. Indeed this was more wonderful. At no time did they make even the slightest attempt to strike at the Maritime Provinces, though they had in New Brunswick a long land frontier exposed to military attack. The only military activity in this quarter was British—the conquest of a considerable portion of Maine in 1814. Turning westward, we find that the second American siege of Quebec, of which there had been loud talk, quickly became a forgotten dream, and the plans for an invasion of Lower Canada collapsed at a touch. True, there was an effort to conquer Upper Canada, but not the oldest and most settled part of it, where the main Loyalist settlements were, and this effort brought precious little result—the American occupation of the small southwest corner of the province. On the other hand, and this was most serious, the whole of the American territory between the Great Lakes and the Mississippi fell under the sway of the British.

Were the Canadian boys right after all, when they cried, "We licked you"? Superficially they were, because the military object of the British in these colonies was to save them from being conquered, and they succeeded. Really, however, these saucy boys were wrong. The meager forces of British North America were on the whole victorious, but over what? Not the United States! One might almost say that there was no such country at that time, except in name.

Serious as it was on the British side, this was actually a "phony" war on the part of the Americans. There would probably have been little left of British North America before Napoleon fell, if division in the United States had not offset the distraction of Great Britain. The American nation was split as it had never been before and, with the exception of the Civil War period, has never been since. The opposition to the war was intense; and it was largely sectional, being concentrated in the North. It divided New York and, what was much more important, it dominated New England, the most solid part of the Republic. Many Americans outside New England were very squeamish about striking Britain in the back while she was fighting Napoleon to preserve her own and Europe's freedom; and to New Englanders the idea was an utter abomination. In their minds the American declaration of war was the betrayal of the whole country, its interests and its honor, by the party in power, who had sold out to the terrible Emperor of France.

Although we know that the government in Washington had entered into no such nefarious pact and was honestly seeking to do its duty under most trying conditions, the opposite belief was hysterically held in New England, and it burst out in all sorts of ways. Massachusetts had a publicly proclaimed fast; flags flew at half-mast in Boston; state legislatures, county conventions, and town meetings passed denunciatory resolutions; and the pulpit, still a power in the land of the Puritans, thundered against the awful thing that had been done in the nation's capital. New England refused to fight and was therefore excluded from the British blockade. The result was that New England actually continued to trade, as if it were a friendly neutral, with its British neighbors. The furious opposition in this part of the country grew as the war progressed, culminating in a serious movement for secession from the Union. Then the governor of Massachusetts sent an agent to Halifax to broach the subject of a separate New England peace and an alliance with Britain; and the Hartford Convention seemed like the beginning of an inde-

The War of 1812

pendent New England confederacy. Fortunately for the United States, at this very time peace was being concluded across the Atlantic in the old city of Ghent.

Returning for a moment to a consideration of the war itself, we can readily see why the Maritime Provinces enjoyed their immunity from attack. New England shielded them. It also largely paralyzed the military strength of the country as a whole, though it could not stand in the way of a drive on Lower Canada and was still farther removed from Upper Canada. But great as were the difficulties created by New England they do not wholly explain the poor showing of the United States in this war. The plain truth is that the mass of the people, even outside New England, were not convinced that their vital interests were in any grave danger, nor were their passions roused by any flagrant national insult. This war was very close to the borderline where a mere severance of diplomatic relations suffices to preserve national integrity and honor. There was little American will to fight.

Nor was this all that was wrong. The fighting resources at the command of the administration were hopelessly mismanaged. "The forces of the United States struck at the leaves and branches of British power in the north instead of attempting to cut it down by attacking the trunk, on the lower St. Lawrence." British agents could not have supported the Indian war in the American Northwest without supplies forwarded from Montreal over the old and expensive route of the Ottawa River and Georgian Bay, or over the newer and cheaper one of the upper St. Lawrence and the Lower Lakes. Upon the latter line of communication, also, all the British forces in Upper Canada, land and lake, were vitally dependent for supplies and reinforcements. It was a single line along the water, and severance at any point meant the loss of everything above. Montreal was the place to strike. There the two routes from the West came together, only a few miles from the American border. There, with one fell swoop, the Americans might have ended the native war in their own country and sliced off the whole of Upper Canada and the richest portion of Lower Canada. There success would have given a strong impetus toward the capture of Quebec, which could not be relieved from overseas until the summer of 1814, and the fall of Canada's

103

citadel would have locked Britain out of the whole land. Everything else should have been sacrificed to strike this decisive blow down Lake Champlain and the Richelieu, over which many expeditions had passed in previous wars. But the military energies of the United States were dissipated in scattered and desultory fighting over the wide region of the Lower Lakes, where there should have been no fighting at all.

What excuse can be found for such astounding stupidity? Did the recurrence of the hideous Indian nightmare serve as a distraction to pull the war westward? Apparently not, for the military operations were mostly centered on Niagara, which was about as far away as the American forces could get from the British line of communications with the American West. A key to the mystery may be found in the proclamation of General Hull when he crossed from Detroit into Upper Canada at the very beginning of the war. Addressing the people of the province, he said, "The arrival of an army of Friends must be hailed by you with a cordial welcome. You will be emancipated from Tyranny and Oppression and restored to the dignified station of Freemen."

Hull and many of his countrymen were thinking in terms of a triumphal progress of liberation rather than of regular warfare, and this seemed the proper place to begin such a pleasant crusade. Lower Canada was much less inviting. The French might have little love for their British rulers but they had less for their American neighbors, as had been shown a generation before. Upper Canada was very different. The only part that was strongly British in sentiment was along the upper St. Lawrence and the Bay of Quinte. The rest, with a small exception at Niagara, was predominantly American; and this fact was well known in the United States. If we may judge from the despairing correspondence of General Brock, who was then responsible for the government and the defense of the province, there was much truth in what was then a common American belief, that Upper Canada was ripening to fall into the lap of the United States. Indeed, the attempt to pluck the fruit might have succeeded if American confidence had not been so overweaning as to scorn proper military preparations.

The secretary of war, a "shiftless politician" whose name is

The War of 1812

now more than half forgotten, actually said that the people in Canada would rise in a body if only American officers would lead them in throwing off the British yoke. As a matter of fact he did send soldiers, but they were badly organized, badly disciplined, and badly led. Therefore the small British forces in Upper Canada were able to hurl back the invasion, and their vigorous action under the bold and able leadership of Brock rallied doubtful elements in the population. There was still disaffection, but the province was no longer ready to fall.

The quality of the American forces, which could hardly have been worse than it was in 1812, was considerably improved in 1813, but this was of little avail because of the defect higher up. Though there was a new secretary of war who aspired to direct the campaigning and had some idea of what should be done, he was incapable of doing it. He lacked the commanding intelligence and the daring to expose the western flank, once it had been engaged, in order to win the war on the lower St. Lawrence, the only place where it could be won. About the only sensible American operation during this year was on Lake Erie, where the little American fleet disposed of the weaker British one. This forced the British to abandon Detroit, which they had taken in the previous year, and to withdraw from the adjoining corner of Upper Canada.

In the same season an American force crossed Lake Ontario and occupied York, now Toronto, for four days. This raid had an important result, though it was not military: Soldiers burned the provincial parliament buildings, and looters entered private houses, the public library, and the church. American officers in command later disclaimed responsibility for these actions. A year and a half after the event General Dearborn protested that the burning was done without his knowledge and against his orders, and when the war was over, Commodore Chauncey at his own expense sent back all the plundered books and plate that he could collect. But these words and deeds could not alter the fact that the invaders had begun in the capital of Upper Canada a disgraceful game that led to the more famous destruction of the capital of the United States in 1814.

In this year the collapse of the big war in Europe, when the Allies occupied Paris and banished Napoleon to Elba, turned this little war in America upside down. Now the military issue was not whether the United States would conquer British North America but whether the British would not reconquer some of the United States. The government in London was set on doing this, partly as a punishment for the attack on the empire in its hour of peril and partly to gain a more defensible frontier on this continent; and the great Duke of Wellington was invited to undertake the task. What shook this determination was the unsettled state of Europe and Wellington's advice that no military conquest of any value to British North America was possible without naval control of the Lakes, which would take some time and effort to win. Thereupon the British government decided to end the war, and on Christmas Eve, 1814, peace was signed with the American commissioners, who had been vainly negotiating with British agents in Ghent for several months.

Though peace was signed there was not yet a real peace settlement. That came afterward. The Treaty of Ghent was a negative thing. It provided for a mutual restoration of territory taken during the war and for boundary commissions to settle differences that had arisen or might arise over the boundary from the Bay of Fundy to the Lake of the Woods. But it did little else except terminate hostilities. It contained not one word about the causes of the war. Impressments and the orders in council, it is true, were no longer practical questions, for they had been a byproduct of Britain's struggle against Napoleon, who was now overthrown. But there were other questions that had arisen and would have to be solved if there was to be real peace between the United States and its British neighbors, and the Treaty of Ghent was silent upon them too. This was not because the authors of the treaty had ignored the questions. These men had wrestled with them desperately but had been able to do nothing with them except leave them. Their failure was perhaps fortunate, for it meant that the treaty did nothing that had to be undone, which is more than can be said for many treaties of peace, and that the problems it left unsolved were settled in an atmosphere of peace rather than of war.

The War of 1812 had results more important than most people realize. It suddenly stopped the peaceful American invasion of Upper Canada and it checked a renewal of this invasion afterward, for it opened British eyes to what had been happening. And too it stifled the potentially American character of the population of the province by purging it of the small minority who were incorrigible republicans and by corraling within the British fold the great majority whose political consciousness had not yet awakened. These changes draw an added significance from the fact that the tide of immigration from the British Isles, though it had begun earlier to pour into this province, did not become a flood until a full fifteen years after the outbreak of hostilities. Then it might have been too late for these newcomers, themselves not very self-conscious politically, to impress a British character upon the country. In other words, the war cut the growing connection between the United States and Upper Canada as if with a knife.

More generally the war left its stamp upon the Canadian spirit as it did not upon the American. It greatly reinforced in Canada the anti-American prejudice that dates from the American Revolution. Canadians have never been able to forget the fight to save their country from being conquered by the United States.

On the other hand, contradictory as it may seem to what has just been said, the experience of this war brought into clear relief a fundamental condition that made for better relations between the United States and its British neighbors, and that was pointed out by the American peace commissioners during the negotiations at Ghent. When the British demanded a drastic revision of the boundary to make the Canadas less vulnerable, the Americans replied that this was not necessary, and the reason they gave is interesting. They said that Britain already had sufficient security against an attack on her empire in the interior of the continent—her undoubted ability to strike a more damaging blow on the Atlantic seaboard of the United States. Whether this argument had any influence in persuading London to end the war, we do not know; but it was so obviously true that there was no denying it, and it undoubtedly explains much that followed. Though these interior colonies lay exposed to an American army, the young Republic was equally vulnerable to the Royal Navy; thus a strong mutual disposition to maintain the peace, now that it was restored, soon became noticeable in

Washington and London. If anyone doubts the significance of this condition, let him look at the opposite side of the United States and see what happened to Mexico after a few years. Americans then took from that helpless country the huge territory they wanted—now a whole belt of states in the Union!

The War of 1812 was like a thunderstorm that clears the air. Of course it would be a mistake to imagine that the spirit of hostility suddenly vanished along the international border. Here and there officious individuals on both sides would have rekindled the flames of war, but these overzealous underlings soon found that they could not engage their principals in a quarrel. The British government and the American government, far from being disposed to bicker, displayed a healthy desire to transform what was little more than a truce into a lasting peace.

One of their most memorable achievements was disarmament on the Lakes. This was not a new idea. John Adams had proposed it during the peace negotiations in 1782, and Jay had done the same in London in 1794. Then it had lain dormant until awakened in a rather unpleasant form by the War of 1812, when first the American government and then the British hankered after a one-sided arrangement to prevent naval competition on these waters by exclusive possession of the Lakes. The American failure to win the war and the British decision not to continue it blocked any such settlement, and the Treaty of Ghent was silent on the question. Yet the war had started a naval race on the Lakes that could not be stopped by the mere termination of hostilities. Though the American vessels were straightway laid up, leaving the British in greater strength, resumption of the race was certain unless the British agreed to call it off. Having taken the initiative with its own vessels, the American government followed it up with a suggestion that Britain agree to put an end to the dangerous game. The immediate reaction in London was a suspicion that the United States was perhaps trying to play a clever trick, for if trouble developed, far-off Britain would be caught at a disadvantage. But the suspicion was quickly brushed aside, and it is not difficult to see why.

Geography had loaded the dice against Britain on the Lakes. The break in navigation, which prevented her from sending in vessels from the sea, reduced the naval command of the Lakes to a question of local building. In this the United States would have the advantage of being on the spot, unless Britain were allowed a superiority in time of peace. But the strategic importance of the Lakes was such that American opinion could not long tolerate British superiority there even in peacetime. For Britain would then be able to strike a deadly blow at will. The conclusion was obvious: Britain could never hope to win the race on these confined waters. Why, then, should she keep any fighting forces on the Lakes? They would be of no use there or anywhere else because of the falls at Niagara and the rapids on the St. Lawrence. In accepting the principle proposed by Washington, London simply bowed to the inevitable. Peculiar conditions rather than peculiar national virtue, American or British, were primarily responsible for the Rush-Bagot agreement for disarmament on the Lakes that was signed in 1817.

More remarkable was the general agreement reached in the convention of 1818. It was the major peace settlement after the War of 1812, and it deserves to be much better known than it is. It settled a number of serious differences that had arisen before the war or were raised by it, differences that had reduced the negotiators in Ghent to an absolute deadlock.

To understand these tangled disputes, we have first to go back to the peace treaty of 1783. This treaty declared that the boundary from the northwest corner of the Lake of the Woods should run straight west to the Mississippi, which was impossible of course, though no one knew it at the time; it guaranteed the British the same rights as Americans to navigate the Mississippi from its mouth to its source, that river then being the western limit of the United States; and it gave American fishermen the "liberty" to ply their calling within territorial waters of British North America, where they had enjoyed a "right" to do this while they were still British subjects. We have also to bear in mind that the third article in Jay's Treaty of 1794 bound the United States not to interfere with the British fur trade in the American Northwest—the price paid for the British surrender of the western posts on American soil. Next we have to recall that after the Louisiana Purchase of 1803 the status of the Mississippi River changed; it ceased to be an international stream. Then we have to observe a general, though not an absolute, principle of international law: that the outbreak of war automatically cancels previous treaty obligations between the warring states and that the restoration of peace does not automatically revive them. Armed with these facts, we can cut our way through the confused struggle at Ghent.

One instruction that the American delegates received from their government forbade them to revive the third article of Jay's Treaty, which by protecting the British trade with the Indians preserved a foreign political influence within the United States and limited American sovereignty. The war had revealed how dangerous this influence might be and had provided what seemed to be a good opportunity to get rid of it by the application of the principle mentioned above. Of course the British wished to renew the article, but they could not do it alone. The treaty was therefore silent on the point, and by inference the Americans thus gained what they wanted—full liberty for their government to sever the historic connection between the British in Canada and the Indians in the United States. But it was by no means certain that Britain would not force a reopening of this question. The principle cut both ways, and she was in a position to turn it against the United States with telling effect in other quarters, as appears from a glance at another problem that exasperated the negotiators of Ghent.

If the Americans could use this principle to recover American sovereignty over American territory, the British could use it to recover British sovereignty over British waters and shores. When the British served notice that their inshore fisheries would not be reopened to Americans except for a just equivalent in a new bargain, the American delegation was frightened and fell to quarreling among themselves. One of them, John Quincy Adams, insisted that the principle did not apply to the sharing of the British inshore fisheries because this was a condition attached to the British recognition of American independence, which certainly did not need to be renewed. Adams' argument drew fire from his western colleague, Henry Clay, who saw that it would restore the British right to navigate the Mississippi, for this had likewise been attached to the recognition of independence. Clay would have let the fisheries go by default in order to keep the British out of the Mississippi, now that both banks were American. The New Englander, on the other hand, would have sold the national character of this river in order to preserve the American share of the British fisheries.

To add to the confusion, the problem of the impossible northern boundary was also tied to the Mississippi question, which thus linked it with the fisheries; and in addition it was snarled with the third article of Jay's Treaty. The British were willing to run the line along the forty-ninth parallel from the Lake of the Woods, which meant giving up the right to run it to the Mississippi accorded in the peace treaty of 1783, but they were not willing to make this concession for nothing. What they demanded in return was free access for British subjects from British territory to the Mississippi "with their goods, effects, and merchandise," and a renewal of the guarantee of free navigation on that river.

It is not surprising that the negotiators at Ghent threw up their hands and signed a treaty that was silent on all these contentious matters. The fisheries question, the Mississippi question, and the impossible boundary question were all left wide open. So also was the question of the third article of Jay's Treaty, for it was tied to all three of the other questions. Altogether they constituted a most unpleasant legacy, but the strong will to peace that soon prevailed in the British and American capitals disposed of it rather easily.

The old problem of British relations with Indians in the United States soon disappeared forever. Taking advantage of the fact that the third article of Jay's Treaty had not been formally renewed, the American government promptly prohibited all foreigners from trafficking with the natives, and the British government raised no objection. The only question that caused any friction was that of the fisheries, but it did not amount to much and it seems to have helped in putting an end to the question itself.

There was little haggling over the negotiation of the convention of 1818, and the story of this agreement is quickly told. The British reopened the fisheries, though on a more restricted basis than in 1783, and the United States renounced its claim to a continuance of the larger liberty. As conditions for their acceptance of the forty-ninth parallel from the Lake of the Woods the British again asked for the free navigation of the Mississippi and an overland access to it. But when the Americans said they would sign no article with these conditions, the British readily agreed to accept the boundary without them, thus allowing the implied claims to lapse by default. The boundary was not carried over the mountains because a dispute that had arisen over the territory beyond could not be settled at that time. But the two parties put the dispute to sleep by declaring that this territory was to be free and open to British and Americans alike for the next ten years. Actually it slumbered neglected for a much longer period.

LA SALLE EXPLORED THE MISSIS-
SIPPI TO ITS MOUTH (CH. 4).

D'IBERVILLE. NO CANADIAN STANDS IN
MORE DESERVED EMINENCE (CH. 4).

LA VÉRENDRYE AND HIS MEN GAZE ACROSS THE VAST CANADIAN
PRAIRIE, BY C. W. JEFFERYS (CH. 4).

AN OLD PRINT OF A
FRENCH CANADIAN HUNTER ON
SNOWSHOES (CH. 4).

A PICTORIAL DESCRIPTION OF THE CAP-
TURE OF QUEBEC, BY HERVEY SMYTH,
AIDE TO GENERAL WOLFE (CH. 4).

VIEW OF QUEBEC FROM POINT LEVY, BY RICHARD SHORT IN 1761 (CH. 4).

THE DEATH OF GENERAL WOLFE, BY BENJAMIN WEST (CH. 4).

LOUIS JOSEPH, MARQUIS DE
MONTCALM (CH. 4).

SIR GUY CARLETON, LORD
DORCHESTER (CHS. 5, 6).

THE AMERICAN REVOLUTION TOOK LAND FROM CANADA BUT GAVE HER
SOME OF THE FINEST PEOPLE IN THE OLD COLONIES. THE COMING
OF THE LOYALISTS, BY HENRY SANDHAM (CH. 6).

FORT CHIPEWYAN (CH. 8).

FRENCH CANADIAN FUR TRADERS
AT A PORTAGE (CH. 8).

"ALEXANDER MACKENZIE, FROM CANADA, BY LAND, THE TWENTY-SECOND OF JULY,
ONE THOUSAND SEVEN HUNDRED AND NINETY-THREE" (CH. 8).

GRAND PORTAGE, RENDEZVOUS BE-
TWEEN EAST AND WEST (CH. 8).

SIR GEORGE SIMPSON, GREATEST
GOVERNOR OF THE HUDSON'S BAY
COMPANY IN CANADA (CH. 8).

"THE OLD CANADIAN PACIFIC EXPRESS," ARTHUR HEMING'S STRIKING
PICTURE OF THE INTREPID VOYAGEURS.

STEAMBOAT WHARF, MONTREAL, ABOUT 1850.

LOCKS ON THE RIDEAU CANAL, SITE OF THE PRESENT OTTAWA; TODAY THE
PARLIAMENT BUILDINGS ARE ON THE RIGHT (CH. 9).

THE CANADIAN FARMER'S WILDERNESS CABIN (CH. 9).

OCCASIONALLY WANDERING MERCHANTS BROUGHT THEIR WARES
TO THE FARMER'S DOOR (CH. 9).

WILLIAM LYON MACKENZIE, FIERY
SCOT, WAS PERSECUTED INTO BEING
THE POPULAR CHAMPION OF
UPPER CANADA (CH. 10).

LOUIS JOSEPH PAPINEAU, FRENCH
CANADIAN LEADER, FILLED THE COR-
RESPONDING ROLE IN LOWER
CANADA (CH. 10).

BURNING OF THE PARLIAMENT HOUSE AT MONTREAL IN THE TORY
RIOTS, APRIL 25, 1849 (CH. 10).

JOSEPH HOWE, OF ALL NOVA SCO-
TIANS BY FAR THE BEST
LOVED (CH. 10).

LORD DURHAM, FATHER OF THE
MODERN BRITISH COMMONWEALTH
OF NATIONS (CH. 10).

HUNDREDS OF THESE CARTS CREAKED OVER THE PRAIRIE TRAIL FROM
THE RED RIVER COLONY TO ST. PAUL, MINNESOTA (CH. 11).

GOLD RUSH IN THE CARIBOO (CH. 11).

MULE TEAM ON THE CARIBOO ROAD, BRITISH COLUMBIA (CH. 11).

THE FATHERS OF CONFEDERATION. MACDONALD STANDS IN THE CENTER; CAR-
TIER SITS ON HIS LEFT; TUPPER STANDS IN FOREGROUND; GEORGE BROWN
SITS WITH KNEES CROSSED (CHS. 11, 12).

LOUIS RIEL, TEMPESTUOUS LEADER OF TWO REBELLIONS (CHS. 11–14).

SIR JAMES DOUGLAS, FATHER OF BRITISH COLUMBIA (CH. 11).

AN OLD SKETCH OF FORT GARRY BEARING THE LEGEND, "DEDICATED TO THE PIONEER SETTLERS OF THE CANADIAN NORTHWEST" (CH. 11).

THREE GREAT LEADERS OF THE NEW CANADA. LEFT ABOVE, SIR JOHN A. MACDONALD, FIRST PRIME MINISTER OF THE DOMINION; RIGHT, ALEXANDER MACKENZIE, CANADA'S FIRST LIBERAL PREMIER; BELOW, SIR WILFRED LAURIER, LIBERAL PRIME MINISTER AND FRENCH CANADA'S MOST DISTINGUISHED SON (CHS. 11–15).

CAMP OF THE NORTH WEST MOUNTED POLICE, SEPTEMBER 1874 (CH. 14).

NORTH WEST "MOUNTIE" ARRESTING AN INDIAN, BY JOHN INNES (CH. 14).

THE PRESENT CENTER OF WINNIPEG, MAIN AND PORTAGE, IN 1872 (CH. 14).

UGLY CUSTOMERS AT SMART'S STORE, BATTLEFORD, 1881 (CH. 14).

THE CAPTURE OF BATOCHE, 1885 (CH. 14).

CHAPTER 8

Furs and the Great West

THE fur trade, to which we have thus far given too little attention, was one of the greatest determining factors in Canadian history. Americans are apt to miss this fact because furs have played a relatively small part in the history of the United States. It was the fur trade that extended the British Empire over the vast region between Hudson Bay and the Pacific Ocean, thereby laying the foundation of the broader Canada of today. Incidentally it was also the fur trade that became the villain in a grim tragedy enacted on the banks of the Red River of the North, and it gave Montreal its first lead over other Canadian cities in wealth and population.

During the French régime Montreal was famous as the chief center of the fur trade in North America, and immediately after the conquest British speculators rushed in to seek their fortunes in this business. From New England, from old England, and from Scotland they came, and they naturally formed connections with the French who had been engaged in the traffic, taking some into partnership and others into their pay. At first they worked only in the region around the Great Lakes, but within ten years they began to invade what is now the Canadian Northwest more extensively than ever the French had done. There they had several advantages over their predecessors. They were free to pocket all their profits instead of having to turn over a goodly share to the government of the colony on the St. Lawrence; they got better and cheaper trading goods from England; and they had more capital, for they were backed by strong commercial houses in England.

The success of the traders operating from the St. Lawrence roused the English company from its slumber on the shores of Hudson Bay. It could no longer wait for the Indians to come down to its establishments on the coast; it had to go to the Indians, and that very quickly, or its trade would be ruined. Then began a memorable race, for the traders from Montreal could not afford to let the men from "the Bay" catch up with them. They could not afford it because there was a big difference in transportation costs. The principal post of the Hudson's Bay Company—York Factory at the mouth of the Nelson—was as close to England as Montreal was, and was about a thousand miles nearer the source of the furs. The heavy expense of carrying trade goods and furs over the enormous distance by canoe and portage made it necessary for the Montreal men to buy their furs more cheaply, and they could do this only by getting in between "the Bay" company and the Indians, who were willing to accept the lower Canadian price because it saved them a long journey or because they did not know of the higher English price lower down. Just as the Montrealers felt the necessity of pushing ahead of the Hudson's Bay Company, so the company felt the necessity of keeping up with them. The result was a race across the continent that led to the further discovery of North America.

At the outset the Montrealers threatened to defeat themselves. In their mad scramble for furs they were trying to beat one another as well as the Hudson's Bay Company, and their competition was vicious, for in all the western land there was no authority of any kind to control it. Though the Hudson's Bay Company had been given by its charter the right to govern the country draining into the bay, it had no means of enforcing its power over any but its own employees. The traders from the St. Lawrence ran wild in a lawless land. On occasion they fought one another with knife or gun, and at times they enlisted the savages in their quarrels. They also debauched the Indians with liquor and cheated them of their furs. As might be expected, there was more than one massacre of white men by red men. In the spring of 1779, in the Eagle Hills on the North Saskatchewan River, a group of traders and their men were having a drinking party. As usual there were Indians around, and they imitated the white men. One of the natives grew troublesome, demanding more and more liquor until an impatient trader gave him some laudanum. This effectively quenched his thirst, and his life too. Then there was a fight, and soon the only white men left on the scene were dead ones. The others had fled, saving their lives but

Furs and the Great West

losing their goods. This incident is perhaps a sufficient illustration of the evil state of affairs that was fortunately ended by the organization of the North West Company in 1784.

The formation of this Canadian company was the combined result of the distance between Montreal and the Canadian Northwest and of the definition of the international boundary by the peace treaty of 1783. Though a trader could leave Montreal in the spring and return in the fall if he went only to the district of the Great Lakes, where the bulk of the Canadian trade still lay, he could not get back until a year later if he went to the region beyond. This meant that roughly twice as much capital was necessary for trading with the more distant country. As few traders possessed this amount, a small group of Montreal merchants got control and were thus able to form the company after the news of the treaty of 1783 brought home the necessity for it. The new boundary cut off the territory south of the Great Lakes from which Montreal had been drawing most of its furs. The only trade left was that of the Northwest, and this was threatened by the way the international line was drawn. It gave the United States the Lake Superior end of the route to the Northwest, including the important rendezvous of Grand Portage to which, early every July, the traders came down with their furs and the merchants went up with their goods.

By forming the North West Company the Montrealers made ready for the continental Marathon; and within ten years or so the rivalry between the Canadian and the English companies resulted in the planting of fur-trading posts along the waterways all over the Northwest. Generally speaking, there was less interest in the prairie than in the wooded region to the north. The chief game on the open plains was buffalo, whose hides brought the lowest price in the European market, whereas the North was the land of the beaver, whose skins fetched the highest. The Canadian company was years ahead of the English one in penetrating two important areas—the far Northwest and the far West —perhaps because the men of "the Bay" hesitated to go outside the territory granted them by the charter, the land draining into Hudson Bay. In the far Northwest was the Athabaska region, the richest of all, and there we come upon the greatest of the fur-trading explorers in this further discovery of North America.

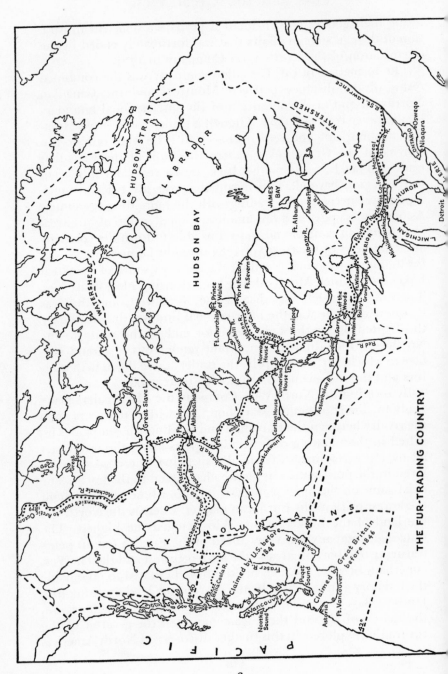

THE FUR-TRADING COUNTRY

Furs and the Great West

Alexander Mackenzie was an intrepid Highlander who as a lad of ten had been sent to Canada and who at the age of twenty-five found himself in charge of the North West Company's trade in the far Northwest with headquarters at Fort Chipewyan on Lake Athabaska. Early in June 1789, having sent off the winter's harvest of furs in a flotilla of canoes, he set out to determine where the great waters of the Athabaska and Peace rivers flowed. At the western end of Great Slave Lake he entered a mighty stream down which his party sped. On and on he went until he saw the midnight sun, and still he pressed on until ice and fog barred the way. When he turned back, Mackenzie had reached the Arctic Ocean though he does not seem to have known it. By the middle of September he was once more at his post, having covered three thousand miles by canoe and having discovered one of the principal rivers of the world, very appropriately named after him—the Mackenzie River.

Three years later, after a trip to the mother country to improve his scientific knowledge and to procure the best instruments for exploring, Mackenzie embarked on another famous expedition. This time he headed west and wintered on the way. He ascended the Peace River through the Rockies and then struck southwest, reaching the Pacific at the mouth of the Bella Coola River. There, in vermilion mixed with melted grease, he inscribed on the face of the rock: "Alexander Mackenzie, from Canada, by land, the twenty-second of July, one thousand seven hundred and ninety-three."

Though Mackenzie was thus the first white man to cross the continent north of Mexico, he was not the first to visit the coast of British Columbia. In 1778 two ships of the Royal Navy under the famous Captain James Cook had come to search for the northwest passage to Hudson Bay that was still believed to exist. Captain Cook could not find what he was looking for, but his men made an important discovery: The Indians had quantities of furs and would sell them for the buttons these white men cut off their uniforms. The news spread, and soon vessels both from England and from Boston came to get the furs the natives gathered. In 1788 a British expedition established a trading station at Nootka Sound, halfway up the western side of Vancouver Island. Then came a Spanish expedition that claimed the whole coast, seized two British ships, and imprisoned their men.

This well-known Nootka Sound incident threatened to light a big war until Spain backed down on learning that the French Revolution had paralyzed her one reliable ally, France. The British government then sent Captain George Vancouver to recover possession and to explore and chart the coast. He came in 1792 and completed his work in the following year, placing on the map many of the names that are still there, such as Puget Sound and Burrard Inlet. The island, which until then was thought to be part of the mainland, was named after him. From this time on fur-trading vessels of many nations haunted the coast. To what country it was to belong remained in doubt for some time, but that doubt was largely removed by traders coming across the mountains.

Herein lies the importance of Mackenzie's journey to the western ocean, although his discovery of new and valuable fur fields in the Rockies and on the Pacific slope was not followed up immediately because his company was rent by quarrels. It split into competing organizations, and the old evils broke loose again, with liquor and blood flowing freely. But in 1804 the Canadian rivals reunited in a new and greater North West Company headed by Sir Alexander Mackenzie—he had been knighted for his explorations—and almost at once his company decided to push over the mountains.

Others were going there too, though not men of the Hudson's Bay Company. In 1805 the famous expedition of Lewis and Clark explored all the way from the Missouri to the mouth of the Columbia River for the American government; John Jacob Astor, the fur king of New York, was endeavoring to establish his company on the Pacific; and Russians from Alaska were working down the coast. In 1807, not knowing that Lewis and Clark had reached their goal, the Canadian company sent an intrepid explorer, a Scot named Simon Fraser, to get ahead of them. Mackenzie had found a great river that he supposed to be the Columbia, and Fraser was ordered to follow this river to its mouth, taking possession of the country as he went. This he did, but when he reached the mouth and took his bearings he was chagrined to find that it was not the Columbia he had descended but another river, which has fittingly been named after him—the Fraser.

Furs and the Great West

Slower but more thorough was the work of another man of the same company, David Thompson. He reached the upper waters of the Columbia in 1807 and spent the next four years exploring its whole system, building posts, and developing the fur trade as he proceeded. The American settlement of Astoria was built at the mouth of the Columbia in 1811; but in the fall of 1813, shortly before the arrival of a British sloop of war sent to capture it, Astor's local representative sold this post to the North West Company. The fate of this place was almost entirely neglected during the negotiation of the Treaty of Ghent and for some little time afterward, but in the fall of 1818, in accordance with the general treaty provision for territorial restitution, it was formally surrendered to an agent of the United States government. The Canadian company, however, was not disturbed in its possession of the post, and, as we have seen, the convention that was signed in this year adjourned the whole question of the disputed national title to this coast.

As we look back over the establishment of the North West Company on the Pacific coast, two things seem to stand out. One is that this company was so much more efficient than any of its rivals that it alone had secured a definite footing there; and the other is that in this way the North West Company saved British Columbia for the British Empire and Canada.

The continental Marathon was over. The Canadian company had won. Its victory was partly due to desperation, for, as we have seen, it had to win or be destroyed. Further reasons for its success may be found in the form of its organization, the character of its employees, and its system of transportation. The Hudson's Bay Company was a permanent joint stock company whose men could never be anything but employees, whereas the North West Company was a partnership that had to be renewed every few years. Each renewal of the Canadian partnership opened the door for particularly successful traders to enter the charmed circle of capitalists in Montreal and become members of its most exclusive coterie, the Beaver Club, whose splendid banquets were a byword. The traders of the North West Company thus had an incentive that their rivals lacked.

There was also quite a contrast between the personnel of the two companies. The men of "the Bay" were ordinarily recruited in the Orkney Islands, which their company's ships passed on the way out from London. These Orcadians, as natives of these islands are called, were hard workers and reliable servants. So also were the Nor'westers, the name applied to the men of the Canadian company, and in addition they had qualities that their stolid Scottish rivals did not possess and could not acquire. Many of the traders and practically all of the canoemen who worked for the Montreal company were French Canadians, who inherited the daring spirit of the old *coureurs de bois,* a genius for dealing with Indians, and a mastery of the canoe.*

Various means of transportation were employed by the two rivals. Toward the close of the eighteenth century the English company experimented with pack horses; but until well on into the nineteenth century there was little travel with freight by land, except in winter, when sledges drawn by dog teams were used. The load varied with the number of dogs in the train and averaged one hundred and fifty pounds for each dog. A man with experience could drive a train seventy miles a day, and, though it is hardly believable, a driver once made that distance without a stop for rest or food. But it was not over the winter's snow that the great bulk of the traffic passed. It went by the water highways in summer, and because the two companies were racing for the trade of the country speed was all-important. This dictated the use of the canoe, in which the Hudson's Bay Company was no match for its competitor. A military officer who traveled with the North West Company has left a full description of the canoes that went from Montreal to Grand Portage and back again.

"These canoes were exceedingly strong and capacious, they were about thirty-six feet in length, by six feet wide, near the middle; and although the birch-bark which formed a thin external coating over their ribs of white cedar, and their longitudinal laths of the same wood, appeared to compose but a flimsy vessel, yet they usually carried a weight of five tons. It may be as well to state that this cargo was very carefully stored, in order to remove any unequal pressure, which would have been fatal to such a vessel. Four poles, three or four inches at their thickest

* A very interesting recent book on this subject is Grace Lee Nute's *The Voyageur.*

ends . . . were laid side by side in the middle of the bottom of the canoe. On these poles, the cargo was carefully arranged so that all the weight rested on them, and none allowed to press against the bare and unprotected sides of the canoe. Every package was made up of the weight of ninety pounds and none heavier.

"The five tons included the provisions for ten men, sufficient to support them during about twenty to twenty-two days. Each canoe was provided with a mast and lug-sail, and also each man had a ten-foot setting pole, of good ash, shod with an iron ferrule at each end, for assisting the men towing with a strong line in ascending the rapids. The paddles were supplied by the canoemen, each bringing his own. Each canoe also had a camp-kettle, provided by the owners, as also a few Hambro lines, a bundle of watap, roots of the pine tree, for stitching up any seam that might burst, a parcel of gum of a resinous nature, for paying over the seams when leaky, a piece of birch-bark for repairs, hatchet, crooked knife, and a few more indispensable articles." The canoes used on all the waters west of Lake Superior were the same in type but smaller in size—the so-called *canoe du nord*. They carried about three thousand pounds of freight and a crew of four or five men, who were proud of being known as "winterers" and scorned the paddlers who plied between Montreal and Grand Portage.

Above and below this most famous of all portages there were many others, and their passage was reduced to a routine. "When arrived at a portage," wrote Peter Grant, one of the chiefs of the North West Company, "the bowman (commonly called the guide), jumps in the water to prevent the canoe from touching the bottom, while the others tie their slings to the packages in the canoe and swing them on their backs to carry over the portage. (A strap or band, called a tumpline, over the voyageur's forehead bore most of the weight.) The bowman and the steersman carry their canoe, a duty from which the middle men are exempt. The whole is conducted with astonishing expedition, a necessary consequence of the enthusiasm which always attends their long and perilous voyages. . . . When they arrive at a rapid, the guide or foreman's business is to explore the waters previous to their running down with their canoes, and, according to the height of the water, they either lighten the canoe by taking out part of the cargo and carry it overland, or run down the whole load."

These French Canadians were astonishingly sturdy. Each carried two packs at once over a portage, and Alexander Mackenzie tells of one who carried seven packs for half a league. According to the military officer already quoted, "No men in the world are more severely worked than are these Canadian voyageurs. I have known them to work in a canoe twenty hours out of twenty-four, and go on at that rate during a fortnight or three weeks without a day of rest or a diminution of labour; but it is not with impunity they so exert themselves; they lose much flesh in the performance of such journeys, though the quantity of food they consume is incredible. They smoke almost incessantly, and sing peculiar songs, which are the same their fathers and grandfathers, and probably their great-grandfathers, sang before them; the time is about the same as that of our military quick marches, and is marked by the movements of their paddles. They rest from five to ten minutes every two hours, when they refill their pipes; it is more common for them to describe distances by so many pipes, than in any other way. . . . They are short-lived and rarely are fit to voyage after they have attained their fortieth year, and sixty years seems to be the average of their existence."

Though the North West Company would have been destroyed if it had been defeated in the race, the Hudson's Bay Company did not have to win to survive, because it could afford to offer the natives more for their furs. But the trade war could not last indefinitely. Sooner or later one rival was bound to break the other. Anything might happen at any time to decide the issue, and in the second decade of the nineteenth century the English company made a move that the Nor'westers believed was a mortal blow aimed at them. This was the founding of the Red River Colony, the beginning of Manitoba.

As a matter of fact, the origin of this settlement had nothing to do with the commercial rivalry in the Northwest. The father of the idea was a Scottish noble, Lord Selkirk, whose motives were philanthropy and patriotism. He wanted to benefit the poor crofters, or peasants, who were then being evicted from Highland estates to make room for sheep runs. Many of these miserable people were migrating to the United States, and he sought to save them for the British Empire by planting them on unsettled land under the Union Jack. In 1803 and 1804 he established some in Prince Edward Island and others in the southwestern part of Upper Canada, but he was not satisfied. He wanted a wider opportunity, and from all the information he could gather he believed it existed in the valley of the Red River that flows into Lake Winnipeg. He saw that he could not make a colony there without the support of one of the rival companies, and for a very good reason he chose to work with the English one. Because of its charter, only from the Hudson's Bay Company could he get the necessary title to the land; and, as the price of its stock had fallen heavily under the pressure of the Napoleonic War, he saw the chance of getting what he wanted by buying his way into a control of the company. By 1811 he had so many shares that he was able to persuade the company to grant him an enormous tract of land covering parts of the present Manitoba, Minnesota, and North Dakota. Some Americans have been startled to discover this; but the territory granted him was covered by the charter, for its streams drained into Hudson Bay, and we must not forget that Britain did not surrender her claim to what was south of the forty-ninth parallel until 1818.

Nevertheless the company was not giving something for nothing, for by this gift it hoped to effect a double saving. Its army of employees was being fed with provisions sent from the mother country, and the European war had raised the price of food so high that this method was becoming most burdensome. The establishment of a colony meant that in a few years food might be produced there more cheaply than it could be bought on the other side of the Atlantic, and the cost of shipping it across the ocean would be saved. Moreover, the company foresaw that a growing agricultural settlement would give a market value to the land it still held.

Though we have no evidence that in forwarding Selkirk's plan the English company intended to strike at its Canadian rival, this is the very thing it was doing, and it was aiming at a vital spot. The Nor'westers drew most of their wealth from the Athabaska country, to which they had as much right as the English company, but to reach this heaven of beaver they had to cross lands that were drained into Hudson Bay and therefore legally belonged to their rival. Therefore the colony might be used to cut their communications. It also threatened their food supply, for they could not afford to support their men in the West with food sent in from the East, and they had come to rely on pemmican made from buffalo slaughtered in the neighborhood of the projected colony. If the settlement were allowed to grow, the buffalo would be driven away. The Montrealers were quick to see that they had to kill Selkirk's plan, or it would kill their company.

At first they tried to prevent the birth of the colony. Over in Britain, where some of their leaders had considerable influence, they used customs officials and recruiting officers to break up the parties of settlers collected by Selkirk. But these efforts failed. The first body of colonists landed at York Factory in the fall of 1811, and late in the summer of 1812 they reached their main destination, the forks of the Red and the Assiniboine, where Winnipeg now stands. A few remained there to break the ground and build houses, while the rest went on to the mouth of the Pembina, on the Minnesota side of the present boundary. There they found such an abundance of fish and buffalo that they were able to send back provisions to feed not only their comrades whom they had left behind but also a second party that arrived in the autumn. In the spring of 1813 the sojourners at the Pembina returned to the forks, where all joined hands and worked with a will under the leadership of their first governor, Miles Macdonell. Thus the colony was born.

The next move of the North West Company was to destroy the settlement. The death sentence was pronounced in the summer of 1814 by the Montreal partners at the annual meeting in Fort William, to which the headquarters of the trade had been moved from Grand Portage in 1803. As one man they resolved that all the colonists were to be removed by fair means or by foul, by temptation or by force.

Temptation was tried first and was the work of the man in charge of the Nor'westers' post, Fort Gibraltar, situated right in the angle of the forks. He was Duncan Cameron, who, because he was a Highlander himself, knew how to approach his new neighbors. Through all the winter months of 1814–15, he played the splendid host to his fellow countrymen. He entertained them after their own hearts with dancing, bagpipes, and whisky, until he persuaded many that their true friend was not the Hudson's Bay Company, which had brought them to die in this bleak land, but the North West Company, which was eager to rescue them. His company would give them free transportation and free food and would settle them in a Christian country down in Upper Canada. He was so successful that he even got some of the innocent people to break into their own storehouses and deliver to him a few little cannons that had been brought for their own defense. But there were some who would not yield to temptation.

To force these obstinate creatures away other Nor'westers prepared an army, the material for which was right at hand in the *métis,* or half-breeds. These people, who were to play a prominent part in the history of the Canadian West until late in the nineteenth century, were just coming to the front of the stage now, for it was only half a century since the Montrealers had begun the serious invasion of the region lying northwest of the Great Lakes. Most of this "new nation," who lived by hunting and trapping, were of French descent. This was because the men from Montreal had been more numerous than the men from "the Bay" and just as they had been ahead of their rivals in penetrating the country and gathering its furs, they had also been ahead in winning the favor of Indian maidens. The largest body of this half-breed population lived in the Red River region, and they were attached to the North West Company by more than ties of blood. From them the Canadian company bought its supply of pemmican, and already they were turned against the colony by the governor's attempt to stop this trade. He had done it to save this food for his own people, their first crop—that of 1813—having been a failure. So all the Nor'westers had to do to raise an army was to tell the *métis* that the land really belonged to them, and that these strangers were stealing it. Little did these Canadians know that they were sowing the wind and that other Canadians were to reap the whirlwind in the Riel rebellions of 1869–70 and 1885, for the half-breeds never forgot the lesson that the country was theirs.

A Short History of Canada

In the early summer of 1815 the settlers discovered that they were living in a hostile place. All their horses were shot or stolen, some of their houses were plundered, and the warlike *métis* forced them to give up every gun. This reign of terror decided Miles Macdonell to abandon the struggle and surrender to the North West Company. Then Duncan Cameron, pretending to be the noble rescuer, set out for Fort William with a fleet of canoes bearing nearly a hundred and forty deserters from the colony. None ever returned. Many settled in Upper Canada, where their descendants are still living. The remainder of the colonists, some fifty people, took to their boats and fled to Norway House, a principal establishment of the Hudson's Bay Company at the north end of Lake Winnipeg. A few days later one of the leading Nor'westers reported: "I am happy to inform you that the colony has been all knocked on the head by the N. W. Co."

But it takes more than a knock on the head to kill a Scot. In the fall of this year, 1815, the refugees came back from Norway House, and a fresh party of settlers arrived under the leadership of one Robert Semple, who came to replace Miles Macdonell. Now the tables were turned for a while. Semple arrested Duncan Cameron, who had turned up again. Nor'wester canoes were stopped; the mail they carried was seized, and when the letters were examined they disclosed a plot to destroy the colony once and for all. Thereupon Semple had Fort Gibraltar destroyed, and he used its materials to strengthen his own fort, which had just been built a mile down the river.

In the early summer of 1816, the Nor'westers struck a greater blow than they had delivered in the previous year. A *métis* army that was gathered up the Assiniboine under Cuthbert Grant, the half-breed son of a well-known Scottish trader of the same name, descended on the colony. When still four miles away it swung off to the north, expecting to meet an expedition that the Canadian company had promised to send from Fort William to join in wiping out the settlement. Semple rushed out with thirty men to face the hostile rabble. There was a scuffle, a shot, and then more shots. The governor and twenty-one of his followers lay dead upon the ground. Grant lost one man. This Massacre of Seven Oaks, or of Frog Plain, as it is called, is a black stain on the page of Canadian history. The crime was committed by a number of half-civilized *métis* at the bidding of lawless Canadian merchants who paid them handsomely and had so much political influence that they prevented any of them from being punished.

Again the settlers went down the river and the lake, seeking a refuge at Norway House, but this was the last time they had to fly. Help was coming. Miles Macdonell, free once more, was on his way west with a small party, and following him was Lord Selkirk himself, with a large party of disbanded soldiers to increase and strengthen the colony. They were German Swiss who had been employed by Britain and were known as the De Meurons, after the name of their old commanding officer. At Lake Winnipeg Macdonell heard of the tragedy and immediately rushed back to meet his chief, whom he found at Sault Sainte Marie. Selkirk had planned to avoid trouble by avoiding Fort William, but now he made straight for what was to him a nest of robbers and murderers, where some of his own men were prisoners. He seized the place, released the prisoners, arrested some leading Nor'westers, and discovered papers that proved their guilt. After spending the winter in Fort William, he proceeded in the spring of 1817 to supervise the third and final establishment of his colony, to which the exiles of course returned from Norway House.

For four months Selkirk managed the settlement, planning roads, bridges, and mills and directing agricultural operations. He was keenly interested in agriculture and, having made a great success of his estates at home, was determined to do the same in this new part of the New World. "So correct and unerring was his judgment that nothing planned at this early date could in after years be altered to advantage," wrote one of the leaders of the community in the generation that followed. Though Selkirk had sunk over half a million dollars in his efforts to plant the colony, he now forgave the settlers the payments they were supposed to make for their lands. He also won the respect of the Indians, who worshiped him as the "Silver Chief." He persuaded them to sign the first Indian treaty of the Canadian Northwest, by which they gave up all their claim to the land lying along the Red and Assiniboine rivers.

This was perhaps the happiest time of Selkirk's life, but unfortunately it did not last long. He had to return to Canada to attend to the lawsuits he had brought against the Nor'westers and they against him, for he as well as they had broken the law. At Fort William he had taken what did not belong to him, the property of the Canadian company; he had resisted arrest when his enemies found a magistrate to sign a warrant for that purpose, for he thought it a fraud. He was to pay dearly for what he had done at Fort William. In September 1817 he turned his back upon the land of his dreams and from that moment knew no peace. He could not get justice in Canada, where the North West Company seemed to be all-powerful, and he therefore appealed to Britain; but even the home government was prejudiced against him, possibly because the Canadian company had served imperial interests by extending British influence in the West. Selkirk's health and spirits were broken and he died in the spring of 1820, really a Canadian martyr. In his death he helped the settlement even more than in his life, for by dying he unwittingly removed its mortal enemy, the North West Company.

The Canadian company, as we have observed, could not operate as cheaply as the English company, and under the strain of fierce competition its profits had been dwindling. Also, by pushing across the Rocky Mountains it had exhausted itself. Its expenses rose with the increase of the distance over which goods and furs had to be carried, and its profits fell because this extra distance added a year to the period of the turnover of the capital involved. When Selkirk started his colony, the Canadian company was already in a rather desperate financial position, which seems to have intensified the strife on the Red River. So desperate was the company's economic plight that its leaders were coming to realize that the only way to avoid bankruptcy was to join their rivals. They made several efforts to do so and they might have succeeded, for it was to the interest of the Hudson's Bay Company to strike a bargain that would end the injurious competition, had it not been for one man who stood in the way of union—Lord Selkirk. He was the most powerful individual in the English company, and he had every reason for hating the whole Montreal crowd. Immediately after he died, however, negotiations were opened, and in less than a year the Hudson's Bay Company bought out the North West Company.

This union of 1821 was a great epoch in the history of the Canadian West, for in addition to removing the enemy of Selkirk's colony, it necessitated a complete reorganization of the fur trade. This was carried out by a young man of genius, George Simpson, who was knighted twenty years later and is today remembered as the greatest governor the Hudson's Bay Company ever placed in charge of its business on this continent. The task he faced was gigantic. Men who had been fighting one another had to be persuaded to work together. Competing posts were no longer necessary; old posts were closed and new ones opened. The method of transportation was revolutionized. Now that speed was no longer imperative, as it had been in the days of hot competition, the swift but expensive canoe gave place to the slow but cheap York boat, propelled by oars and sail, as a regular conveyance for goods and furs. The great channels of trade were also changed. Thenceforth all freight entering or leaving the country east of the Rockies went by Hudson Bay, and the trade beyond the Rockies was no longer conducted overland but by ship around Cape Horn. Except for expresses bearing mail and passengers, the more expensive route by way of Fort William was abandoned. The great fur trade of Montreal was a thing of the past; but happily Montreal no longer needed it.

CHAPTER 9

A Half Century of Growth

THE general growth of British North America in the first half of the nineteenth century presents some interesting contrasts to the growth of the United States in this period, though of course there are many similarities. The population increased in about the same proportion but, being much smaller, it expanded over a correspondingly smaller space. During this period the mighty march of the pioneers doubled the settled area of the United States, pushing the western frontier line out to Minnesota in the North and Texas in the South. It was a gigantic movement. North of the border, however, there were no important changes in the British territory west of the Great Lakes until about the middle of the century, and meanwhile the extension of settlement was confined to a relatively narrow region east of the Lakes. The Maritime Provinces were filling out, and so were the southern portions of the present provinces of Quebec and Ontario, known as Lower and Upper Canada until 1840 when they were combined to form United Canada. Like the United States these provinces were being fed by immigration from across the sea—very little during the war era and not very much during the first decade of peace, but very greatly during the second quarter of the century. A rough analysis of this migration may shed light on the present character of British North America.

As might be expected, practically all the immigration to the colonies was from the British Isles, whereas only the majority of those who entered the United States came from those islands. The minority, which was considerable, came mostly from Germany. Here then was one important difference between the movement to the United States and that to its northern neighbor: Some Germans have settled in Canada, but there they never constituted the important element that they have been in the United States.

A Half Century of Growth

Turning to those who left the British Isles, we have to be careful to distinguish between English, Irish, and Scottish. ("Scotch" is a word that is abused more often than is the product it stands for!) As England possessed a much larger population than Ireland and Scotland combined, one might suppose that it would send a proportionately larger number of people to this continent. But it did not. The English who entered the United States in this period were only half as numerous as the Germans and lost their identity much more quickly. The percentage of English among the new settlers in British North America was much larger than in the United States, and their English character was more persistent; but in Canada too they were overshadowed by other immigrants from the British Isles.

About half of all the immigrants who came to North America between 1800 and 1850 were Irish. Their parents and their grandparents, together with the potato blight, were responsible for this; for the Irish population had multiplied far beyond the point where it could support itself at home in any other way than by growing potatoes. During the first third of the century quite a number of Irish people migrated, but they were the veriest trickle compared with the human stream that began to flow around 1834, when the potato blight robbed them of food, and this stream in turn was as nothing to the flood let loose by the utter ruin of the crops of 1845 and 1846. Those rotten potatoes reduced the island's population to half its former size!

Here we should notice something that may surprise many Americans who have imagined that all these pitiable refugees came to the United States, where they planted a new Ireland— Roman Catholic and anti-English. They settled in British North America too, and there likewise they upheld the Pope and denounced Britain. The addition of the Irish to the French has made the percentage of Roman Catholics about twice as large in Canada as it is in the United States. Yet the strength of the Roman Catholic church in Canada is not so great as its numbers might suggest. It is weakened by division between the French and the Irish, whose competition for control is always active and often bitter. In the West, for example, when a French archbishop died and was succeeded by an Irishman from the East, the latter confessed that he went "to clean out the French."

What French parishioners openly said when he replaced their French priest with an Irish one was far from edifying. It is reported that disputes between the Irish and the French are frequently referred to Rome, where the Irish usually win with the argument that the appointment of a French Canadian, by interposing a language barrier, would be bad for the propagation of the faith. Indeed it is perhaps true to say that there is less mutual love between Irish Roman Catholics and French Roman Catholics in Canada than there is between English-speaking Protestants and Roman Catholics.

British North America also welcomed from Ireland another appreciable class of immigrants who have been almost unknown in the United States. They were not paupers, nor papists, nor Anglophobes but people of some little property, of stern Protestant faith, and of stout loyalty to their sovereign. They brought with them their own peculiar institution, the Orange Order, with which all Canadians but very few Americans are familiar. The Ku Klux Klan is perhaps the nearest American parallel of this organization. It gets its name from the Protestant William of Orange who drove the Catholic James II out of England and smashed his forces in Ireland at the Battle of the Boyne in 1690. Orangemen annually celebrate the anniversary of this victory over "popery, slavery, knavery" on July 12, with public processions led by bands of fifes and drums and bearing appropriate banners. Of late years they have been more discreet in their damnation of the Pope, but nothing can shake their worship of the empire. For a whole century these sons of Ulster have been a political power in Canada, and the only thing they have in common with their fellow Irish is the desire to keep the French in their place.

More marked has been the influence of the Scots who went to British North America in this period. There has been nothing like it in the United States. The Scottish strain in the American people is almost microscopic, but when you cross the Canadian line you run into Scots everywhere, particularly in high places, for there is no keeping them down. They have not been so well organized as either of the Irish groups, nor has their division into Highlanders and Lowlanders, Catholics and Protestants, cut so deep as the schism between Irish Canadians. As agricul-

A Half Century of Growth

turalists, they did some of the toughest pioneering work in the country (some say because the soil of Scotland is so poor), and they have been outstanding in education, business, politics, and other professions. Sir William Dawson, a Scot born in Nova Scotia, was the dean of Canadian geologists and head of Mc-Gill University, which he made a leading institution. Principal George Munro Grant, a prominent divine who did the same for Queen's University, was another Nova Scotian Scot. Sir Hugh Allan, the greatest shipping magnate in the history of the country, was a Scottish immigrant. So was George Brown, the founder of the Toronto *Globe* and the father of the Liberal party. So also was Sir John A. Macdonald, the father of the Conservative party, the chief architect of the Dominion, and its first premier.

Shortly after 1800 Scots began to migrate into Nova Scotia in such numbers that they gave its name a real meaning and pretty well filled up the eastern portion of the province. Cape Breton, which was reunited to Nova Scotia in 1820, received about twenty-five thousand Gaelic-speaking Highlanders, both Catholic and Protestant, during the first quarter of the century, and to this day their native tongue is spoken there.

The movement of immigrants into New Brunswick was slower. After Waterloo, however, considerable numbers began to come from the north of England, from Scotland, and from Ireland. By the middle of the century the southern third of the province was pretty well occupied, and there was continuous settlement up the St. John and Madawaska valleys, up the Miramichi to tributaries of the St. John, and from the lower Restigouche right around the coast to Bay Verte.* Prince Edward Island failed to attract as many people as it might have done, because immigrants could not get titles to land there. In 1767 the whole island had been granted to a few speculative proprietors who lived in the mother country and had enough influence to get it erected into a separate colony two years later and also to keep possession of the land, though they did not pay the quitrents they had promised.

When Lower Canada was separated from Upper Canada it had much less need for immigration. Its French population,

* For these and other places mentioned in this chapter see the map of Railways in 1860 in Chapter 11.

doubled since the conquest, greatly outnumbered all the other settlers in the whole of British North America, a fact overlooked by those who say the French ought to have been assimilated, or Anglicized. Yet Lower Canada still had land that attracted newcomers. Unmindful of Haldimand's advice to reserve the Eastern Townships for French Canadians, the government in Quebec decided to open this district to all who wanted to come. It was immediately filled with English-speaking people whose descendants have since been gradually squeezed out by the expanding French population. Until the War of 1812 the Eastern Townships were settled by people from across the line in Vermont and New Hampshire—pioneer farmers like those then pressing into Upper Canada—and after the war by people from across the water.

Upper Canada was of course the province most affected by the War of 1812. Like Nova Scotia, which was first French, then American, and finally British in character, Upper Canada experienced the same number of changes. In the beginning it was British, or Loyalist, but it soon became American. Then it lost this character and became again a solidly British colony, as immigration poured in. Thither went the bulk of those who left the mother country to live under the old flag in the New World —English, Irish, and Scots, for there they found the most space for settlement.

Many immigrants were drawn to Upper Canada by the promise of aid from Colonel Thomas Talbot, who had secured an enormous tract of land on Lake Erie and had just commenced placing settlers upon it when the War of 1812 interrupted his work. This former gay young officer was the virtual ruler, and a very autocratic one, of the country around the present cities of London and St. Thomas, Ontario—the latter named after him, though he was certainly no saint. The success of the Talbot settlement may have helped to suggest the more elaborate scheme of the Canada Company, to which the government, in 1826, sold a huge block of a million acres, known as the Huron Tract. The company, formed by the Scottish novelist and poet John Galt, sold the land to immigrants, built roads for them, and promised to pay half the cost of any bridge, school, or other improvement they undertook. Galt spent three years in Upper Canada directing the colonization of the district. This was the origin of the towns of Guelph, Galt, and Goderich. In 1825 Peter Robinson, a Loyalist descendant of the prominent Virginian family, brought out a party of more than two thousand Irish people to Cobourg on Lake Ontario and thence over a rough road, which he hastily made passable for heavy wagons, to Rice Lake. There he had three large boats carried on wheels from Lake Ontario, and for navigation up the shallow Otanabee River he slapped together a large, flat-bottomed craft in eight days. Thus came the people who settled Peterborough, Ontario, named out of gratitude to Robinson.

Ten years earlier (1815) the Perth settlement was founded halfway between Kingston and Ottawa, largely by retired soldiers placed there by the government to make sure that a loyal military population would live along the new Rideau Canal. The building of this canal was then begun because the late war had shown the danger of Upper Canada's depending solely on the St. Lawrence for communication with Montreal. Incidentally, the canal at one end helped Kingston and at the other gave rise to Ottawa, first called Bytown after Colonel By, the military engineer in charge of construction.

Between the War of 1812 and the middle of the century, the population of Upper Canada increased tenfold, to 950,000. This was about 60,000 more than Lower Canada then possessed and nearly twice the combined population of the Maritime Provinces. Nova Scotia's population at this time was 275,000, New Brunswick's a little over 190,000, and Prince Edward Island's about 63,000. As yet there was no British Columbia, and Selkirk's colony, which later grew to be Manitoba, was still an infant. It had been fed by no immigration since its birth, for it was too cut off from the outside world. Less than 1,000 white people dwelt on the banks of the Red and the Assiniboine, and for neighbors they had about five times that number of half-breeds.

The figures for New Brunswick and more particularly for Nova Scotia would have been larger if a considerable number of the immigrants that these provinces received had not been attracted on to the United States. There were complaints of a similar loss from the two Canadas, but this was offset by a movement in from the United States, not so much of Americans as of people from the British Isles who took advantage of the greater facilities to sail for New York and to proceed thence over the improved inland water route, after the Erie Canal was opened in 1825.

Life for the immigrant and his children was not quite the same in British North America as it was in the United States. Except in Quebec and Montreal, where ships unloaded swarms of Irish with no money and much disease, to be a public burden and a public menace, the newcomers encountered less hostility than was common south of the line. North of it there were no large cities or expanding industries—there were practically no industries at all—in which the workers saw their standard of living threatened by the competition of strangers from across the sea. Nor were the English, Irish, and Scots regarded as foreigners. Only the French thought of them as such, which also accounts for some trouble in Lower Canada. In the rest of British North America there was no old stock of any considerable size and little ground for antagonism between the new arrivals and those already settled there. The latter were immigrants too, and they welcomed the latest comers as cooperators, rather than competitors, in opening up the country.

The society of British North America was more completely agricultural than it was in the United States, and conditions in Upper Canada, where by far the greatest expansion of British settlement occurred, resembled those of the earlier American frontier in the Ohio Valley before it moved on to the more open lands beyond. Land was cheap, whether immigrants got it from private individuals, from companies that had large tracts for sale, or from the government. Of course every man had to make his own farm, and before he could get at the soil he had to attack the forest. With the first trees that he felled he constructed a house—a log cabin roofed with bark and provided with a fireplace and chimney built of stones gathered in the neighborhood. Few of these early dwellings had glass windows or even wooden doors. Blankets served instead. Only with the growth of settlement did sawmills appear, providing the materials for new and better homes.

Clearing the land was a hard battle. The trees were huge, men were few, and fewer still were horses or oxen to haul away the enormous trunks felled by the axe. To speed the work and to make the heavy toil seem lighter, neighbors often combined to help one another. Frequently the pioneer called fire to his rescue. By girdling the trees he killed them, and when they dried they burned like tinder. But even then he had to get rid of their gaunt remains that cumbered the ground. It was usual to till fields with the stumps still standing, their removal being the work of years. In the middle 1820's by far the most important Canadian export was ashes, then extensively used in the textile industries in the Old World. Obviously the chief activity of the population was clearing the land.

Farming was then very different from what it has since become. There was no farm machinery, and agricultural implements were crude, for they were homemade. The plough that tilled the ground in Upper Canada was commonly fashioned out of wood that had grown on the same land, and was shod with iron. Not every pioneer had even this kind of plough; many a first crop sprang from land prepared by spade and hoe and perspiration. Horses long remained a luxury, for oxen were the ordinary beasts of burden. Though often stubborn, they were proverbially strong, and in the end they made good, if tough, eating. The only reaper then used was a sickle or a scythe wielded by hand, and the binders were usually the women and children. Threshing was still done as in Biblical times, by spreading the sheaves upon the floor of the barn or stable and beating them with a flail. In the earliest days much of the grain was ground by pounding it with a wooden pestle, called a stamper, in a hardwood stump hollowed out with hot iron to form a mortar. It was called a hominy block—a reminder that at first the principal crop was corn. Grinding by hand was gradually abandoned as gristmills, run by water, were erected throughout the country.

In those days, unlike our times, farming was not a business. The average farmer now sells most of what he produces and buys most of what he needs—and can pay for. In those days he could sell little and therefore could buy little, and money was a strange sight to him. Like the habitant, though less and less as time passed and settlement thickened, he and his family produced most of what they consumed and consumed almost all they produced. Even their soap and their sugar were made on the farm, the latter from the sap of maple trees and the former from fat boiled with lye extracted from wood ashes. Clothes were family-made until traveling tailors appeared and undertook the fashioning of the "best" suits. Each tailor had his circuit, which took a year to get around. His pay was chiefly board and lodging in the houses where he tarried to ply his trade. Even then the materials were still homemade. What little surplus the farmer had he exchanged not for money but for the goods that he and his family could neither make nor do without. Occasionally he was served by wandering merchants who brought their wares to his door. Otherwise he had to carry his produce to the storekeeper in the nearest town or village. With all the development down to the middle of the century, the total annual export of wheat and flour from Upper and Lower Canada combined did not then amount to two bushels a head, and there was as yet no export of meat or of dairy produce. This is a measure of the extent to which these new settlements in the interior were still self-sufficing. The common occupation of the people was subsistence farming.

At the same time the Maritime Provinces were actually importing wheat and flour, for the new society there was not predominantly agricultural, like that of the two Canadas. The dwellers by the sea had other opportunities and a less fertile soil. The neighboring waters abounded in fish, for which there was a good market in the West Indies and in Europe, and fishing villages grew in size and number. The combination of forest and sea led to another development little remembered today, except locally, though it was once widely known all over the world. For a great shipbuilding industry arose in this little region. Some of the finest vessels that furrowed the ocean in those glorious days of wood and sail came off the stocks of Nova Scotia and New Brunswick, as well as New England. These British colonial ships sailed the seven seas, bearing a goodly share of the world's commerce, and the ports of Nova Scotia and of New Brunswick, particularly Halifax and St. John, were busy centers of trade. When steam began to supplant sail, it was quite natural that an enterprising Halifax merchant should start the first line of transatlantic steamships. He did it with the aid of a mail subsidy

A Half Century of Growth

from the British government. In 1840 his paddle-wheel steamers opened a regular service between Liverpool and Boston via Halifax. He was Samuel, later Sir Samuel, Cunard, and this was the beginning of the famous Cunard Line.

The St. Lawrence also had its shipping industry, but it was not so large as that of the Maritime Provinces, and it played a much smaller part in the life of the two Canadas. Geography explains the difference. The Maritime Provinces were thrust out into the ocean, whereas the Canadas were withdrawn from it; and winter closed the navigation of the great river for five months out of the year's twelve, while it never locked up the ports of Halifax and St. John. What was true of shipping was also true of lumbering. Though there was a considerable development of this business in the St. Lawrence Valley, it was small compared with what took place in the Maritimes. But lumbering would never have grown as it did in the provinces down by the sea had not the mother country experienced a serious alarm at the beginning of the century.

Britain's sea power, the main prop of the empire, was threatened. Her own forests had long since been used up, and she had come to depend on her Baltic trade for masts, spars, timber, and other articles as essential to the navy as coal and oil became later. In 1800, for a second time in twenty years, the countries bordering on the Baltic combined to exclude British ships from that sea. Though the trade was soon reopened, Britain was determined never to be caught again; it was too dangerous. To develop another and surer source of supply the government in London turned to the colonies in America, giving them a heavy preference for these articles in the British market.

The act of Parliament that changed the duties in favor of the colonies roused vigorous echoes from the woodman's axe in the forests of the Maritime Provinces. Nova Scotia began to export quantities of lumber, but the industry there had nothing like the proportions of the business in New Brunswick, where the greatest stands of timber were. The profit was so high that it drew many men from the farms, and agriculture languished. Fathers and sons disappeared into the woods to cut and log. They ripped the logs into lumber, some of which they used to build the ships on which they loaded the rest. The same energetic men sailed their ships to England, where they sold them with their cargoes, and then took passage home to repeat the process.

Less thriving but quite vigorous was the coal industry. The French had worked the rich deposits in Cape Breton, and those of Pictou County were discovered in 1798. Thirty years later, after a period of makeshift mining, the extraction of coal from both fields began in a businesslike manner according to the best methods of the day.

Throughout the different colonies, villages, towns, and cities grew with the country to meet its business and professional needs. Each of the numerous villages always had a store, and it might also have a church, a school, a blacksmith's shop, a wagon-maker, a carpenter, a cobbler, and even a mill. Towns were fewer, with larger stores carrying a greater range of goods. They also had millers, weavers, tailors, furniture-makers, carpenters, masons, surveyors, doctors, lawyers, and sometimes judges.

The only urban life in these colonies was commercial. Halifax, of course, was now well established, and there were other thriving towns around the indented coast of Nova Scotia. New Brunswick had less commerce, but most of it was concentrated in St. John, which was quite a busy place. Upper Canada for many years had only one real town of any size—Kingston. Its location, in the midst of the main settlement of the Loyalists and at the eastern end of Lake Ontario, explains its early importance. But it is more than a century since what was long known as "little muddy York" outstripped Kingston and became the city of Toronto. The center of gravity of the population of the province had shifted westward.

In Lower Canada Montreal had surpassed Quebec at the time of the American Revolution, and in the first half of the nineteenth century it leaped ahead. It lay in the midst of a much larger and richer agricultural country, but this accounts for only a small part of its growth. The improvement of the St. Lawrence channel left Quebec with only a local trade and made Montreal the commercial capital not only of the better part of Lower Canada but of the whole of Upper Canada as well. Between 1800 and 1850 its population jumped from 9,000 to about 57,000, and the impetus it then gathered has since continued. In further con-

A Half Century of Growth

trast with Quebec, which remained almost exclusively French, the larger center was nearly one third English-speaking. Practically all the big business of the city was in the hands of this minority, the French having been much less zealous in the pursuit of mammon. Here in 1817 appeared the first bank in British North America, still the largest in the Dominion, the Bank of Montreal.

Turning from this examination of material growth to glance at other concerns of the people of those days, we should notice the developing religious pattern of British North America. This was largely governed by immigration. It spread Roman Catholicism beyond the French settlements. The Scots led in this change, beginning with the establishment of the Loyalists on the upper part of the St. Lawrence, for this body of refugees included quite a number of Catholic Highlanders who had gone to northern New York shortly before the outbreak of the Revolutionary War. Then, as we have seen, other Catholic Highlanders went directly to Nova Scotia and Cape Breton. Not until well on toward the middle of the nineteenth century did the Irish Catholics flock in. The religious balance of the whole population, however, was swinging strongly in the Protestant direction, for an overwhelming proportion of immigrants to British North America was Protestant.

The first Protestant settlements were in the old Nova Scotia, where the pre-Revolutionary migration introduced the Baptist and the Congregational churches from New England. The Church of England, as a popular organization, entered this province with the Loyalists. The proportion of Anglicans among the Upper Canadian Loyalists was much smaller, as might be expected from the different character of these people. The established, or official, church in England and Ireland, it was favored by the government in the colonies, though technically it was not established there; and of course it was the church of the official class. It did not grow as rapidly as rival churches, for the immigration from the mother country was more Scottish and Irish than English, and the English immigrants were commonly Nonconformists. It was this predominantly Scottish and Irish character of the immigration that made Presbyterianism a power in the land, particularly in Nova Scotia and Ontario.

There were two Methodist churches, the Wesleyan and the Episcopal, the former British and the latter American. The Episcopal appeared only in Upper Canada, where it was introduced by the post-Loyalist migration from the United States. It seems to have been for a long time about the most vigorous branch of British North American Protestantism, which is not surprising when we examine the conditions. The principal frontier of British settlement was then in Upper Canada, and this church was peculiarly well adapted to frontier life. Its clergy were not required to possess the expensive education essential in other churches. Its lay preachers cost nothing, and its circuit-riding ministers could serve such a widely spread "connexion" that they cost little more. The appeal of such a clergy was emotional rather than intellectual, and that was just what pioneer people wanted.

After the War of 1812 the British Wesleyans, loath to lose their immigrating fellow countrymen, pushed into Upper Canada, where there was a rather un-Christian conflict between the two Methodist churches until 1820, when the British Wesleyans agreed to withdraw under the threat of an Episcopal Methodist invasion of Lower Canada. Twelve years later the Episcopal Methodists, having cut their ties with the United States and having thereby become a less formidable foe, the Wesleyans returned. This time, instead of fighting, they were married—in the union of 1833. In its organization the new church followed the British model more than the American one with its bishops, and the union brought larger numbers of English-trained ministers. But it was not identified with the church in the mother country. Fusing English and American practices and attitudes, it soon became distinctively Canadian in character, a development that appeared later in the other Protestant churches.*

Egerton Ryerson, the son of a New Brunswick Loyalist who had moved to Upper Canada, was the leader of the Methodists there. He was editor of their church paper, the *Christian Guardian,* which was founded in 1839 and had a much larger circulation than any other paper in the country. From his editorial

* There are no Methodists in the country now, and no Congregationalists. They disappeared in 1925 when with most of the Presbyterians they combined to form the United Church of Canada, the largest Protestant church in the Dominion.

chair he wielded an enormous influence in politics as well as in religious affairs. He could swing an election for or against the government. In later years he won fame as superintendent of public education and as the father of the Ontario school system. He was one of the makers of this province. He has been called an ecclesiastical statesman, a distinction he shares with only one other man of the period. This was John Strachan, a Scot who came to the country as a poor Presbyterian schoolmaster and prospered when he joined the clergy of the Church of England. He became the "fighting bishop" of Toronto and the most dominant personality in the government circle in the second quarter of the nineteenth century.

The history of education in British North America was very different from that in the United States, though it was likewise strongly colored by religious influences. From the time of the conquest the policy of the home government was to provide each locality with a schoolmaster. For his support he was to have the use of a conveniently located farm lot, and to make sure he would lead the youth in the way they should go, he was required to be a communicant of the Church of England, whose head was the king. This policy failed miserably. Teaching and farming did not well agree, and the majority of the people were not Anglicans. A new system had to be worked out, and this took many years and much trouble. Not until after the middle of the century was the present plan finally established, with its free schooling in tax-supported schools run under the rather close direction of the provincial government. Meanwhile there were schools of various kinds in growing numbers. At first they were mostly private institutions connected with a church or organized by voluntary groups of individuals whose children formed the classes. Then the government made grants for schools here and there, and the principle of public support, applied in different ways, gradually spread. Generally speaking, the Maritime Provinces were ahead of Upper Canada, while Lower Canada was the most backward of all.

For this state of affairs in French Canada the English-speaking minority were chiefly responsible. They managed to get a law passed providing for a public educational system that alarmed the religious and racial sensibilities of the great majority of the people. A scheme rather than a system, it was designed to force the English language down their throats and was headed by an Englishman—the *Protestant* bishop of Quebec. It was a tragedy that public education was first presented to the French Canadians in this suspicious guise, and there was another tragedy a few years later, when the racial minority, who controlled the government, blocked the efforts of the assembly to establish public schools under local control. This experience confirmed the suspicions already aroused. Many Protestants in Canada, not being familiar with these facts, have blamed the Roman Catholic clergy for trying to keep their people ignorant.

Though the vain attempt to establish an Anglican monopoly of teaching in British North America has left no mark upon the schools, it has left a deep and permanent one on higher education. Anyone may see it today if he compares the Canadian universities west of the Great Lakes with those in the older parts of the Dominion. In each of the four western provinces, where a lesson was learned from what happened in the other provinces, higher education is concentrated in one state university, and no other degree-granting institutions are allowed; whereas in the other provinces higher education is split up among many colleges and universities, most of which are religious in origin.

This was perhaps inevitable in Lower Canada, where differences of race and religion cut deep. There Laval University grew out of the Quebec seminary established in 1668, "classical" colleges under clerical control sprang up all over the province, and one of the Scottish merchants who made a fortune out of furs, James McGill, left the means for the founding of McGill University in 1821. McGill has long been the strongest privately endowed institution in the Dominion. It should not be confused with the French university in the same city—the University of Montreal—a recent refoundation of a branch of Laval University.

In Upper Canada and the Maritime Provinces, on the other hand, the multiplicity of degree-granting institutions was unwittingly forced upon the people by the narrow policy of the government. Each province would long have remained content with its one original state institution, as in Western Canada today, if the government had not insisted on making its teaching body a close corporation of Anglican clergy. This drove the people, who belonged mostly to other denominations, to create their own institutions of higher learning. The best known of these, Queen's University in Kingston, was Presbyterian but has since been secularized. The state institution of Upper Canada, chartered in 1827, was made completely nondenominational in the middle of the last century, after a bitter political fight, and its name was changed to the University of Toronto. Since then it has been the outstanding state institution in the Dominion. The best known institution in the Maritime Provinces was of different origin. When the British occupied part of Maine in 1814 they established a "British" customhouse there and collected duties on the heavy traffic with New England. The proceeds were used to found the nonsectarian Dalhousie University in Halifax.

Schools and colleges were not the only means of education. The newspaper has often been called the university of the public, and there were a number of these "universities" in British North America before the others were founded. For many years all the newspapers in British North America were called gazettes.* The Halifax one was the first, appearing in 1752. The next was the bilingual and semiofficial Quebec *Gazette* in 1764. St. John had a *Gazette* in 1783, the very year the city was founded. The Montreal *Gazette,* which still survives as the leading conservative organ of Canada, commenced publication in 1785, though it claims to have been founded in 1778, when an ephemeral French sheet bearing the same name was produced by a printer imported by Benjamin Franklin two years before. In Upper Canada, Newark (Niagara) had a *Gazette* in 1793, and shortly afterward, when the capital was moved to York (Toronto), there had to be a *Gazette* there. The Newark paper died early, and the York *Gazette* was killed by Americans when they destroyed its office during the incursion of 1813; and for some years the Kingston *Gazette,* born in 1810, was the only newspaper in Upper Canada. In the various provinces other papers followed, with other names that broke the monotony.

These little sheets resembled our larger papers of today in

* One of the first papers to appear in Europe was published in Venice, where it sold for a small Venetian coin called a *gazet.* As often happens, the price came to be used to designate the thing, and *gazette* became the commonest name for newspapers to adopt.

conveying news and in carrying advertisements; but they also resembled our better magazines, for along with news and advertisements they published purely literary articles. To the reader of today their old, yellow pages are very revealing, and among other things they show that in the second quarter of the century public interest became more and more centered on the problem of government.

CHAPTER 10

The British North American Revolution

As THE middle of the century drew near, the most interesting development in British North America was a revolution in government. In the history of the British Empire it stands only second in importance to the American Revolution, with which it is more closely connected than most people realize. In the long run the United States was greatly, though unconsciously, responsible for emancipating the colonies that stayed in the empire. Contrary to this ultimate effect, however, the immediate result of the American Revolution was to make British colonial policy more reactionary rather than more liberal, and this policy prevailed for two generations.

Naturally the home government was intent on avoiding the mistakes that had produced what was to almost all thinking Britons the greatest tragedy in the history of the empire. But according to the common British diagnosis of the day these mistakes were first letting the colonies develop practically free of control and then attempting to tax them. Consequently it became the settled purpose of the imperial government never to tax a colony again and never to let the remaining colonies get out of hand. These quickly became the two cardinal principles of colonial management. The first, of course, was not reactionary at all, but the second was wholly so.

The method by which the mother country tried to keep her children in leading strings was simply a more rigid application of two old systems that she had more or less neglected. One was commercial—the Old Colonial System, which is so well known that it need not be explained here. The other was the system of government by governor, council, and assembly; and though this may seem familiar too, it needs closer examination.

Assemblies were more necessary than ever because of the British decision never to tax a colony. But now assemblies were to be kept strictly in their place and never allowed to grow independent, as they had in the old colonies. No assembly was to have more than a limited power over colonial legislation, or any power whatever over a colonial executive. The legislative will of the popular chamber was subject to a triple check—first by the council acting as an upper chamber, then by the governor, and finally by the home government. No assembly had even a voice in the way the government of a colony was administered. That was the business of the governor or lieutenant governor. With the advice of the council, which he selected, he ruled the colony and could dismiss every government official in it. They were all answerable to him, and he in turn was responsible to the government in London.

On the whole this system worked well in the beginning, for it suited the character of the empire as it had been altered by the American Revolution. From being an empire composed chiefly of colonies that were not only populous and wealthy but also mature enough politically for the fullest measure of self-government, it had suddenly become an empire of poor and weak colonies, unable to stand on their own feet for a long time to come. The grown-up family was gone, and the mother was starting over again with a new family of little children.

The time came, however, when things began to go wrong. The system was not static, and neither were the colonies. It degenerated and they developed. Either of these changes would have produced friction. Occurring simultaneously, they produced such a serious situation that some kind of revolution was inevitable.

The degeneration of the system was quite different from what had been allowed to occur in the American colonies before the Revolution. In the old days, by a neglect that was not to be repeated, the assembly had grown to upset the established balance of government. Now something else happened, something much less healthy—an ossification in the executive department. The disease began before the American Revolution, which eradicated it from the "old thirteen," but it became much more pronounced in the remaining colonies afterward. When the governments of these colonies were established, it was not easy, except in New Brunswick, to find local men with the necessary education and ability to staff them, and some importations were necessary. Once found, these men were too valuable to lose, and thus they became entrenched in the service, their permanent tenure of office hardening into custom. The one exception was the highest official of all, the governor or lieutenant governor. He could be only a temporary sojourner because he was almost invariably a military officer sent out from England or transferred from another station. If his administration was a failure, he was naturally recalled; if it was a success, he was just as naturally rewarded by being promoted to a more important command elsewhere. The man who replaced him, likewise a stranger to the land and its people, had to lean on the permanent officials for advice on how he should carry out his orders from London. Moreover, these orders had to be based on some information about the colony; and this information was secured from him and his predecessors, who in turn had got it largely from this very group of permanent officials.

Thus it came about that the government of each colony, though theoretically controlled by the mother country through the governor or lieutenant governor aided by the councilors whom he could select and remove, fell into the hands of a close little oligarchy in each provincial capital—the members of the council, who, with their friends and relatives, filled every important office except that of the chief executive. Legally they were responsible to him and through him to the home government, practically they were not, because he was a stranger and London was far off; and neither legally nor practically were they responsible to the assembly.

This perversion made the system doubly intolerable as the colonies approached what might be called the adolescent stage in their development, and the inevitable result was a rising demand for self-government. At first it was not clearly formulated. Here and there a popular leader hinted at copying the American pattern with its election of the executive as well as of the legislature, its separation of powers, and its checks and balances, but these suggestions made little headway. Gradually the movement became focused upon securing a form of government like that of the mother country with its fusion of powers in the Cabinet, its executive chosen from the legislature and responsible to it. The movement thus came to be known as the struggle for responsible government, and those who supported it were called Reformers.

Strange as it may seem now, the Reformers did not have the backing of the whole people. Their demands met with serious resistance in each of the provinces and in London as well. As might be expected, the members of the ruling clique in each province would not yield to the popular outcry. They were, of course, clinging to office and power, but their motives were by no means wholly selfish. They held two honest convictions which, being shared by many others in the community and by the home government, made them the leaders of a real Tory party and gave them the support of the authorities in Britain. One of their convictions was that self-government would be bad government because the majority of the people could never be entrusted with the control of public affairs, and to prove this the contemporary workings of American democracy were freely cited. This attitude of mind is not surprising if we remember that, in the awakening and triumph of democracy, the colonies lagged behind the United States but anticipated the mother country, where the mass of the people did not get the vote until the latter part of the nineteenth century. The other conviction was that colonial self-government would lead straight to colonial independence and thus to the breakup of the empire. Here was the greatest obstacle in the path of the Reformers. They had to fight the invulnerable ghost of the American Revolution.

The agitation for self-government and the resistance to it troubled British North America for a good many years. New Brunswick and Nova Scotia were the least disturbed, for there the issue lacked the exasperating complications that appeared in the other provinces, and there also the ruling clique was not quite so narrow as it became elsewhere. On more than one occasion a man who had gained the public confidence and become a leader of the assembly found himself appointed to an important government position in these provinces. Apart from a little friction now and then there was tolerable harmony until 1830 in Nova Scotia and even later in New Brunswick.

The Nova Scotians were roused by the eloquent preaching of the greatest Reformer in all British North America, Joseph Howe, a man of remarkable ability and magnetic personality. Of all Nova Scotians from the beginning down to the present day, he was by far the best loved—and by the men as well as by the ladies. He is reputed to have kissed nearly every girl in the province, and there are still a few old men who stand an inch or two taller for having once "held Joe's horse" when they were lads. It was he who ended the tolerable harmony in 1830, when he began his crusade in the columns of his newspaper, the *Nova Scotian*. Six years later he was elected to the assembly, where he soon became and long remained the dominant figure. He was just succeeding in rallying the majority of the population in his native province when he was suddenly embarrassed by developments in other provinces and the angry feelings that had been let loose there.

In Prince Edward Island the land question complicated the issue. The absentee proprietors clung to their titles and would pay neither quitrents nor taxes. The people, through their assembly, were constantly attacking this abuse, but they were as helpless as children crying for the moon. This, however, was not what embarrassed Howe. He was concerned over the situation in the two Canadas, where rebellion had raised its head.

The most dangerous complication was the division of races in Lower Canada. The English-speaking residents of Quebec and Montreal had long worked for an assembly, expecting to control it; but they were alarmed when they got it, for it was accompanied by the separation of Upper Canada, which placed them in a hopeless minority in the Lower Canadian chamber. Their fear of being crushed by the overwhelming weight of the French majority quickly turned their political principles upside down. Now they denounced popular government and rallied behind the ruling group, for it was chiefly composed of men of their own blood who were likewise fearful of what a French assembly might do. In self defense the local executive and its supporters developed a strong anti-French policy. They wanted to Anglicize the French, to make them learn English. They wanted to check the powerful influence of the religious organization of the French, the Roman Catholic church. They knew that the French assembly would lay the main burden of taxes on commerce, which was largely in their own hands, whereas they wanted the weight to fall on the owners of land, the French. Were not these the majority of the people, and would not commerce enrich the province? Finally, back of all this lay the feeling that the interests of the race that had conquered the country should be supreme.

Meanwhile the French, to whom representative government was something utterly strange, were slow to realize that they possessed the assembly. Nearly fifteen years elapsed before they awoke, and then they too were alarmed by what they saw. Their assembly was blocked by the upper chamber, and the government was in the hands of men who were hostile to their language, their religion, and their economic interests and would treat them like a conquered people.

The two races were thus pitted against each other by the system of government. There is no point in blaming either of them, for both did what was most natural under the circumstances. Driven by mutual fear they closed in a bitter struggle, each fighting for self-preservation. The results were little short of tragic. We have seen how the conflict prevented the province from having any public school system. It also retarded the economic development of the country. The English-speaking minority were the progressive element in the population. Anxious to encourage commerce and industry, they sought the reform of outworn French laws and the expenditure of provincial funds upon public works. But they could not budge the assembly. Even the improvement of Montreal harbor was stopped. Generally speaking, the machinery of government was thrown out of gear. It could not work without the cooperation of the assembly, and the assembly would not cooperate.

Governor after governor was sent out to wrestle with the ugly situation. The first was Sir James Craig, an old soldier of over forty years' service who believed in attacking things boldly. Because he was out of patience with the French assembly he scolded it severely and then dissolved it. He was going to teach public opinion a lesson and thereby get a more reasonable house, but his method produced only a more obstinate chamber. This too he dissolved in anger. Then he arrested some of the popular leaders on charges of treason, for they had been very outspoken in their attacks upon the government. The French retaliated by eagerly electing every man whom he had lodged in jail. Craig retired in 1811, a broken man.

Some of his successors had more tact, but few had more success,

The British North American Revolution

and on the whole the situation grew worse, until by 1832 the public temper had become almost explosive. In that year when troops were used to suppress election riots in Montreal, Louis Joseph Papineau, the fiery champion of his race, burst out with the statement that while Craig had merely imprisoned men, Lord Aylmer, who was now governor, shot them down in the streets. It was twenty years since Papineau, a young lawyer, had joined his father as a member of the assembly, seventeen since he had been elected speaker, ten since the assembly had sent him to England to fight a proposal of the British government to re-unite Upper and Lower Canada, five since he had grown so offensive to the governor of the day that the latter had refused to accept his reelection as speaker, and he was now approaching the climax of his stormy career. The idea of armed revolt began to simmer, and soon a few extremists on both sides were drilling quietly. Of course each side started it. Meanwhile something interesting was happening throughout the province. Though the Roman Catholic clergy had good reason for fearing the policy of the racial minority, they grew even more fearful of the way Papineau was leading their people, for it seemed to them that this demagogue was following a dangerous road. This explains why the revolt, when it came, was not widespread.

The rebellion of 1837 in Lower Canada was not a rising of the French people. If it had been, the situation would have been terrible, for the French still numbered more than half the population of Upper and Lower Canada combined. But as a people they remained quietly at home with their curés when Papineau sent forth his call to arms in the fall of 1837. Only a few hundred answered the call, and the disturbance was limited to two small localities. Papineau fled in panic to the United States even before the authorities restored order, which they did quickly and with little loss of life. Nevertheless both races had received a great fright, and the shock did not improve their tempers.

In Upper Canada the rebellion of 1837 was only an echo of the small explosion in Lower Canada. Although there was no conflict of nationalities in the upper province, there were other complications. We have seen how this province was becoming Americanized until the War of 1812 checked and reversed the process. But it would be a mistake to imagine that American influences did not survive. As late as 1824 the largest religious body in the province was a real part of the church south of the line, not just an offshoot of it. Until that year, when the Upper Canadian Methodists organized a separate conference, their preachers belonged to a conference in the United States, and there were many suspicions that they mixed some American gospel with their religious gospel as they wandered about the province. In many other ways, too, much of the American character of the population was being preserved, and this condition naturally intensified the political strife in Upper Canada. To the minds of the Family Compact, as the local oligarchy was called, the popular agitation for self-government took on the shape of American democracy and republicanism, which had to be crushed.

Geography, which was largely responsible for this American character of the population, contributed in still other ways to the bitterness of Upper Canadian politics. Being an inland province, its only contact with the outside world was through the United States or Lower Canada, where its imports paid duties. All that Upper Canada could recover of this tax upon its own trade was a portion of what was collected on the lower St. Lawrence. This was regulated at first by an interprovincial agreement that broke down and later by legislation in London, but even then Upper Canada got less than its just share. While geography thus cramped the revenue of the province, it also swelled the public expenditures, for Upper Canada was dependent upon the development of roads, bridges, and canals, and it undertook more than it could afford. The cost of the Welland Canal, upon which work commenced in 1824, proved to be many times what was expected. The result was that Upper Canada, alone among the provinces, approached bankruptcy, and naturally the people blamed the government for it.

Still more exasperating was the land question, which was also peculiar to the province. One seventh of every township was reserved for the support of the Church of England and another seventh for the support of the government.* These Crown and clergy reserves, wild lands scattered everywhere, prevented solid settlement and increased the natural difficulty of building and

* Lower Canada also had clergy and Crown reserves, but only in a small portion of the province, whereas they were general in Upper Canada.

The British North American Revolution

repairing roads and of organizing schools and churches. To make matters worse, almost everyone connected with the government, every friend and relative of every official, seems to have got a generous grant of land to hold for speculation. All these lands held for private profit or public gain were like a millstone round the neck of the people. This situation alone created such a spirit of discontent as was never known in the Maritime Provinces except in Prince Edward Island—and the discontent in Upper Canada had a strong religious flavor that was lacking in the Island. The clergy reserves belonged to the church of the governing group and not of the people. In them, the sight of a clergy reserve often stirred feelings that were not very Christian.

The leader of the popular cause in Upper Canada was William Lyon Mackenzie, a hotheaded Scot whose outspoken newspaper, the *Colonial Advocate,* so enraged the Family Compact that they persecuted him into becoming the most popular man in the province. In 1828 he was elected to represent York in the assembly, but the Tories, who then had a majority, expelled him. Five times they did it, and each time he was reelected. In 1834, when the Reformers got control of the chamber, he finally took his seat and became the stormy petrel of the legislature. He was the Papineau of Upper Canada, and naturally the two men fell into correspondence, by which means they egged each other on, each persuading the other that the people of his province were solidly behind him and would rise in revolt when necessary.

There would probably have been no rebellion in Upper Canada if the lieutenant governor had not sent all his little garrison to Lower Canada to help suppress the disturbance there. Thus left unguarded, Toronto had a considerable stock of arms and ammunition, and the temptation was too great for Mackenzie. He decided to seize the capital, to overthrow the government, and to establish a republic in this British colony. Fewer than five hundred desperate farmers gathered at a tavern north of the city, while more than twice that number of loyal citizens offered their services to defend the capital and crush the rebels. A skirmish between a small loyal party and the main body of insurgents ended with both sides running away. Two days later, in an engagement that lasted only twenty minutes, the rebellion was snuffed out. Like Papineau, Mackenzie fled to the United States, where he breathed fire and thunder. Meanwhile, as in the lower province, the shock of the explosion unsettled people's nerves.

But these two uprisings had one good result. They startled London into sending out Lord Durham, with wide powers to take charge of the whole situation in British North America. Durham was one of the outstanding British statesmen of the day and perhaps the ablest of them all. He had been a power in the Cabinet of his father-in-law, Lord Grey, and was the principal author of that Cabinet's greatest work, the famous Reform Bill of 1832. Though an aristocrat, and one of the wealthiest, he was politically too radical to remain in the Whig Cabinet, and now that he was no longer in it he was feared as the man who could turn the ministry out of office whenever he wished. He hesitated to accept the Canadian mission, yielding only after a strong personal request from the young Queen Victoria. His arrival on this side of the water marks the beginning of another era.

On reaching Quebec in May 1838, Durham was brought face to face with two nasty problems that demanded immediate action. Refugee rebels, assisted by numerous American sympathizers, threatened Canada from the United States. The tension along the border was most acute at Niagara, where two "invasions," one from each side of the river, had occurred the previous December. Canada was "invaded" when Mackenzie, with a body of American followers under Rensselaer Van Rensselaer of Albany, took possession of Navy Island, and the United States was "invaded" when some British seized and burned the steamer *Caroline,* which had been engaged by the rebels, and in the process killed an American. Realizing that any day might bring serious trouble and perhaps war with the United States, Durham straightway communicated with Washington to remind the American government that it was in duty bound to stop this border threat against a friendly people. His reminder stimulated quick action, and American officials soon broke up the nests of plotters.

The other pressing problem was how to deal with the captured rebels. A few had already been hanged in Upper Canada, and in both provinces excited people were crying out for wholesale execution. A handful of the prisoners were guilty of murder, and of course the law would have to take its course with them. But what should be done with the others who were held on charges of treason? Feeling was so tense that it was impossible to find impartial juries. Innocent men would be executed and guilty men set free according to the prejudices of the jurymen. Some other solution was necessary, so Durham promptly opened the doors of the prisons to all the ordinary rebels except eight leaders, for whom he felt some punishment was necessary. These he dispatched to Bermuda for detention, instead of sending them to a penal colony, which he judged would be too heavy a disgrace.

Durham's stay in Canada lasted only five months. It was cut short by the news that the home government, then tottering under the assaults of the opposition, had deserted him. This forced his resignation. But he had already done much, and he was yet to accomplish far more. The report that he submitted on his return is perhaps the most famous government report in the English language. It is the cornerstone of the present British Empire, or Commonwealth of Nations.

Durham's report, submitted early in 1839, insisted upon a complete change in British colonial policy. The fear of letting the colonies have too much freedom lest this freedom destroy the empire, he argued, was both false and dangerous. Trying to hold back the colonies would only irritate them into wishing to break away, and their people would cease to be British if their British birthright were withheld from them. There was only one way to keep them attached to the mother country, and that was to give them the same liberty to govern themselves that the people at home enjoyed. Instead of a policy of force inspired by fear he demanded a policy of freedom inspired by faith. This, he proclaimed, was the sovereign cure for the ills that had been troubling British North America. This was the magic that would bind the empire together. He was the first British statesman to see this fundamental principle, and seeing it he gave the idea to the British world. In this lies the supreme greatness of his report.

In other parts of this memorable document Durham advocated the federation of British North America. This, he said, would enable the colonies to attack their common problems together; it would give their public men a wider outlook and higher ambitions; it would inspire the people with self-confidence; and it would make them grow into a real nation. Here too he was a prophet.

But Durham knew that the time had not come when his

dream of a Dominion could be fulfilled. The Maritime Provinces were not yet willing to be united with Canada. Then, too, there was the peculiar situation in Lower Canada, which he described as "two nations warring in the bosom of a single state." Something drastic had to be done to still the racial strife or it would rend the colony more than ever, and the only way he could see to do this was to reunite the Canadas. Incidentally, this union would rescue Upper Canada from bankruptcy. In urging such a step, however, Durham's main motive was to prevent the revival of the troublesome French assembly, which the British Parliament had suspended before sending him out. In its place he would put a larger assembly with an English-speaking majority. He did not see how the French could be fitted into his scheme of self-government so long as they retained their separate nationality. Their only hope, he believed, was to become Anglicized, and he would hasten the process by union.

Here was Durham's blind spot, and it was a big one. At different times in various lands, races have been assimilated. But this has occurred only when the assimilated people did not possess an old and fixed civilization, or when they were such a small or such a scattered minority that they all came into personal contact with those who absorbed them. Neither of these basic conditions existed in Canada. The French belonged to a civilization as ancient and as established as that of the English. Far from being a small and scattered minority, they were still perhaps a majority in the two Canadas, though Durham seems to have doubted it, and they were already settled in too big and solid a block ever to be broken. They were bound to survive.

The union of the two Canadas was the only part of Durham's report that was adopted immediately. In 1840 the imperial Parliament passed the Union Act. It was most unjust to the French. In the first place, Upper Canada had piled up a huge debt, while Lower Canada had contracted only a small one. The act combined them as the debt of United Canada and thereby shifted a heavy financial load from English to French shoulders. Even more distasteful to the French was another provision of the act making English the only official language and thus depriving the French tongue of the status it had shared equally with English in Lower Canada. Greater still was the injury that the act inflicted by giving to Upper Canada the same number of seats in the new legislature that it gave to Lower Canada, though the population of the former was scarcely three quarters that of the latter. This was to prevent the French, who were still perhaps the majority of the total population, from having anything more than a helpless minority in the assembly, for they were out-numbered in the English-speaking districts of Lower Canada. They were gagged and crushed. Small wonder they cried out for the repeal of this act as an iniquitous and un-British measure!

Without denying the injustice of the Union Act many writers have defended it on the ground that it was necessary at the time and wise in the end. They have argued with Durham that any assembly with a French majority would have run wild and was therefore out of the question. They have also argued that the only way in which the French could learn how to operate the British system of government was by being yoked with those who had grown up in the British tradition, and so the restraint imposed was good for all concerned. Yet however sound these arguments may seem to those who speak English as their native tongue, it is hard to find any French Canadian who has accepted them.

Durham died in the summer of 1840, and he had lain in his grave for several years before London allowed the colonies to have responsible government. It was an intellectual difficulty that stood in the way of adopting his prescription. He had pro-posed that the colonies have the same kind of government as Britain; that just as the king followed the advice of his ministers, who were the leaders of Parliament, so should a governor follow the advice of ministers who were the leaders of his legislature. But this raised a nice question. How could a governor be like the king, who was in a very different position? There was no one above the king, whereas the king was above a governor, who was only his representative. When the ministers in London told the king what to do, he did it without demur, because no one else had any authority to advise him. But ministers in a colony might advise their governor to do something that conflicted with his orders from London. Then what would he do? If he obeyed his ministers, would he not become an independent sovereign and his colony a separate state? It certainly looked as if the granting of responsible government would put an end to the empire.

Though the authorities in London shrank from adopting

Durham's principle, they wished to give the people in the colonies every possible satisfaction, and a blow from above was now struck at the local oligarchies. In 1839 the home government condemned the custom of permanent tenure of office. Thenceforth each governor was to be free to change any of his officials as he saw fit. By judicious dismissals and appointments he was expected to keep the executive in harmony with the will of the people as expressed in the assembly. In other words he was to be prime minister as well as governor of his colony. This arrangement was a hybrid between the American system, with its separation of the executive from the legislature, and the British system, with its fusion of these two branches of government.

The failure of this new hope of harmony was soon apparent in every colony but New Brunswick, where no serious demand for responsible government had arisen. At first glance it is rather puzzling to find one province so different from all the others, but an explanation may be found in the Maine border dispute which, after simmering for many years, boiled up in the so-called Aroostook War of 1839. Lumbermen from both countries clashed in the disputed area, and soon British and American troops faced each other across a stream only thirty yards wide. Fortunately no nervous finger on either side pulled a trigger, and a truce ended the crisis. The upshot was the well-known negotiation between Daniel Webster and Lord Ashburton and the final settlement of the boundary by the treaty of 1842. Meanwhile the people of New Brunswick, realizing how dependent they were upon the backing of Britain in this dispute, were bursting with patriotism and were therefore little inclined to challenge her control of their government.

In the other provinces, where there was no such restraint upon the natural urge of the people to get possession of their own governments, trouble quickly developed. The beloved Joseph Howe persuaded the members of the Nova Scotian legislature to declare that they had no confidence in the executive, and when the governor replied that *he* had, Howe carried a motion demanding his recall. London acquiesced but sent out a successor who was no more acceptable. He was a proud noble who could never forget that he had held an appointment at court as lord of the bedchamber. Howe lampooned him in verses that be-

MONTREAL YESTERDAY AND TODAY. ABOVE, THE OLD TOWN EARLY IN THE
NINETEENTH CENTURY, WITH BEAVER HALL HILL AND THE HAY MARKET.
BELOW, MODERN MONTREAL; PANORAMIC VIEW FROM MOUNT ROYAL,
SHOWING VICTORIA BRIDGE ACROSS THE ST. LAWRENCE RIVER.

TORONTO'S GROWTH OVER A HUNDRED YEARS. ABOVE, THE CITY IN 1834.
BELOW, THE METROPOLIS OF TODAY.

CALGARY, ALBERTA: THE GROWTH OF A PRAIRIE CITY. ABOVE, IN 1881.
BELOW, THE CENTRAL SECTION OF THE CITY TODAY.

VANCOUVER, FROM WILDERNESS TO METROPOLIS. ABOVE, BURRARD INLET,
THE SITE OF MODERN VANCOUVER, 1861. BELOW, THE CITY OF TODAY.

gan "The lord of the bedchamber sat in his shirt" and got him recalled also. If the new system could ever have been worked, it would have been in United Canada, where even the finest type of governor failed. The difficulty was in the system itself, which attempted to combine the incompatible roles of governor and prime minister. The only government that would satisfy the people was one controlled by them through their elected representatives, not by the mother country through a governor.

At last the home government decided to let the colonies have what they wanted. The way was prepared by the adoption of free trade by Britain in 1846. This revolution in fiscal policy, which was brought about by the needs of the mother country, carried with it implications of importance to the colonies; for the abandonment of protection meant the end of the closed economic system of the empire. This economic emancipation of the colonies was quickly followed by their political emancipation.

It is interesting to probe into the motives behind such a change. The colonial secretary, Lord Grey,* was inspired by the faith of his late brother-in-law, Lord Durham, but in this he was peculiar. His colleagues in the Cabinet, including the prime minister, were still obsessed by the logical conflict between imperial unity and colonial self-government. They had not conquered their fear of another American Revolution; it had finally conquered them, and now it turned them face about. They realized that continued resistance to the colonial demand would sooner or later drive the colonies into revolt and that no imperial force could then hold them within the empire because they were too close to the United States. As the colonies were apparently destined to go, was it not much better to have a peaceful and friendly parting than a violent and bitter one? Such, it seems, was the decision these men of little faith thought they were making. Then Durham's magic began to work, though it took some years to show its strength.

No legislation was necessary to effect this momentous transformation in the government of the colonies. A simple instruction from the colonial office that the will of the assemblies should no longer be resisted was sufficient to establish the cabinet system of government in the colonies, and this was done quietly

* The son of Lord Grey of the Reform Bill.

in the Maritime Provinces. In United Canada, however, it was accompanied by another convulsion, because there it meant much more than it did in the provinces down by the sea. It meant the end of the effort to keep the French Canadians down, as well as the end of the governor's control of the administration. Though more and more English-speaking politicians had been coming to see that responsible government was impossible in Canada unless it were shared equally by the two races, the extreme Tories still believed that no French Canadian could be trusted with the affairs of government. These Tories were the cause of the convulsion, which occurred in Montreal, the capital of the united province.

The governor general who was sent out to inaugurate the new era in Canada was Lord Elgin, an ideal choice. He had married Durham's daughter and had imbibed Durham's faith. He also learned a lesson that his father-in-law had missed. He saw that the French Canadians could never be Anglicized and that any attempt to crush their nationality would only strengthen it. With a noble vision that recalls Carleton at his best, he maintained that there might be no British subjects more loyal than the French Canadians if their loyalty was rooted in real British liberty—the liberty to be themselves. Early in 1848, when the government of the day resigned because a majority of the assembly was opposed to it, he called upon the two leaders, French and English, of this majority to form a new administration. To carry still further the principle of racial equality, he persuaded the home government by an amendment of the Union Act to restore French as an official language, and in the following year the legislature was opened with speeches in French and English.

To the extreme Tories the presence of French Canadians in the new government was like a red rag to a bull. Their rage mounted in 1849, when the government proposed a measure known as the Rebellion Losses Bill. Its purpose was to compensate people for damages they had suffered during the rebellions, unless they had been convicted or transported. As this exception covered few of those who had risen in arms, it was plain that many who did not deserve payment would get it. The government knew this but believed that some injustice could not be avoided, for an examination into the loyalty of every claimant would reopen old sores.

The British North American Revolution

The Tories fought the bill, accusing the government of introducing it in order to pay rebels for having rebelled, and when the measure passed they clamored for the governor general to veto it. But he was true to the principle of responsible government and signed the bill. Then the loyal rage of the extreme Tories exploded in disloyalty. They stirred up a mob that burned the Parliament buildings, wrecked the French leader's house, and hurled rotten eggs, hard stones, and harder words at the governor general as he drove through the streets of Montreal.

These Tory riots of 1849 have left their mark. Montreal would probably be the seat of the Dominion government today had not these disgraceful outbursts of violence made it impossible for that city to remain the capital of United Canada. The honor that Montreal then lost was given alternately to Toronto and Quebec until 1865, when Ottawa became the permanent capital of United Canada.

In these riots also the Tory party rushed toward political suicide. Its leaders were now as guilty as Papineau and Mackenzie had been. Though it is not true in arithmetic, it is true in Canadian history that thirty-seven equals forty-nine. The sheet of the past was balanced, and Canada could begin a new page. But as if to make sure that there could be no doubt about it, some of the Tory leaders almost immediately took another step that was to complete the ruin of their party. They openly declared for annexation to the United States!

The publication of the Annexation Manifesto in Montreal in the fall of 1849 was due to more than blind fury against Elgin. The chief reason for it was economic. When Britain adopted free trade, she did not repeal her ancient navigation laws, and the combination injured the colonies generally and Canada in particular. By abandoning protection, the mother country abolished the generous preference that colonial goods had enjoyed in her markets. This hurt Canada especially because it destroyed a valuable trade that the preference had drawn through Canada from those parts of the United States that touched the Great Lakes. Thus the trade advantage of being a colony disappeared, while the trade disadvantage remained, for the navigation laws confined the trade to British ships. Therefore the businessmen of Montreal, the commercial capital of Canada, saw the ruin of their own and the country's prosperity. In despair they proclaimed that the only way of salvation was to cut the tie with Britain and to join the neighboring republic.

This Annexation Manifesto misfired. No welcoming hand was held out from the United States because of the fear of precipitating war with the South by adding to the free states of the North. (It has therefore been suggested that the cities of Canada should be adorned with statues of a negro slave!) But the slavery issue was not the only reason for the disappearance of the annexation movement in Canada at this time. The offending navigation laws were actually repealed just before the manifesto was published, and after much negotiation, in which Elgin played a prominent part in a visit to Washington, the Reciprocity Treaty of 1854 gave the principal exports of Canada and the Maritime Provinces a free market in the United States. This treaty killed what was left of the 1849 annexation movement.

Meanwhile the Tories had practically disappeared, and a new party had arisen—the Conservative party, which has continued to the present day. Its members called themselves Liberal Conservatives, because they included many old Reformers as well as Tories, and this is still the official name of the party. The man who gathered it together was one of the younger and more moderate Tories who had refused to sign the manifesto. As a lad he had come with his parents from Scotland, and as a young man he studied and practiced law in Kingston. When only twenty-eight, he was elected to the city council, and a year later he was chosen to represent Kingston in the Canadian assembly. This was in 1844. Young as he was, his influence quickly grew, for he had remarkable ability and a rare personal charm. His rapid rise is not surprising, because he was none other than the man who was to be chiefly responsible for the union of British North America in the Dominion of Canada—John A. Macdonald, who dominated the political life of the Dominion until his death in 1891.

Before proceeding to examine the next great transformation in Canadian history, the formation of the Dominion, we should point the moral and adorn the tale of the British North American Revolution by glancing at what happened in 1859. When responsible government was granted, the recent triumph of free trade in Britain seems to have obscured the fact that the colonies might use their new liberty to impose protective duties against the mother country. This was precisely what the united Province of Canada did in 1859, and it naturally stirred great surprise and indignation in England. Manufacturing interests vigorously denounced the new Canadian tariff and called upon the government in London to veto it. There was quite a little tempest in the imperial teapot. The home government remonstrated with the Canadian government, but the latter remained firm and London had to submit because, in the last analysis, British North America was living in the shadow of the United States. Only ten years had passed since the specter of annexation had arisen, and it was only too obvious that if Britain would not allow her North American colonies to go their own way in the empire they could go their own way out of it. The British North American Revolution was an accomplished fact.

CHAPTER II

Dominion from Sea to Sea

THE American Revolution sowed the seed that the American Civil War brought to fruition in the formation of the Dominion of Canada. The idea appeared on the morrow of the Revolution when the British government sent Dorchester out to salvage what had been left of the imperial wreck. Though he failed to draw the fragments together, the idea never quite died. Every now and then some prominent individual in one colony or another came forward with a proposal to realize it, and when Durham visited Canada he too became a convert. Here it is well to remember something that is often forgotten: that the American people, impelled by necessity, rehabilitated an ancient but long discredited form of government and inaugurated the rather striking growth of federalism in the modern world. In other words, the United States demonstrated the practicability of the formula by which British North America might be united.

The example of the United States also suggested more and more strongly that British North America ought to be united. The suggestion sprang from the phenomenal growth of the Republic as it strode like a young giant across the continent. If the lost colonies could thus become a great nation, why could not the remaining ones unite and build another? If they did not seek strength in union, could they avoid in the end being drawn under the expanding Stars and Stripes? Such thoughts inspired most of the advocates of federation for these colonies. Little attention was paid to them, however, until the middle of the nineteenth century, when new conditions opened people's eyes and changed their minds.

The condition that first compelled a large number of men to think seriously about federation developed in United Canada. The Union Act, which gave equal representation to Canada East and Canada West, as the old Lower and Upper Canada were now called, pinched first one and then the other. By 1850 Canada West had the larger population, and as it continued to grow, people there began to cry out for a larger proportion of members in the legislature. They demanded "Representation by Population"—a clumsy phrase that was commonly shortened and given a flavor of profanity as "Rep. by Pop." The cry threatened to wreck the union. But even if it had never risen there would have been trouble.

Government broke down under the weight of the union. The existence of two peoples divided by race, religion, language, social customs, and systems of law, each inhabiting a separate part of the country, made self-government increasingly difficult. Every cabinet had to have two heads and two distinct halves, one from Canada West and the other from Canada East. Otherwise it would be turned out of power. Also it had to have the support of each half of the legislature. A majority of the members from Canada East could not make up for a minority from Canada West, and the opposite was equally true. Neither half of the country would submit to rule by the other. Between 1854 and 1864 there were ten changes of ministry. The parliamentary system was ceasing to work.

One thing was now clear to the public men of the province; the Union Act had to go. French Canadian nationalism and English Canadian nationalism were too distinct and too strong to be squeezed together under one government and one parliament. They needed separate governments and parliaments, and yet they could not part completely. A simple repeal of the Union Act would revive the financial difficulties of Upper Canada. More important still, United Canada had undertaken certain responsibilities that could not well be divided. They were too big, and they were vital to both parts of Canada—railways and canals, for example. Therefore, although each section ought to have its own government to manage its own affairs, there should also be a government to look after customs, railways, canals, and the other interests they had in common. It was impossible to go back to mere division; it was necessary to go on to establish a federal system.

While people in United Canada were coming to see that this was the only way of escape, they lifted their eyes to look beyond the limits of their province. On the eastern horizon and on the

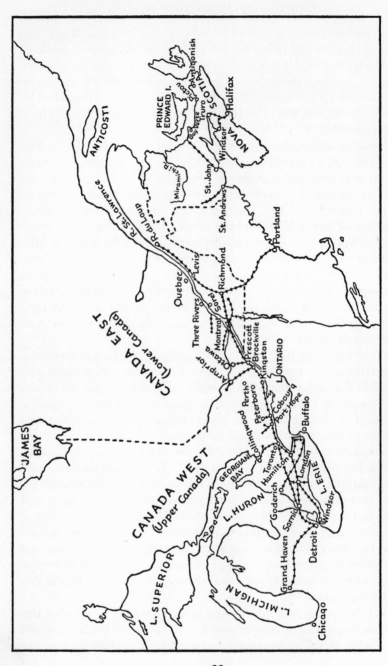

BRITISH NORTH AMERICAN RAILWAYS IN 1860.

168

western horizon they saw visions that made them believe it was not only possible but also desirable and probably urgent to organize a much greater federal union—one stretching from sea to sea!

It was the coming of the railway age that lifted the union of British North America out of the land of dreams. Before 1850 there were scarcely fifty miles of railway in all British North America. Then came a great change. By 1860 United Canada had two thousand miles of railroads—all she needed and more than she could afford. Her greatest system was the Grand Trunk Railway, which ran from Sarnia, at the foot of Lake Huron, to Rivière du Loup, on the south side of the St. Lawrence a hundred and twenty miles below Quebec, and had an outlet to the ocean through the United States at Portland, Maine. The Maritime Provinces had three small railways that had no connection with one another. If only these railways could be joined together and linked with the Grand Trunk by a road filling the gap to Rivière du Loup, British North America might have a real railway system.

Still other changes were giving men larger views. In Canada West, as we have seen, the expansion of settlement had been proceeding rapidly. Around the middle of the century it ran up against the wilderness of rocks that runs from east to west about a hundred miles north of Toronto. Blocked in this direction the surplus population poured across the international border to take up good land in the northern Middle Western states, then growing by leaps and bounds. The great frontier movement that had once surged into Upper Canada had now passed beyond, into a newer and larger West in the United States. Immigrants were still crowding into Canada, but she could not keep them. Her growth was being stunted, and her public men were coming to feel that she must have a West of her own for expansion. So they looked to the part of the Northwest that was still under the Union Jack, and there they saw unlimited possibilities, likewise brought within reach by the coming of the railway.

The Hudson's Bay Company was losing its hold over the huge empire of the West. Who would get possession of it? Already there was a change that was ominous to British eyes. It will be recalled that in 1818 the international boundary had been run along the forty-ninth parallel to the Rocky Mountains, and the territory beyond had been left free and open to British and American traders on equal terms. As the years passed, the Hudson's Bay Company proved to be more than a match for every American rival that appeared; and by 1840 it looked as if this British company, with its headquarters at Fort Vancouver on the Columbia, opposite the present city of Portland, Oregon, had established practical British control over the whole country. Then American settlers entered the country in the wake of American missionaries, reopening the question that time and the Hudson's Bay Company had been closing: Who would have this territory? The American answer was "Fifty-four forty or fight," in other words, American possession of everything between California and Russian Alaska. But common sense prevailed in London and Washington alike, and negotiations led to the Oregon Treaty of 1846, which carried the boundary along the forty-ninth parallel to the sea. But though this crisis had passed its lesson was clear. Sooner or later the tide of American settlement would encroach upon the empty British land in the West unless the way were barred by British settlement. Canada determined to get this empire; she needed it for her own growth.

The section that first attracted the attention of a number of people in Canada was the prairie country. At its eastern corner the little Red River colony demonstrated the rich agricultural value of the soil. Until the middle of the century the settlement grew slowly, for it was too remote from the rest of the world to attract immigrants. The only increase of population came through the cradle or through the settlement of those who were already in the country—retired employees of the Hudson's Bay Company and *métis,* of whom the latter were the more numerous. In 1850 there were only about five hundred white people and nearly ten times as many half-breeds living along the banks of the Assiniboine and the Red rivers. But the outside world was creeping close, as the settlement of Minnesota moved north. Hitherto the only way into the country had been through Hudson Bay; now another opened, a prairie trail of five hundred miles to St. Paul, along which hundreds of Red River carts creaked back and forth. The opening of this door to the wide, fertile prairie lands led both to the development of the colony and to the downfall of its government.

Dominion from Sea to Sea

As the Hudson's Bay Company possessed the right of government by its charter, it had appointed a governor, a council, and various other officials. They had managed fairly well as long as the people had no temptation to sell their furs to any except employees of the company. But private trade began as soon as it became possible to smuggle furs out by Red River cart over the border, some sixty miles away. The government, acting in the interests of its master, the company, tried to stop this trade by searching houses, chasing carts, and confiscating furs. But the result was failure and worse. It soon became apparent that the authority of the government was broken and that the days of company rule were numbered.

The restlessness of the settlers grew as Americans and Canadians appeared in their midst. The white people of this company colony began to talk of getting a free government of their own either by becoming a regular British colony or by annexation to the United States or by joining Canada. In the winter of 1856–57 nearly six hundred of them signed a petition asking Canada to take over the country. This was great encouragement to Canada, and greater still soon came from England, where public criticism of the company led to the appointment of a parliamentary committee to examine into all its doings. Many witnesses were called, and the inquiry was almost like a trial. The committee concluded that "such territory as may be useful for settlement," particularly the "districts of the Red River and the Saskatchewan" should be "ceded to Canada on equitable principles." In other words, the prairie country ought to belong to Canada.

Then came startling news from the Pacific Coast, where the Hudson's Bay Company was likewise losing its grip. Beyond the territory drained into Hudson Bay it had owned no land until 1849, when the British government, reading the lesson of the Oregon crisis, had given Vancouver Island to the company to build a colony there. But it was then at the end of the earth, too far away to attract settlers from Britain or anywhere else. It had only a handful of people, most of whom had been or still were connected with the company, and though a governor and council were appointed and a diminutive assembly was elected, the government of the colony of Vancouver Island was really in the hands of the company. The first governor, sent from England, soon resigned and was succeeded by James Douglas, the company's chief factor in that region. The mainland remained a no man's land until 1858, when the discovery of gold on the Fraser River attracted a swarm of fortune seekers from every quarter of the globe, particularly from California. Thus a new and real colony arose, but one without a government. Douglas straightway assumed authority over the rabble on the mainland, and later in the year Britain created the colony of British Columbia, appointing Douglas its governor.

The gold rush did on the Pacific Coast what the opening of the St. Paul cart trail did on the Red River—and more. It destroyed the company's monopoly of trade, which there rested not on its charter but on a later grant by the British government, and it immediately killed the company's little power of government, instead of letting it linger in a sickly state, as on the Red River. The British government bought back Vancouver Island and forced Douglas, now governor of two colonies, to sever his connection with the company.

These sudden developments in the Far West were another reason why Canada wanted the whole domain of the Hudson's Bay Company. A railway could be built to connect the Atlantic with the Pacific, as had already been done in the United States, and this possibility, like that of linking Canada with the Maritime Provinces, raised hopes of great profits for businessmen already interested in the railroads of British North America. Eager to seize the prize and encouraged by the crumbling of the company's authority, the Canadian government tried to get the West without paying for it, claiming that the country had always belonged to Canada since the days of the French explorers. The Canadian contention was that the charter was worthless and that, if it had given the company anything, it was only a strip of land lying around the bay. To the company, therefore, Canada became an enemy seeking to rob it of its heritage. The hostility between the two delayed the taking over of the West and contributed not a little to the serious trouble that was shortly to arise.

On top of all these changes—first, the political situation in Canada necessitating some new form of government; second, the possibility of uniting the old British North American colonies by a railroad; third, the undermining of the Hudson's Bay

Dominion from Sea to Sea

Company's position; and, fourth, the vision of a dominion reaching from sea to sea—there came another that was more influential than any of these in bringing about a realization of the old dream. This was the American Civil War, which like the American Revolution was one of the most important events in the shaping of Canadian history.

If it had not been for the Civil War the United States, not Canada, might have been the heir of the Hudson's Bay Company. In 1861 Northerners were on the point of reaching farther north to the lands beyond their own prairies—but just then conflict with the South drew their energies in the opposite direction. In other words, the war pulled back the American arm stretched forth to seize what is now the Canadian Northwest. It is doubtful if the old United Canada, however reorganized, would have been strong enough to acquire and hold this huge territory, but the larger Dominion of Canada was able to do it, by how much margin we cannot say; and it is more than doubtful if there could have been a Dominion of Canada then or for a long time afterward, if at all, without the Civil War.

The Dominion was born, as it was conceived, in fear. The Civil War gave a new meaning to the old argument that the great Republic would sooner or later devour the little adjoining British colonies if they remained divided. That the government of Great Britain, by openly favoring the South, incurred the bitter hostility of the United States during this war is well known. That alone endangered British North America. It is perhaps less well known that these American colonial hostages of the empire gave further offense to the fighting Republic. Halifax and St. John were notorious bases for Southern blockade runners, and the Canadian border was alive with Confederate plotters whose threats to Americans across the line kept them in an almost constant state of alarm. These pin pricks from Canada developed into a nasty jab at St. Albans, Vermont, when the raiders shot up the town, looted the banks, and escaped back to Montreal where, though arrested, they were freed on a legal technicality. With the subjugation of the South, the United States had ample justification to make war on the neighboring parts of the British Empire; and it had the strength to succeed in this quarter, for in 1865 it had become what most people have forgotten—the greatest military power in the world. The obvious menace welded British North America together.

As late as 1864 the question of federation was still undecided, though it had been much discussed in the press and on the platform. There seemed to be no practical way to bridge the railway gap south of Rivière du Loup. New Brunswick could not pay for it, nor, it was feared, could all the provinces together. It could be done if the mother country would lend financial aid, and many efforts had been made to reach an agreement between the different provinces and the government in London, but all these efforts had failed. At last the Maritime Provinces, despairing of the larger union, decided to consider one of their own. They appointed delegates to meet in Charlottetown, the capital of Prince Edward Island, on September 1, 1864.

Meanwhile Canada had reached the end of her tether. The difficulty of working her parliamentary system had grown so great that it forced her opposing political leaders, John A. Macdonald and George Brown, to form a coalition government that was pledged to find a way of escape through a federal solution. This coalition had two plans. One was to reorganize United Canada on a federal basis; the other, which its members agreed would be better and therefore should be tried first, was to include the provinces down by the sea. The railway would come after the union—somehow. Seizing the opportunity of the coming Charlottetown meeting, the Canadian government asked permission to send a delegation there to discuss the question, and the request brought a cordial invitation. The Canadian delegation arrived on September 2, the plan of the Maritime Union was promptly shelved, and it was agreed to have a great conference in Quebec to work out the details of a federal scheme for all British North America, including Newfoundland. The Quebec Conference met in October and, as many men had already studied the problem closely, took less than a fortnight to complete its task. Almost everything in the British North America Act, which created the Dominion in 1867, was settled in the resolutions passed at Quebec in the autumn of 1864.

The next step was to get the consent of the several colonies that were to unite. When submitted to the Canadian legislature, the plan roused serious opposition only from Canada East, where the Roman Catholic church and the French population were afraid of what the English and Protestant majority in the new central government and Parliament might do to them. There was some danger of the French being stampeded into wrecking the proposal, but this was averted by their far-seeing leaders, particularly the bishops. The church quickly reversed its attitude, fearing that the rejection of federation would lead to annexation, which seemed a much greater evil. As it was, nearly half the French members voted against federation.

There was more opposition in the Maritime Provinces. They had been talking of annexing Canada; but now that they came face to face with the issue it looked as if Canada was going to annex them, for its population was nearly four times that of all the Maritime Provinces combined. Would not Canada be the body and they be the tail of the proposed federation? Moreover, the fact that these provinces were maritime made their people less apprehensive of danger from their great neighbor. The knowledge that Britain ruled the waves gave them a feeling of confidence that people in Canada could not share. Newfoundland, which had been represented at Quebec, would have nothing to do with the plan, though its governor favored it. The legislature of Prince Edward Island rejected it offhand. The New Brunswick government, which favored it, was defeated in a general election. Neither the legislature nor the people of Nova Scotia ever voted on the Quebec resolutions, or they too would have turned the scheme down. Therefore the government in Halifax, eager to achieve federation, stalled for time.

While federation was thus held up, strong forces were quietly at work to bring the Maritime Provinces into line. The government in London, fearing for the future of the colonies lying beside such a dangerous neighbor, determined to do everything possible to unite them and in many ways brought pressure to bear on public opinion where it was needed. Washington also helped by denouncing the Reciprocity Treaty. The people in the Maritime Provinces then saw themselves seriously injured by the loss of the American market for their produce. Federation offered them a substitute in Canada.

Another American influence was provided by the Fenians. When the Civil War was over, these Irish Americans, who hated

England with a consuming hatred, gathered on the border to invade and conquer British North America, and the United States seemed to smile upon their enterprise. In 1866 they invaded Canada in two places, across the Niagara River and the Vermont boundary, inflicting considerable damage before they were chased out. But their influence was greater where they did not actually appear—in New Brunswick. There the militia was called out and regular troops were sent from Halifax to defend the frontier against four or five hundred Fenians, many of them veterans of the Civil War, who had gathered for an invasion that never came off. Meanwhile the threat stirred a great wave of loyalty through the province and inclined many doubting minds to seek strength in union.

The tide turned in the spring of 1866. The shrewd premier of Nova Scotia, Dr. Charles Tupper, the man who had kept the legislature and the people from voting on the Quebec scheme, saw an opportunity for a clever stroke. He proposed, and the assembly passed, a resolution that, without mentioning the Quebec Conference or its work, authorized the provincial government to arrange with the British government a scheme of union that would protect the rights of each province. A few weeks later, just as the fear of a Fenian invasion was reaching a climax in New Brunswick, another general election was held in that province and a government in favor of federation was returned to power. Prince Edward Island was still obstinate, but United Canada, New Brunswick, and Nova Scotia felt that they could go on without it. In December their delegates met in London, adopted the Quebec resolutions with only slight changes, and decided what the new country was to be called. "The Kingdom of Canada" was the name that Macdonald then urged in vain. Many Canadians have since regretted that it was not adopted, for they believe that it might have led to a much earlier recognition of the present status of Canada as an equal partner in the empire. Macdonald's proposal was vetoed by the British government out of the fear of offending republican sensibilities in the United States. Thereupon the colonial delegates fell back upon the old term *Dominion*. In every other respect the British North America Act, which will be examined in the next chapter, was drafted exactly as they wished, and the "mother of parliaments" passed it without any question.

Dominion from Sea to Sea

On July 1, 1867, the Dominion of Canada came into existence. Quite naturally Macdonald became prime minister of the new country, and it was soon announced that he had been knighted. Thenceforth until his death in 1891 the political history of the Dominion is the history of this man. During all this time, with the exception of a five-year interlude, he remained at the head of the government. He was not a great speaker, but he had a ready tongue that seldom if ever wounded anyone. He had one notorious weakness—an unquenchable thirst, which has inspired countless tales about "the old man." According to one story still current, a young reporter was sent to get a verbatim record of a much advertised speech, got it, found it so bad that it made no sense, and was afraid to send it to his paper. Next morning he brought it to Macdonald with an apology for reporting him so badly and a request for his correction. He was then given a copy of the important speech that alcohol had wrecked, and with it the merry warning, "Young fellow, let this be a lesson to you! Never report a public man when you are drunk!"

Macdonald had a rare genius for handling men and was a consummate politician. Having organized the Conservative party when the old Tories rushed to their destruction, he now organized a coalition government on the plea that the old party issues had no meaning in the new Dominion. But it was not long before the party division asserted itself in federal politics, the coalition having served to strengthen the Conservatives at the expense of the Liberals. It would be a mistake, however, to suggest that Macdonald was nothing more than a politician. He was a statesman of fine quality—so fine that many Canadians regard him as the greatest their country has ever produced.

The Dominion of 1867 was only one tenth as big as the Dominion of today. It had only four provinces, Nova Scotia, New Brunswick, and the two provinces into which the old Canada was again divided, Quebec and Ontario. The last two were a mere fraction of their present size, for all the land draining into Hudson Bay still belonged to the great English fur-trading company. Yet small as the new Dominion was, it was at first in danger of becoming smaller still. Nova Scotia threatened to withdraw, and the threat greatly worried Macdonald.

The secession movement in Nova Scotia is not to be compared with the movement of the same name in New England or in the

177

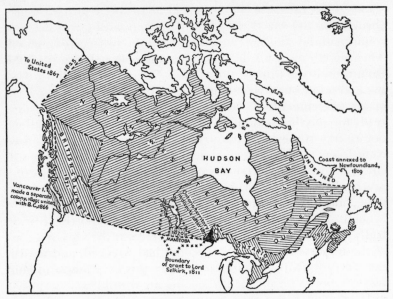

THE DOMINION OF CANADA IN 1873.

South. It was largely the work of one man who had preached federation when it was still a dream but fought it when it became a practical issue—the eloquent, impulsive, and beloved Joseph Howe, hoary champion of responsible government. He was passionately devoted to his native land, Nova Scotia, and he saw it being bound and delivered to Canada by his younger political rival, Charles Tupper. He did his best to keep his province out of the union, and when he failed he became desperate and determined to pull it out. He would have succeeded if the people of Nova Scotia had been allowed to decide. They had never voted for federation, and as soon as they had a chance, in the first elections after the Dominion was created, they voted strongly against it. Though this was largely the result of Howe's fiery appeals by tongue and pen, we should not overlook the fact that the geographical position of Nova Scotia gave full force to them. The sea insulated her from the fear that operated in the provinces lying close by the mighty Republic.

The antifederation government that was now established in Halifax sent Howe with a delegation to London to demand the release of the province from its new bonds. But the imperial authorities turned a deaf ear to all Howe's pleading. For safety's sake British North America had been united and must remain united. Nova Scotians grew angrier and angrier until the new premier of the province began to talk of annexation. His words frightened Howe into changing his course. Opening negotiations with Macdonald, he secured a larger Dominion subsidy for Nova Scotia and thenceforth he courageously supported what he had so bitterly denounced. For a short time the storm down by the sea continued to rage furiously—and then blew itself out.

Geography also explains what happened to the two island colonies represented at Quebec—Newfoundland and Prince Edward Island. It prevented the fear of the United States from pressing strongly upon their people, and it allowed them to escape the experience of the Nova Scotians, who were brought into federation and held there against their will. Newfoundland has continued to remain outside the Dominion because, being farther away, it has felt less attraction to join. But the Dominion was most eager to get Prince Edward Island. Lying close to New Brunswick and Nova Scotia, it threatened to cause trouble if it remained outside. In addition to agriculture and fishing, the islanders might develop a third industry—smuggling. Moreover, the proper control of the fisheries would always be difficult, if not impossible, as long as there were two authorities instead of one. So the Dominion made every effort to persuade Prince Edward Island to join, offering an extra financial allowance to assist in buying out the absentee proprietors. The island rejected all proposals until it got into further difficulty by building a railway it could not pay for. Then, on receiving from Ottawa a hint that the federal government might help, the provincial government opened negotiations. Terms were quickly arranged; the federal government took over the railway and also provided money to buy out the proprietors. On July 1, 1873, Prince Edward Island became the seventh province of the Dominion, the fifth and sixth having meanwhile been added in the West.

At about the time the Dominion was born, the public men of Canada abandoned their effort to get the West without paying for it. To do so would have meant lawsuits against the Hudson's Bay Company, which might have ended in Canada's being forced to pay full value for the land in addition to the heavy expense of litigation. Moreover, the courts might have taken years to reach a final decision, and immediate action seemed urgent. Americans were openly talking of annexing the country north of the forty-ninth parallel, and in 1866 a bill to that effect was actually introduced into the American Congress and debated there. In the following year the United States bought Alaska, and there was talk of this being a move to prevent the Dominion from reaching the Pacific.

As soon as the Canadian government was prepared to negotiate, it found the English company ready to do the same. They came to terms in the spring of 1869. The company agreed to give up all its rights under the charter—its monopoly of trade, its ownership of the land, and its authority to govern. In return, Canada promised to pay the company £300,000; to allow it to keep blocks of land around its trading posts and one twentieth of the land in the "fertile belt," that is, one twentieth of all the land lying south of the North Saskatchewan from the mountains to Lake Winnipeg and Lake of the Woods; and to permit the company to continue its business as a private organization. The company was to hand back to the Crown the land that Charles II had granted in the charter, and the British government was to give both this land and the remainder of the Northwest to the Dominion on December 1, 1869.

When that day arrived the Dominion refused to accept delivery because a rebellion had broken out in the territory that was to have been handed over. For this outbreak, however, the Canadian government was much to blame. In buying the country it had paid no attention to the people living there, although they were certainly the most concerned in what was happening. They felt as if they had been sold with the land like so much livestock. The white people, numbering about fifteen hundred, had hoped for self-government but learned that they were to be ruled by a lieutenant governor and council appointed in Ottawa and controlled from Ottawa.

The half-breeds, of whom there were nearly ten thousand, had further grounds for fear. The few Canadians in the country had treated them with scorn, boasting that the land would soon be swarming with other Canadians. Then what would happen to the *métis?* The French Canadians of Quebec, on becoming part of the Dominion, had insisted upon laws to protect their language and their religion, but the French-speaking and Roman Catholic people on the banks of the Red River, who formed the greater part of the *métis,* were to be herded into the Dominion without any such protection in their own, their native country. The *métis* also suspected that their lands were to be stolen from them, and they became sure of it when they saw surveyors, sent from Ottawa, beginning to run their chains all over the countryside. The federal government received warnings from many men, even from the head of the Roman Catholic church in the West, Bishop Taché, who visited Ottawa in June, and yet did nothing to quiet the suspicions that spread like wildfire along the banks of the Red River.

The rebellion broke out in the fall of 1869. It was the work of the *métis,* not of the white people, who stood aside out of fear or sympathy. The leader of the movement was Louis Riel, a well-educated and clever, though unstable, young man of twenty-five. He and his people believed that the country was really theirs. Had not other Canadians told them so, long ago? Determined to keep it, they stopped the lieutenant governor at the border—he had had to travel up through the United States—and they seized Fort Garry, the headquarters of the Hudson's Bay Company. They were in control, and they arrested all who would not submit to their authority. For eight months theirs was the only government in the country, and during this time they forced the Dominion to do what it should have done in the beginning—negotiate an agreement with the people of the colony.

This agreement was embodied in the Manitoba Act, which the Canadian Parliament passed in May 1870 and which came into force on July 15, the day the Dominion received the territory from the British government. By this agreement the Province of Manitoba was created, with the same rights of self-government that the other provinces enjoyed.

Meanwhile Riel continued to rule the settlement. Though no other government was possible, he had no legal authority. Some of the white settlers showed signs of resistance, and one of them, an Ontario youth named Thomas Scott, was tried and shot. His death was one of the greatest tragedies in Canadian history. It set Ontario and Quebec by the ears, the people in the former province crying out for the blood of Riel as a murderer, and those of the latter province rallying passionately to the defense of one of their own race and religion.* In the West it left bitter memories that are dying only now. But for the death of Scott, there might have been no second Riel Rebellion, which occurred in 1885, and Louis Riel, instead of being execrated by English-speaking Canadians as a criminal whose hands were stained with blood, might have been remembered as a hero in the fight for constitutional government—for his first rebellion was successful in forcing the birth of the Province of Manitoba and cost only one other life, and that perhaps by accident. By putting Scott to death, Riel unwittingly threw away the amnesty that had already been granted him for his rebellion.

The Canadian government naturally decided to run no risks in taking over the country. There was a Fenian in Riel's government, and other Fenians in the United States hoped to seize the opportunity of capturing this British colony. It was doubtful, too, if Riel would step down from the place of authority when the time came. Therefore an expedition of twelve hundred men, British regulars and Canadian militia, set out for the West. Being a military force, it could not pass through the United States as ordinary travelers did, but had to sail over the Upper Lakes and march from Fort William. As it approached Fort Garry on the morning of August 24, 1870, Riel and a few of his friends slipped out and fled across the border.

When the Province of Manitoba was born, its northern boundary was level with the southern end of Lake Winnipeg, its eastern side was thirty miles short of the Lake of the Woods, and on the west it extended only eighty miles beyond Winnipeg. It was often called "the postage stamp province," because it was so small. In 1881 it was enlarged somewhat, but its appearance on the map was not much changed. It did not become the large province of today until 1912, when Ontario and Quebec also reached their present proportions. The huge remainder of the new country acquired by the Dominion in 1870 had then no

* This is how it appeared, and still appears, to French Canadians. It was enough for them that he had French blood in his veins and a French tongue in his head.

population except wandering tribes of Indians, a few half-breeds, and a small number of fur traders. In accordance with the plans of 1869 it became the North West Territory, controlled by Ottawa through a lieutenant governor and a council.

When by this transfer of territory the Dominion reached the Rockies in the summer of 1870, arrangements were already being completed to push its borders over the mountains and down to the sea. Meanwhile James Douglas had retired as Sir James Douglas. He had done his work so well that he is known today as the father of British Columbia. Of the two colonies over which he ruled the one on the mainland caused him the greater worry. Many of the miners had found poverty instead of the gold they had come to seek, and he had to care for them. Then, too, as prospectors pushed farther and farther inland, discovering new deposits of the precious metal, the nature of the country made roads absolutely necessary and yet very difficult to construct. Mining meant a fairly continuous and bulky traffic, quite unlike that of earlier days. Moreover, snow often blocked the old fur traders' tracks for more than half the year. Highways must be built over rocky gorges and boiling mountain torrents. Machinery could not be tied up in neat little packages to fit on men's backs.

Fortunately the British government sent Douglas a contingent of the Royal Engineers, whom he employed in the laborious and skilled task of building roads. One of these highways, running through the Fraser canyons, had to be blasted out of solid rock. In later days comfortable railway travelers could catch glimpses of it clinging high up on the face of the cliff across the river, and the sight caused many a gasp of wonder. This was part of Douglas' most famous road, the Cariboo Trail, which was nearly four hundred miles long. The visible presence of these engineers of the British army and the invisible presence of the British fleet (Esquimalt on Vancouver Island became a naval station in 1855 when Britain was fighting Russia in the Crimean War) assisted Douglas in maintaining order. But the greatest power in the land was Douglas himself, a man of solid character, keen mind, and iron will. He gave the mainland colony the government it then needed.

Such a government, however, was not what the colony wanted.

Douglas lived in Victoria, the capital of his older but smaller colony, and the people of British Columbia wanted a government seated in their own capital of New Westminster, near the mouth of the Fraser River. They also wanted self-government. Petition after petition went to London, and by 1863 the colonial office decided to give the mainland colony a completely separate and partly representative government. The people were to elect one third of the legislative council, which was to replace the little nominated council that had advised but had not controlled the masterful governor. In the following year Douglas opened the new legislature and gave up both his offices, which were filled by men sent out from the mother country.

The separation of 1864 lasted only two years. By 1865 the golden days were gone. The rich deposits of yellow sand in the river valleys were being worked out, and no new ones were being discovered. People were leaving, though not so fast as they had come. Hard times hit both colonies, for the gold rush had brought a business boom to Victoria, and the two governments were sinking deeply into debt. Expenditures had to be cut, and the only way to do so was to unite the colonies. In 1866, therefore, London combined them under the name of British Columbia, and two years later, after much wrangling between the island and the mainland, Victoria became the capital.

From the time of the union the people of both parts of this colony, who numbered about twelve thousand, were dissatisfied with their government and doubtful about their future. The island had lost its assembly, and the new legislature, like the one that had existed for two years on the mainland, had more appointed members than elected ones. How could the people get the self-government they desired so strongly? By remaining a little colony in one of the far corners of the earth? The prospect offered little hope. Then why not join the United States? That would bring them both freedom and prosperity! So in 1866 an annexation movement began, and local conditions seemed to favor it. Most of the mainland population had come from California, and even some British-born residents of the island were ready to welcome the Stars and Stripes. But other groups began a strong countermovement to join the Dominion, which was opposed in turn by the appointed councilors, who feared for their offices, and by the governor, who controlled the administration. His sudden death in the early summer of 1869 removed one obstacle. The other was overridden by his successor, who was picked for the purpose—the profederation governor of Newfoundland whom Macdonald persuaded the home government to transfer to the other side of the continent.

In 1870 the legislative council voted for union with Canada and sent delegates to Ottawa to discuss the conditions upon which British Columbia might become a province of the Dominion. The federal government gave them a warm welcome and promised practically everything they sought. The most pressing demand was for a highway to link British Columbia with the rest of the country. The delegates asked for a wagon road within three years and for the survey of a line along which a railroad might be built sometime in the future. The Canadian cabinet undertook to commence the building of the railway within two years and to complete it in ten. On July 20, 1871, by an order in council passed in London, British Columbia became the sixth province of the Dominion. Two years later, when Prince Edward Island was added, the geographical expansion of the Dominion was completed.

CHAPTER 12

How Canada Is Governed

THE members of the Quebec Conference of 1864, which was Canada's constitutional convention, were more or less familiar with the American proceedings of 1787 and with the subsequent history of the Constitution drawn up in Philadelphia. Some of the leaders at Quebec, particularly Macdonald, were close students of the American Constitution, and their minds were quite clear on what they would copy, what they would alter and how, and what they would reject for something else. The other model before these "fathers of confederation," as they are called, was of course the British constitution. So a broad analysis of these quite different models, showing how the Canadian constitution resembles now one and now the other, is a necessary introduction to the subject of this chapter.

Anyone who reads the Constitution of the United States and its various amendments can get a fair idea of how this country is governed, for its government functions largely according to the letter of the law. Britain, on the other hand, has no such document and is governed quite differently from what the letter of the law asserts. Although according to law the king still rules, everybody knows that he does not rule but merely reigns. The United States has what political scientists call a *written* constitution, Britain an *unwritten* one. The Canadian constitution is both written and unwritten. The written part is the British North America Act and its amendments, but these documents do not tell the whole story of how Canada is governed. Taken literally they would mean that the country is ruled by the king, acting through the governor general of the Dominion, whom he appoints, and the lieutenant governors of the provinces, whom the governor general appoints—which is not at all true. A vital part of the constitution does not appear in the letter of the law; it is unwritten, but none the less real. Indeed the written part of the constitution is subordinated to the unwritten. This must be so, for, as we shall see, the government of the country could not otherwise be carried on.

The American constitution is also what is known as a *rigid* one, because it cannot be altered by the ordinary process of legislation, and the British as a *flexible* one, because it can be changed at any time by an ordinary law passed by Parliament. Here again the Canadian constitution resembles both. Most, but not all, of the written constitution is rigid, and of course the unwritten part is flexible.

Another striking contrast is between the separation of powers in the American system and the fusion of powers in the British. Here the unwritten part of the Canadian constitution resembles the British model, in which the heads of the executive departments, instead of being excluded from the legislature, are actually its leaders. This cabinet form of government, of which more anon, had already been established by the British North American Revolution and was regarded by the members of the Quebec Conference as so superior to the American form that they took for granted that it would be continued in the provinces and applied in Ottawa. No written constitutional provision was necessary for this.

On the other hand, the Canadian constitution resembles the American in being *federal*. Macdonald wished to make it a *unitary* one, like that of Britain, where Parliament is supreme, its acts being subject to no judicial review. His desire was natural, for in the history of government the federal form has been adopted only when the unitary form was impracticable. The prime reason for Canada's being a federal country is its dual nationality. The French were to be a permanent minority in the new central Parliament, and this they would not tolerate unless its powers over the government of their own province were limited. The Maritime Provinces, having enjoyed a separate existence for over three quarters of a century, also insisted on being allowed to retain a measure of their individual independence, but the issue was really decided by the French.

The Dominion legislature is not only called a Parliament, after the British original, but is also patterned upon it, though there are some interesting variations. Legally, the king is the head of the federal Parliament, but as he cannot fill this role in person he is represented by the governor general. Parliament is summoned, prorogued, and dissolved by the governor general, and its bills are transformed into acts by his signature. In the beginning, his office was nearly, but not quite, that of a constitutional sovereign; and now it is nothing else, except that his term expires at the end of six years unless it is renewed.

With one early exception, the governor general has always been a British peer. He is, of course, formally appointed by the king. For a long time this appointment was made on the advice of the government in London, but now he is selected by the government in Ottawa, which has always paid his salary and provided him with an official residence, Rideau Hall. No Canadian has ever been appointed, though there is nothing to prevent such a selection and there has been a growing movement in favor of it. The custom of choosing an outstanding man from the mother country has been followed partly because it has been the tradition and partly for other reasons. It has been felt that a Canadian would not be such a visible and personal link with the center of the empire and that it would be much more difficult for a Canadian to fill the role of a constitutional monarch, who must be aloof from party politics.

The Canadian Senate bears a distant resemblance to that of the United States in that its composition has a geographical basis intended to protect sectional interests. Originally it had seventy-two members, twenty-four coming from each of three geographical divisions—Ontario, Quebec, and the Maritime Provinces. When Prince Edward Island joined the Dominion in 1873 it was given four members, and Nova Scotia and New Brunswick each lost two. But the westward spread of the Dominion upset this geographical balance. For many years the four western provinces had all together only fifteen senators. In 1915, however, when they were allotted six senators each, making a total of twenty-four, the original balance was restored, with four divisions instead of three. Having watched the example of Washington, the framers of the Canadian constitution were anxious to guard against deadlocks between the two houses of Parliament, and they were afraid that the Senate, if elected, would be encouraged to challenge the House of Commons. Therefore they decided, after much debate, that the members of the upper chamber should be appointed for life by the governor general, which means that the government really appoints them. Here it may be interesting to observe that Alexander Hamilton, whose ideas greatly influenced Macdonald, wanted American senators to be appointed for life.

Because the party in power fills vacancies in the Senate as they occur, the majority in the Senate is of the same party as that which forms the majority in the Commons except after a change of government, when it may take some time to bring the upper chamber into political harmony with the lower one. Thus there is friction between the two houses only after a change of government, and then it is usual. For three reasons, however, this friction is seldom serious or taken seriously by the Commons. First, the Senate, without the historic background of the English House of Lords, has never dared to hold out resolutely against the clearly expressed will of the people. Second, the hostile Senate majority seldom lasts long, for death eats it away, most of the senators being old men. Third, the party that has just come into power finds consolation in the thought that when it falls it may then play the same game of obstruction. Indeed the opposition of the two chambers, whenever it occurs, operates to soften the transition between two governments of different parties, and some people aver that a hostile Senate is a good excuse for not carrying out rash election promises. Throughout the country there has long been a considerable sentiment in favor of abolishing the Senate, the last second chamber to survive in Canada, as will shortly appear.

The House of Commons is very much like that of Britain. The chief difference is in the redistribution of seats according to population, which is effected only at long and undefined intervals in the mother country but periodically in Canada, as in the United States—every ten years. The provision in the British North America Act, however, is different from that of the American Constitution. To prevent an unwieldy growth by the mere addition of new members for new population, Quebec always has sixty-five members, the number which that part of the country had in the old assembly of United Canada, and the other provinces are allotted seats in proportion to that number. Each of the other provinces thus retains its old number of seats only if its population grows at the same rate as that of Quebec. Roughly speaking, Ontario has stood still, while the western provinces have gained and the Maritimes have lost. As in Britain, members of the lower house do not have to be resident in the constituencies for which they sit. Men of one province have often been elected in another.* Nor are they elected for a fixed term, as in the United States. A general election must be held at least every five years, but it is unusual for Parliament to last that long and, as constitutional lawyers say, "expire by the effluxion of time." The governor general may dissolve it at any time that his government advises. Parliaments have commonly lasted for about four years, but several have been shorter. The one elected in 1925 lived for less than a year.

Money bills must originate in the lower chamber, as in Washington and London, but in contrast to American law and practice, British custom has restrained the Canadian Senate from amending such bills. It is also interesting to observe that the House of Commons is expressly prohibited from voting the expenditure of money for any purpose that has not been first recommended by the government, which therefore controls all spending.

In addition to being the titular head of Parliament, the king is also legally the chief executive of the Dominion, all the laws being administered in his name. The real head of the executive, however, is neither the king nor the governor general who acts for him but the prime minister, who is also the real head of Parliament. His office is not even mentioned in the British North America Act or in any of its amendments. Only of recent years, and only incidentally, has any law recognized his position; and no law defines it. Because the governor general, being a constitutional monarch like the king, cannot conduct the government himself, he must get others to do it for him. These ministers of the Crown, as they are called, are the members of the Cabinet, the heads of the executive departments, and though the governor general appoints them he cannot select them, for as a constitutional sovereign he can have no choice. Therefore he has to get someone to form the Cabinet, and because the Cabinet

* One striking example is that of the present prime minister, Mr. W. L. Mackenzie King, an Ontario man who sits in Parliament as the member for Prince Albert, Saskatchewan.

could not carry on without the support of Parliament, the governor general must ask the leader of the majority in the House of Commons. It is he who picks the Cabinet and is its head as first, or prime, minister.

By the very nature of his position the prime minister must control the Cabinet, for he is responsible to Parliament for everything done by the Cabinet or by any of its members. If in any way, such as by the rejection of a government bill (that is, one sponsored by the Cabinet), or a hostile amendment of it or by a straight vote expressing want of confidence, his Cabinet loses the support of the majority in the Commons, he must resign or appeal to the people in a general election, and after the election he must resign unless his party has secured enough seats to assure him the support of the new house. No written law states that he must resign, but something more powerful requires it: Parliament would go on strike, stopping all the wheels of government.

When forced to resign because he is in a minority, the prime minister advises the governor general to call upon the leader of the successful opposition party to form a new government. If for any reason he resigns while his party still controls the House of Commons, he advises the governor general to call upon the man whom he knows his own party has chosen, or would choose, to succeed him. His resignation, whether forced or voluntary, automatically dissolves the Cabinet. Because the prime minister may at any time decide to have a general election, he has a disciplinary check upon irresponsible followers in the House, and because the members of his party can force him out of office whenever they wish, they have a corresponding check upon him. This balance makes for greater and more continuous responsibility all round.

To conclude, the prime minister possesses a great concentration of power, for he is the controlling head of both the legislature and the executive, and he holds this power for an indefinite period of time—as long as he has the desire and the ability to keep it. But the moment he fails to command the confidence of the majority in the Commons, he falls from his high office, dragging his government with him, and a successor steps up into his place.

The members of the Cabinet are also members of Parliament

and leaders of it. No law says they must be, but this is not necessary for the simple reason that no government could otherwise carry on. The House of Commons would turn it out. If, as occasionally happens, the prime minister wishes to include in his Cabinet a man who is not a member of Parliament he can appoint him but to keep him he has to get him into Parliament by election to the Commons or appointment to the Senate. Senatorial members of the Cabinet are limited to one or two ministers of lesser importance, and when they exist they do so only by the tolerance of the lower house.

In the provinces, which have the same form of cabinet government, the representative of the Crown is the lieutenant governor. There is no governor in all Canada—just the governor general of the Dominion and the lieutenant governors of the provinces. The office of lieutenant governor in each province is always held by a Canadian, who is picked by the Dominion government and is formally appointed by the governor general. Here again we may suspect the influence of Alexander Hamilton, who favored federal appointment of state governors. The provincial lieutenant governors are of course constitutional sovereigns.

The provincial legislatures, which are sometimes incorrectly called parliaments, have a history that might be profitably examined by those who are interested in the recent Nebraskan innovation of a one-house legislature. When the Dominion was formed, one province broke away from the bicameral tradition; Ontario was launched without a second chamber. When Manitoba was organized it was given a second chamber, like Quebec and the Maritime Provinces, but British Columbia entered federation without one, and then Manitoba soon got rid of its upper house. Nearly fifty years ago New Brunswick and Prince Edward Island adopted the unicameral system, and Nova Scotia did the same in 1928. Saskatchewan and Alberta were established in 1905 with unicameral legislatures. Quebec was thus left as the only province with two chambers, and in 1940 its government decided to eliminate the upper one. As a whole the Canadian people see little sense in second chambers.

In the division of powers between the federal and the provincial legislatures, the "fathers of confederation" made some important departures from the American model. The Civil War was an object lesson to them. They could not avoid seeing the constitutional cause of that tragedy, and they were determined to keep the cloven hoof of state sovereignty out of Canada. So instead of leaving the provinces with all the authority that was not specifically transferred to the Dominion Parliament in accordance with the American principle, they did the very opposite. They also invested the Dominion with certain controls over the exercise of the powers left to the provinces.

Sections 91 and 92 of the British North America Act define the authority of the federal and provincial legislatures, and these sections have given a headache to many a student, for at first glance they seem to be unnecessarily complicated. One might expect a single enumeration of the subjects on which a province can legislate and a general statement that Parliament can legislate on anything else. But there is a double enumeration, the former section detailing a list of subjects for exclusive Dominion legislation and the latter section a list for exclusive provincial legislation.

The puzzle of this apparent duplication is actually quite simple. The framers of the act realized that by merely vesting general power in the Dominion Parliament they might prevent the provinces from legislating on subjects which, though not specified as within their jurisdiction, ought to be left to them. Therefore at the end of the list of provincial powers, section 92 has a general clause authorizing the provinces to legislate upon "all matters of a merely local or private nature in the province," but to prevent this clause from being stretched to cover what was intended to be left to the Dominion, section 91 sets forth the list of exclusive federal powers and states that the general clause of section 92 can never be interpreted as touching any of these. Section 91 also gives Parliament power "to make laws for the peace, order and good government of Canada" on all matters not within the scope of the subjects assigned exclusively to the provinces, and expressly states that this general power is not to be restricted by the list of specified federal subjects and was added "for greater certainty."

The division of legislative powers, it will be observed, is not geographical but topical. Parliament cannot legislate on any enumerated provincial subject, such as municipal institutions or property and civil rights, even though it might make the statute Dominion-wide in its application; nor can a province legislate on a federal subject, such as banking or bankruptcy, even though its act would be only local in operation. Conversely Parliament can legislate on any of its subjects and limit the application of the law to any part of the country, such as the seacoast and the inland fisheries. If legislation on any provincial subject is needed over an area larger than one province, such as the organization of a wheat pool for the Prairie Provinces, it must be accomplished by concurrent provincial legislation. Sometimes it also happens that exclusive federal powers and exclusive provincial powers are bound up in one question, requiring both federal and provincial action to achieve the desired end. In 1921, for example, Ottawa appointed a royal commission to investigate the marketing of grain, only to find that interested parties blocked the work of the commission by appealing to the courts on the ground that provincial jurisdiction was being invaded. The difficulty was surmounted by joint Dominion and provincial action to invest a new commission with all the necessary authority. No one could challenge it, for the feature of the American system that withholds certain powers of legislation from both federal and state legislatures is foreign to the Canadian system, as it is to the British. Questions of divided authority also arise in the United States, but it is easier to deal with them in Canada because of the cabinet system. When the premiers of the governments concerned, a group that can never exceed ten men, agree upon what is desired and possible, the job is as good as done.

The actual allotment of powers between the federal and the provincial legislatures is much the same as in the United States. Almost the only noteworthy exceptions are the disposal of residual powers, as already explained, the definition of banking and criminal law as subjects on which only the Dominion Parliament can legislate, and a peculiar, though natural, provision for education that must now be explained.

Education has a section all to itself, section 93. It is one of the longest in the act and can be understood only by first examining the school system established before federation in United Canada. The key to the system is to be found in the nature of the

population in Canada East. It was only natural that ordinary
public schools in that part of the country should be under
French and clerical control and that in consequence the English-
speaking Protestant minority should demand a separate tax-
supported set of schools for their own children. This the
majority were willing to grant at a price—the same privilege for
their fellow Roman Catholics in Canada West. The price was
paid, with much grumbling in Canada West, and at federation
French Canada was able to insist upon this right of a religious
minority being put into the constitution, with some additional
matter on the subject. Section 93 gives the provinces exclusive
power to legislate on education but bars any law from prejudi-
cially affecting "any right or privilege with respect to denomina-
tional schools" enjoyed by any class of persons at the time of the
union. The limitation would of course be guarded by the courts,
but this control was not considered sufficient. So the section also
provides for an appeal direct to the governor general in council,
which means the Dominion Cabinet, by any Protestant or Roman Catholic minority against any invasion of the educational
rights they possessed at the time of the union, or even acquired
afterward. It empowers the federal government to issue a reme-
dial order to an offending province, and, if this is not fully
obeyed, it authorizes Parliament to pass such legislation as may
then be necessary. It was around the terms of this section that
one of the principal storms of Canadian politics revolved in the
early 1890's, as will appear in the next chapter.

The federal right to check the exercise of provincial powers is
not confined to education. The British North America Act gives
the Dominion government the right to disallow any provincial
legislation within a year of its passing—another reminder of the
fact that Macdonald was fond of reading Alexander Hamilton.
For some years after the Dominion was formed, Macdonald's
government wielded this axe rather freely to kill provincial legislation that seemed to be unconstitutional or otherwise bad.
Then for a long period the heavy instrument was very sparingly
used. The prevailing opinion was that the federal Cabinet
should not usurp from the courts the function of judicial review,
for the courts were better qualified to perform it. Nor, by the
same opinion, should it protect the people of any province from

the folly of their own legislators, for the way to educate electors is to let them pay for their own mistakes. For a while there was some question whether the federal right of disallowance had not already become what the royal veto had long been, an empty form. But experience has shown that occasionally there is a necessity for its employment when a provincial act that may be constitutional, and therefore not liable to be upset in the courts, threatens to do serious damage outside the province. Recently it has also been used against some of the social credit legislation of Alberta which, though obviously unconstitutional, might have wrought great havoc before a judicial decision could be reached.

The financial relations between the provinces and the Dominion offer another contrast between Canadian and American federalism. Under the British North America Act, the Dominion has possessed unlimited powers of taxation, but the provinces have been allowed to levy only direct taxes. Because the municipalities derive all their authority from the provinces, they too were automatically bound by this restriction. As compensation for this limitation upon the provinces, the act transferred their public debts at the time of federation to the Dominion and bound the Dominion to pay them annual subsidies. The amount of the subsidies was calculated to cover so much of the expenses of the provincial governments that they would not need to raise very much by taxation. There was also a general belief that the federal government, with a good customs and excise revenue, would find little or no occasion for invading the field of direct taxation, which would therefore be left to the municipalities without much competition from the provinces.

Time has played sad tricks with these comfortable plans made three quarters of a century ago. With the evolution of society, the pressure of public demand enormously enlarged the sphere of government. Much of the increased financial burden fell upon the provinces, because the new duties lay within the limits of provincial activity as defined by the act. The provinces were consequently driven to raise more and more money by direct taxation, and the municipalities, faced with the same necessity, felt the growing competition. Then the stupendous cost of the First World War forced the Dominion to burst into the field of direct taxation, which is now badly trampled. It is not surprising that the depression brought some provinces face to face with default. They were saved by generous loans from the Dominion, but it cannot continue to play fairy godmother to distressed provinces without some control over their expenditures. The problem has recently been explored thoroughly by an able commission, whose report proposed such a readjustment of governmental responsibilities and taxing power that some of the provinces balked. It was observed by many people, however, that the Dominion might apply its superior financial power to force the recalcitrant provinces into line; and now the public spirit created by the war has weakened provincial resistance and enabled the federal government to achieve, for the duration of hostilities and a year afterward, substantially what the commission proposed.

The organization of the judicial system of Canada bears only a distant resemblance to that of the United States. There are only three purely Dominion courts, but most Canadians have heard of only one of them. This is the Supreme Court, which consists of a chief justice and five puisne, or associate, judges. Two of the judges must be from the bench or the bar of Quebec, to ensure the court's familiarity with the civil law introduced by France, which still prevails in that province. This is the highest court of appeal for both civil and criminal cases in Canada. It has also an advisory function. Either house of Parliament may ask the court for an opinion touching any private bill under consideration, and the Dominion government may request its advice on any important question of law or fact.

The other courts are called provincial, but this term is misleading to an American, for they are not the conterparts of state courts in this country. They administer both provincial and federal law. The provinces regulate civil procedure; the Dominion, criminal. The provinces are severally responsible for the organization of the courts, and the Dominion for the appointment and payment of the judges, whose tenure is permanent. Really these Canadian courts are neither provincial nor federal, but both; and one might almost say that the Dominion and the provinces are there married.

The highest court of appeal is outside Canada, in London. It is the Judicial Committee of the Privy Council, popularly known as the Privy Council. Appeals may be taken to it either directly from the highest court of a province or indirectly through the Supreme Court in Ottawa. Criminal appeals are no longer carried to London and, as will be observed in a later chapter, civil appeals may also be stopped whenever Canada wishes.

Another striking thing about government in Canada is that the provinces have no constitutions like those of the various American states. There has been no need for them. By the express terms of the British North America Act a provincial legislature can change the whole structure of the government of the province in any way it wishes by simple enactment, so long as it does not touch the office of lieutenant governor or invade the powers reserved to the Dominion Parliament. That was the way the provinces got rid of their second chambers—by just legislating them out of existence.

The amendment of the British North America Act is another and more difficult matter. When the Commonwealth of Australia was established in 1900 and the Union of South Africa in 1909 by imperial statutes, these statutes provided for the amendment of the written constitutions of these dominions by themselves; but the imperial statute that established the Dominion of Canada did not confer this power, for the concept of Dominion autonomy had yet to develop to the point where such a concession was possible. It had reached this point by the turn of the century, as Australia demonstrated, but still the Dominion of Canada cannot amend its own constitution without going to London for another imperial act to change the British North America Act. That it has not done so is for the simple reason that the people of Canada have not yet found a method of amending it themselves that would be satisfactory to the provinces.

CHAPTER 13

Uniting the Nation

ALTHOUGH the new Dominion stretched from sea to sea in the early 1870's, it was yet a disjointed country, depending on the United States for connection between its parts. The regular route for passengers and mail between the Maritime Provinces and Quebec was through Portland, Maine. The only communication between Ontario and Manitoba was through Chicago and St. Paul, and it took ten days for a letter to reach Winnipeg from Toronto. The journey from Central Canada to the capital of British Columbia required three weeks, and the way was over American railroads to the Pacific and then up the coast in American vessels. Under such conditions the Dominion could not hope to survive, much less become a united land. The attractive influence of the United States upon each of its parts would slowly but surely tear it asunder. Canada had to have its own communication from the Atlantic to the Pacific. Because of its vast extent and its widely scattered population, railways have been more important to the Dominion than to almost any other country in the world, for they were the rivets that fastened the parts together.

The Maritime Provinces refused to enter federation without the guarantee of a railway linking them with United Canada. Therefore the British North America Act required the Dominion to build a railway to join Halifax with Quebec. The motherland, anxious to help the new country onto its feet, lightened the burden by lending financial aid. This decided a question that had been argued for many years. Where would the line run? Only its two ends were known, Truro in Nova Scotia and Rivière du Loup in Quebec. The cheapest way to unite them would have been to use the railways already constructed in New Brunswick. The people in the western and southern parts of that province clamored for it, because they would then be on the main line. But this meant running the road along the upper St. John Valley, where it would hug the Maine boundary, and the government in London insisted that this vital British communication should nowhere be at the mercy of possibly hostile Americans. That is why a more expensive route was adopted. Running up the eastern side of the province, along the Bay of Chaleur, across to the St. Lawrence, and up to Rivière du Loup, it would almost everywhere be within reach of the sea and the British navy.

The building of this railway, which was begun in 1867, took more time and much more money than had been expected. The construction of the road was let out to private contractors, many of whom went bankrupt or broke their contracts when they encountered unforeseen difficulties. Again and again the government had to step in and complete a section by day labor. Not until July 1, 1876, when the Dominion was nine years old, was the whole line opened. Together with the railways that the governments of the Maritime Provinces had built and the Dominion had already taken over, it formed the Intercolonial Railway. It never paid; it could not pay; it was not intended to pay. It was a great public work, built to draw the country together.

So also was the Canadian Pacific Railway, which cost the Dominion still more, though in another way. For years men had talked about building a road to the West, but it did not become a practical problem till 1871, when it became a necessity. It was the price the Dominion promised to pay for being allowed to reach the Pacific. At once the chief government engineer set about finding a route, and for some years he was in charge of the surveys. He proposed to run the line across the narrows of Lake Manitoba, along the North Saskatchewan to the Yellowhead Pass, and down the Fraser, much as the Canadian National runs today.

Meanwhile the government in Ottawa was wrestling with the problem of how to construct the railway, and there were great political storms. Sir John A. Macdonald originally intended to build the road as a public work, but this was a task many times bigger and more difficult than the Intercolonial, and it frightened his colleagues. Therefore the government decided to pay a private corporation to take over the whole business of building and operating the road. At once two companies appeared, both eager to secure the contract. Behind their competition stood the rivalry of the two leading cities of the Dominion, Montreal and

Uniting the Nation

Toronto, each wanting to be the headquarters of the road. The Montreal company was organized by Sir Hugh Allan, the foremost businessman of the country, and the founder of the Allan Steamship Line, which has since been taken over by the C.P.R.* Allan had much more wealth at his disposal than did his Toronto rival and so would be less likely to fail. But much of this capital was provided by Americans, chiefly by Jay Cooke, the "financier of the Civil War," and the government would not allow foreigners to control this most important railway. Allan was told that he would have his share of the business if he would cut his American connections and join the men of Toronto. But the rivals would not unite.

Then came the general election of 1872, and it was a hard fight between Macdonald's Conservative government and the Liberal opposition. Since the Liberals insisted that Canada could not afford to build the railway as quickly as the government had promised, Allan feared a Liberal victory, and he gave the Conservatives large sums to help pay their campaign expenses. The government won the election, and Parliament gave the contract to a new company that Allan formed. Feeling that he had betrayed them, his American friends betrayed him, informing the Liberals that he had paid to keep the government in office. A great scandal resulted, the famous Pacific Scandal of 1873. To many it looked as if Allan had bought the government; consequently the Conservatives had to resign, and Allan had to give up the contract.

During the next five years the Liberals were in power under Alexander Mackenzie, another native of Scotland. Though bearing the same name, he was not of the same family as the noted explorer. He was a building contractor who had begun life as a stonemason, and his principles were as solid as the stone he had once cut. Unfortunately for him, he entered office at the very time that Canada, as well as the United States, was hit by the great depression of the 1870's. The hard times of course made it more difficult for the Dominion to keep its promise to British Columbia, and instead of constructing a through railway, the new premier proposed to use the waterways between the Rockies

* The Allan Line did not lose its identity until the First World War, several years after the C.P.R. had bought the control of it.

PACIFIC PASTIMES; or. THE HARD "ROAD TO TRAVEL."

"The Reform Government took up the Pacific Railway scheme, but initiated a new policy with regard to it. Sir John Macdonald had pledged the country to complete the entire work within ten years. Mr. Mackenzie characterized this as a physical impossibility, and proposed, as the cartoon has it, 'to tak' the distance in sensible like jumps, ye ken!' *Grip*, May 16th, 1874."

J. W. Bengough (1851–1923) is still remembered as the greatest cartoonist of Canada. In 1873 he founded *Grip*, a humorous Toronto weekly, in which he published the cartoons that made him widely known. In 1893 he severed his connection with *Grip* to become cartoonist for the Montreal *Star* and later for the Toronto *Globe*. Selections of his cartoons were republished in book form first in 1875 as *Grip's Cartoons*, and then in 1886 as *A Caricature History of Canadian Politics*. The cartoons reproduced here are from the latter and include the explanation that accompanied each.

and Lake Superior as a means of transportation and to build connecting lines only where they were absolutely necessary. These lines were to be owned by those who built them, and as an inducement the government offered a bonus of ten thousand dollars and twenty thousand acres of land for every mile of track completed—about half the rate promised Allan's company for the whole contract. These terms attracted no one, and the government had to proceed with the construction as an ordinary public work.

Because Canada was not keeping her word, British Columbia grew restless and threatened to withdraw from federation. Thereupon Lord Carnarvon, the colonial secretary in London, offered to arbitrate between the Dominion and the aggrieved province. They accepted his offer, and the conditions he laid down, known as the "Carnarvon terms," put off the date for completing the railway until 1890 but required the federal government to do some definite building in the province right away. Still Canada did not live up to her promise, and feeling in British Columbia grew angrier until Lord Dufferin, the governor general, a man of remarkable diplomatic ability, went out to the Pacific and persuaded the people to be more patient.

When Macdonald came back into power in 1878, his Cabinet continued the policy of government construction for two years, hoping to get assistance from the mother country on the ground that the railway across the continent would be a valuable link of empire. This hope failed, and the gigantic nature of the undertaking was more alarming than ever. Time was passing, and little more than seven hundred miles were completed or under construction.

The government was eager to get rid of the burden when a new group of men appeared to shoulder it, men who were familiar with railway building and management and who at the same time knew enough about the West to have confidence in it. They were three Scottish-born Canadians and two native-born Canadians, one of them James J. Hill, who had settled in the United States. Having come together by accident in St. Paul, these men had secured control of a bankrupt and half-built railway in Minnesota and were making fortunes out of it. (This, by the way, was the beginning of the Great Northern Railway.) "Catch them before they invest their profits," said one of Macdonald's advisers, and the Cabinet did.

These men formed the Canadian Pacific Railway Company, on which the government unloaded the whole task, with the consent of Parliament, in 1881. The Dominion gave the company the sections of road already built or being built and twenty-five million dollars in cash and twenty-five million acres of land in the fertile belt, as well as certain exemptions from taxation. This was the price that the government paid to persuade people with capital to invest in building the road. As a matter of fact, the group of men who formed the Canadian Pacific Railway Company added little to their fortunes by this venture. Only their experience and their energy saved them from losing heavily by it.

The new company pushed construction vigorously and, finding a more southerly route through the mountains, ran the line straight west to the Kicking Horse Pass instead of to the Yellowhead. This shortened the line, thereby reducing the cost of building and hastening the day when it could be opened for traffic and would begin to earn money; but it also meant running through the dry belt instead of along the North Saskatchewan with its plentiful rainfall. Many people regard this as the great mistake of the Canadian Pacific, but, after all, the railway paid for it. In November 1885 the last iron spike was driven in the line that tied British Columbia to the rest of Canada.

Now federation had united the country politically and the railways had riveted its parts together, but something more was needed. The provinces had long led separate lives, and there was a strong provincial patriotism before ever the Dominion was born. The Dominion had to develop a life and a spirit of its own, or it would remain an artificial body that might fall apart in time. The common interests entrusted to the federal Parliament and government, as well as direct communication by railway, helped to build up this new life, which would of itself create and strengthen a larger patriotism. But the process was bound to be slow, and there were fears that it might be too slow to achieve the end for which the Dominion was formed—to counteract the pull of the United States on each of its parts.

Therefore a conscious and widespread effort was made to stimulate this growth and to place the Dominion beyond peril.

Uniting the Nation

Many public men throughout the country, politicians and others, did their best to stir the different people of the Dominion to think and feel as one nation. They had least difficulty in Ontario, where public opinion for federation had been keenest and where the inhabitants had not called themselves Ontarians but Canadians. They had merely to throw out their chests and expand the meaning of the word. In Quebec the way was not so easy. Though the people there had been called Canadians for a much longer time, divisions of race and creed cut deep. But the greatest French Canadian of the day was optimistic and encouraging. This was Macdonald's friend and colleague, Sir George Cartier, the man who was perhaps chiefly responsible for persuading the heads of the church to support federation. Referring to the way in which English, Scots, Irish, and Welsh had united to form a great people, he pointed out to his fellow French Canadians that the new nation would be richer and finer because it comprised both English and French elements.

The task was difficult, too, in the Maritime Provinces, where federation had been most strongly opposed and where it still aroused suspicion. Nova Scotians, New Brunswickers, and Prince Edward Islanders were loath to admit that they were Canadians, for to them a Canadian had always been someone who lived in Quebec or Ontario. It was not so hard in Manitoba, a new province that owed its life to the action of the Dominion Parliament. People who had always been Canadians flocked west to this province, and the other inhabitants did not become Manitobans until they became Canadians. To most British Columbians, however, years passed before Canada meant much more than a promise that was not kept.

Of all the efforts to rouse a national feeling throughout the land, the most interesting was a movement begun by five young men who chanced to meet in Ottawa in the spring of 1868. These men, whose individual names are far less important than what they did, came from different parts of the Dominion, and they fell into the habit of meeting frequently to discuss its future. They were of one mind in believing that a soul had to be breathed into the new body, and when they separated to go to their several homes they pledged one another to do all in their power to rouse the people to think and feel as one nation. They adopted the motto *Canada First*—not the old but the new Canada. They set out to cultivate a positive loyalty to the Dominion, a belief that the whole is greater than any part and worth whatever sacrifice might be necessary to uphold and strengthen it. The Canada First movement, which was thus launched, was well organized. It grew until it seemed about to become a regular political party, though if it had, the cause for which it stood might have suffered from the opposition of the Conservatives and the Liberals. In 1875 the organization began to break up and it soon disappeared, but its influence lived on. It did much to awaken a national consciousness, and the principles it proclaimed were adopted by the two historic parties in the rivalry to win the support of the growing national feeling throughout the Dominion. Durham's prophecy was at last being fulfilled.

More than once the United States unconsciously helped to stimulate this spirit—even from the very beginning of the Dominion. Fishing rights provided the first occasion, but to understand it we have to go back to the convention of 1818. That agreement gave Americans the right to share the inshore fisheries only of Newfoundland, Labrador, and the little Magdalen Islands in the Gulf of the St. Lawrence. It expressly canceled their right to fish within three miles of any other British North American "coasts, bays, creeks, or harbors." There, however, Americans were allowed to enter "for the purpose of shelter and repairing damages therein, of purchasing wood, and of obtaining water, and for no other purpose whatever," under such restrictions as might be "necessary to prevent their taking, drying, or curing fish therein," or in any other manner abusing their liberty. There was little trouble until about twenty years later when the mackerel inconsiderately deserted the New England coasts and took to frequenting the bays of the neighboring British waters. American fishermen followed them, and there were lively disputes, intensified by some seizures, over what was a bay and what was not.

This unpleasant business was brushed aside by the treaty of 1854, which provided for reciprocity not only in natural products but also in the use of inshore fisheries. This arrangement made things worse after the Reciprocity Treaty came to an end in 1866, for the treaty had freely admitted Americans to inshore fisheries from which they had formerly been excluded and they were determined not to be excluded again, treaty or no treaty. The new Dominion, born in fear of a hostile United States, thus inherited a difficult problem. For a while the Canadian government tried to compromise by requiring Americans to buy licenses for fishing in Canadian waters. But this system quickly failed, as American fishermen invaded Canadian waters "without leave or licence," and in 1870, after consulting London, Ottawa decided to shut all foreigners out of the Canadian fisheries and to defend them with a small fleet of cruisers. Violence ensued, and there was angry talk of more violence.

Unfortunately for Canada the fisheries question was then tangled up with the Anglo-American dispute over the *Alabama*, whose depredations during the Civil War had given the United States a good excuse for war against Britain. Anxious to keep the peace, the government in London agreed to negotiate a settlement of both questions together in 1871 at Washington, whither Macdonald went as the representative of Canada. He had hoped to checkmate the American claim against Britain by pressing a Canadian claim against the United States for allowing the Fenians to invade Canada; but through some oversight in London the Fenian business was already excluded from the negotiations in which he was to participate. Macdonald was thus placed in a most difficult position. He could not present the Fenian claim, nor could he refuse to open the fisheries without wrecking the conference and perhaps bringing on a war between the United States and Britain, in which the Dominion would probably suffer most of all. He saw that he would have to yield, but he wrung two promises from the British government. One was that Britain would pay Canada for her Fenian claim if the other questions were settled. The second was that the fisheries would not be surrendered without the Dominion's consent. Then he tried to get the best possible terms from the United States for opening the fisheries. His first desire was a renewal of reciprocity, but he found that this was impossible. Finally he secured an agreement for a money payment, the amount to be decided, like the *Alabama* claims, by arbitration.

The negotiation of the Washington Treaty of 1871 marks an important stage in the growth of Canadian nationality. It left a

ANCIENT TROY TACTICS
OR

"This was still another repetition of the opinion that the Tory Party, in adopting the National Policy, had in view the one grand object of 'getting in' to office. The allusion is of course to the familiar classic story of the method adopted by the Greeks to gain admission to Troy. *Grip*, July 6th, 1878."

suggestion that Canadian interests had been sacrificed for British interests. This thought rankled in the minds of many Canadians, who failed to see that the sacrifice was the price paid for being able to call upon the British navy whenever necessary. They also overlooked the fact that the mother country bought out Canada's Fenian claim by guaranteeing a large Dominion loan. But much stronger than the feeling against Britain was the resentment against the United States for forcing open the Canadian fisheries and refusing to open the American market for Canadian produce, and this resentment greatly stimulated the growth of national sentiment in the Dominion.

The hard times that began in 1873, just when the Liberals under Alexander Mackenzie came into power, caused Canada to hanker after the lost market south of the border, and soon there came a glimmer of hope of regaining it. George Brown, already mentioned as the father of the Liberal party and the founder of the Toronto *Globe,* visited Washington, where he was welcomed because he had been a stout champion of the North during the Civil War. On this visit he heard a number of things that made him believe reciprocity was still possible. Thereupon he was appointed to act with the British ambassador to the United States in negotiating a new treaty. The negotiation proceeded smoothly and resulted in an agreement that would have renewed the old treaty and enlarged it by the addition of an important list of manufactures. It was submitted to the United States Senate two days before adjournment in June 1874 and was quietly buried in that graveyard of treaties. This rebuff stirred national feeling in Canada.

Meanwhile manufacturing had been springing up in central Canada, and those who were engaged in it did not grieve over Brown's failure. They were suffering from the depression, and they feared they would suffer still more from the competition of large American industries. The Dominion then had a low tariff, and manufacturers complained that Americans were dumping their goods north of the border to destroy the growing industries in Canada. As conditions became worse, the public did what it normally does under such circumstances; it blamed the government for the hard times. Taking advantage of this, Macdonald made one of the cleverest moves in his clever career. He urged changes in the tariff to restore prosperity—always so easy to capture! He was advocating protection but was careful to avoid using the word because there were then too many free traders in the country. Instead, he called it the National Policy.

The selection of this name was a stroke of genius. It implied what many in the country were ready to believe—that the government was neglecting the national interests. It suggested that prosperity was within easy reach. It helped people to forget the Pacific Scandal, which had turned Macdonald out of power. Most important of all, it reached out after the national spirit cultivated by men of the Canada First movement and others and stimulated by current anti-American feeling. Macdonald shrewdly judged that the Dominion was developing a spirit of its own, but even he seems to have underestimated it. When the general election of 1878 came, the National Policy swept the

HIS BEST FRIEND DESERTING HIM

"The main hope of the Opposition in view of the general election was in the capital that was being made out of the depression of trade. A slight improvement was noticeable in the business outlook at the date of this cartoon. *Grip,* October 20th, 1877."

Uniting the Nation

country and carried Macdonald back into power, where he remained until his death thirteen years later.

The readjustment of the tariff, which the Conservative government proposed and Parliament passed in 1879, was a thorough going protectionist measure. Why should Canadians buy from foreigners what they could make for themselves? That was the question of the day. The Liberals fought the adoption of the new policy, saying that it was better to export what Canada could raise most cheaply, her natural produce, and with it purchase what she needed of the things that other countries could make more cheaply. Protection, they urged, would be taxing the farmer for the benefit of the manufacturer. But they might as well have tried to prove that black was white. The great majority in the country and in Parliament were against them, and for a very good reason.

The people of the Dominion had awakened as a nation; and whether protection would be financially profitable or not they felt it would be nationally profitable. A high protecting wall around the country would make it become more diversified economically, more self-sufficient, more unified. Trade outside the country was to be discouraged in favor of trade that would knit the country together. Almost every other self-governing people except those of the British Isles were doing this very thing—none more vigorously than the Americans next door—and in self-defense it seemed necessary for Canada to become a protectionist country. The change came at a most auspicious moment for Macdonald and his policy. The depression was lifting, and reviving prosperity raised the National Policy into a sort of political religion. Under the National Policy Canada developed a strong life of her own, and this reacted to strengthen her spirit. But it would be a mistake to imagine that the feeling of national unity was complete. It was to pass through a number of trials.

The fears that Sir George Cartier had tried to explain away were not groundless. In the early 1870's, the death of Thomas Scott (see page 181) roused such angry passions in Ontario and Quebec that the government feared for the unity of the country if Riel were captured and tried for murder. So it secretly advanced him money to remain in the United States, and, when he came back, banished him. Passions flamed up again in 1885,

THE VACANT CHAIR
A RIEL bond of union

"Louis Riel, the leader of the Red River Rebellion and alleged murderer of Thomas Scott, had been returned for Provencher, Manitoba, to the Dominion Parliament. He prudently failed to take his seat in the House, while the unanimity with which both sides cried for his arrest made 'the vacant chair' a bond of union for the time being. *Grip*, April 4th, 1874."

after Riel had returned to lead his second rebellion, the story of which will be told in the next chapter. This time he was caught and condemned to death for treason. The sentence rent the country in two, and the government faced an awkward dilemma. Should it satisfy Ontario by letting him die, or Quebec by letting him live? After much hesitation Macdonald's Cabinet chose to please Ontario, but from that moment Quebec began to turn against his party, which has never recovered its once strong hold in this province.

Public attention was then distracted by another question that in the end drew the country together again. In the late 1880's hard times returned, bringing a revival of the old hankering after the American market. To satisfy this longing the Conservative government once more tried to get some measure of reciprocity with the United States. But the United States would not open its doors to Canadian raw materials unless Canada opened her doors to American manufactures, and the government in Ottawa would not listen to such a proposal. Many prominent Liberals, however, felt that the country needed reciprocity so badly that it would have to pay the American price. They talked of abolishing the tariff between the two countries and having only one customs barrier around both. The Conservatives denounced this suggestion of "commercial annexation," insisting that it would lead to political annexation, and in the general election of 1891 they were victorious. Then the Liberals realized that they had defeated themselves by running against the national spirit of the country, and they held a convention in which they formally rejected the policy of "unrestricted reciprocity."

While the Canadian people were thus demonstrating that they would not sell their national birthright for a mess of commercial pottage, their family quarrel again broke forth. Shortly after the Province of Manitoba was created, it established a public educational system like that of Quebec, with two sets of schools, one French-speaking and Roman Catholic and the other English-speaking and Protestant. This system was subsequently undermined by immigration, which upset the balance of the population. By 1890 the province had become so overwhelmingly English-speaking and Protestant that its legislature abolished the separate schools supported by taxes and at the same time did away with French as an official language. Quebec raged and Ontario rejoiced, and for six years this Manitoba school question was the storm center of Canadian politics.

That the Conservative government in Ottawa had been growing weaker with age was noticeable before Macdonald's death in 1891, and afterward it became more obvious, as the Conservatives had no one ready to take his place. During the next five years they had three premiers. The last was the worst, and his own Cabinet turned him out early in 1896. In a desperate plight, the Conservatives sent to London for Tupper, who was now Sir Charles. After bringing Nova Scotia into federation, he had been Macdonald's righthand man in Ottawa until he went to England as high commissioner for Canada. Though an old man, the new prime minister was still vigorous, and he courageously sought to carry through the Dominion Parliament the policy his government had already formed, which was to force Manitoba to restore separate schools, a policy that had the official support of the Roman Catholic church. It hurt the Conservatives in Protestant Ontario without doing much good in Quebec, where Riel's ghost still haunted the minds of the people and Roman Catholic voters defied their bishops' political dictation.

In the Dominion election of 1896 the Conservatives were defeated by the Liberals under their young leader Wilfrid Laurier, who, knighted in the following year, is best known as Sir Wilfrid Laurier. He had pleaded for a reasonable settlement with Manitoba, and now, as prime minister, he achieved it. Though separate schools were not revived, provision was made for the separation of Protestant from Roman Catholic pupils so that each group might have its own religious instruction, and the regulation that English was to be the only language used by teachers was modified.

The Liberals had earlier suffered from want of proper leadership. Many of them feared they had made a mistake in 1887 when they chose Laurier as their head, and not until the victory of 1896 did their doubts disappear. In forming the new government, he gathered an unusually strong body of men into his Cabinet. Three veteran provincial premiers, those of Nova Scotia, New Brunswick, and Ontario, resigned their posts to join him in Ottawa, and he also secured the strongest man of the

Manitoba government. But the greatest strength of this Liberal administration, which lasted for fifteen years, was Laurier himself, who has often been compared with Macdonald.

Laurier may never have risen to as great heights as a statesman, though there are many intelligent people who think he did, but neither did he sink to as low a level in the game of politics. There is a suggestion of asceticism about the ever immaculate and courtly Laurier, though he could be mellow after a good dinner. On one such occasion, when a waspish member of the opposition—a teetotaler—tried to sting him, Laurier brushed the attack aside by rising in his place, beaming upon the house, and quoting from *Julius Caesar,* "Yon Cassius hath a lean and hungry look." Laurier was a scholarly man and one of the most eloquent and effective speakers in Canadian public life. No other man save Macdonald has gained such a hold upon the country. French Canada almost worshiped him, its greatest son, the only one to become prime minister of the Dominion; and, what is more remarkable, English Canada had great confidence in his leadership, in spite of the fact that he was French and Roman Catholic.

Here we should perhaps glance at an unpleasant chapter in Canadian political history. For a quarter of a century the church in Quebec had been working hand in glove with the Conservative party in that province. Rome had condemned liberalism— continental European liberalism, which had a distinctly anticlerical flavor—and this action had cast a shadow over political liberalism in French Canada, where the Conservatives astutely managed to confuse these two quite different movements that had the same name. Laurier, therefore, had been forced from the beginning of his career to combat the interference of his own church in the political field. The climax came in 1896, when the bishops threw all their weight behind the Conservative party, hoping thereby to force separate schools back upon Manitoba. Laurier emerged victorious, and he and a number of other Roman Catholics appealed to Rome against the bishops. A special agent was sent out to investigate, and thenceforth the Roman Catholic clergy in Canada eschewed politics. All this of course saved Laurier from falling under English Canadian and Protestant suspicions as a possible tool of his church. Incidentally, the election of 1896 reveals the limitation of the power possessed by the church. The curés, who have always lived very close to the people, swung with them against the dictation of the hierarchy.

Laurier was a firm believer in the British Empire. He introduced the policy of imperial preference, a policy that has been continued by his successors in both parties, and when the Boer War broke out in 1899 his government sent a Canadian contingent to South Africa, thereby establishing a precedent for Canada's active participation on the outbreak of war in 1914. But he steadily resisted the pressure of British statesmen to establish in London some form of imperial government in which the self-governing dominions and colonies would have a share. This pressure was strong in the years around the turn of the century, and it had the support of many thinking people of British extraction in Canada. It is possible, as some believe, that Laurier saved the empire from being centralized in London and kept the way open for it to become what it is today, the British Commonwealth of Nations. This achievement, says one of his biographers, "is his chief claim to an enduring personal fame."

Within Canada Laurier's greatest accomplishment was his settlement of the Manitoba school question, stilling the bitter strife that had torn the country. Racial harmony, thus restored in the beginning of his administration, he strove to preserve and to develop in the years that followed, though his task was not an easy one. The outbreak of the Boer War put him in an awkward position. He was pulled in opposite directions by the two races. The decision to send a Canadian contingent to South Africa was largely due to pressure from English Canada. No such pressure existed in French Canada where a noisy minority cried out against the country's being dragged into distant British wars. This was the beginning of the French Canadian Nationalist movement led by Henri Bourassa, who until then had been one of Laurier's ablest lieutenants.

Ten years later Laurier was placed in a still more awkward position by the naval question. The rapid creation of a huge German navy caused an alarm in Britain, and echoes of the alarm were heard in the Dominion. French Canada was not much concerned over the danger, but the rest of the country was. Many English Canadians felt that Canada was not playing the part of a self-respecting nation, that it was sponging on the mother country by enjoying the protection of her navy without paying a penny for it. In 1910 the government introduced into Parliament a bill for the construction of a Canadian navy that, if need be, might be used as part of the British fleet. The bill stirred much criticism—in French Canada because it went too far and in the rest of the country because it did not go far enough. Many English Canadians insisted on an outright gift of money to Britain, while Bourassa's Nationalists asserted that the government in Ottawa was becoming the tool of the government in London. As might be expected, the expression of these opposite opinions mutually exasperated those who held them. In Ontario Laurier was attacked as too Canadian to be British, and in Quebec as too British to be Canadian.

When the country was all agog over this question the government sprang another—reciprocity. Farmers in the East and in the West had been urging it, and as in days gone by Ottawa privately approached Washington to see what could be done. The result was quite unexpected in Canada. Conditions of living in the United States had so changed that the American government gladly agreed to just such a measure as both Canadian parties had earlier sought in vain. But time had brought changes in Canada as well. The Conservatives discovered that they no longer wanted reciprocity, and many Liberals agreed with them that it would be the undoing of the country. They argued that after a few years Canada would become so dependent on the American market for the sale of its natural produce that it would be at the mercy of the United States. When President Taft urged the people of the United States to seize this opportunity for establishing closer commercial relations with Canada, because if they did not they might miss it forever through the tightening of imperial preference, and when he summed up the situation by saying, "Canada is at the parting of the ways," he did not realize how his words would react in Canada, where they were used as a powerful argument for choosing the British way. And when Speaker Champ Clark openly advocated reciprocity as a step toward annexation, he could not have done more to defeat reciprocity in Canada.

From the Atlantic to the Pacific there was such an outburst of patriotic sentiment as had never been witnessed in the Dominion. The navy and reciprocity were the two main issues in the general election of 1911. In Quebec the chief interest was in the naval bill, and the Nationalists put up such a fight that Laurier lost many seats in his own province. But he still had a majority there, and he would have remained premier had he not suffered a much greater loss throughout the rest of the Dominion, where the naval bill was almost forgotten in the excited feeling over reciprocity and its danger to Canada both as a nation and as a member of the empire.

This reaction may seem incomprehensible to many Americans. Few citizens of this Republic have ever been able to understand why English Canada has always shied away from annexation. This failure to understand is partly the result of blind prejudice, just as the shying has been. But this is not all. There is something deeper, something more spiritual, and because it is a thing of the spirit it is very difficult, if not impossible, to define or explain. As two persons may look alike and yet be different in spirit, so is it with these neighboring nations. There is much in the Canadian spirit that is American, but there is also much that is not. This is partly the product of the British tradition, which, as the election of 1911 illustrates, is an important factor in Canada. Whatever the other causes may be, the plain fact of the matter is that there exists a distinct quality of life in Canada of which Canadians are more or less conscious and which discerning Americans or Englishmen sometimes perceive. The Canadians would no more like to lose it than would citizens of this country like to lose their own American spirit.

With the defeat of Laurier, which was decisive, the Conservatives came back to power after a long spell of opposition. The disorganization that had weakened that party after Macdonald's death had continued after its fall in 1896. But in 1901 Tupper resigned, and another Maritime Province man was selected in his stead. The choice was wise, for the man who headed the new government in 1911 soon became famous as Sir Robert Borden, the wartime premier of the Dominion. He was to lead Canada through the next stage of her development to national maturity.

CHAPTER 14

Filling Out

Fᴿᴏᴍ the time of federation down to the outbreak of war in 1914, the Dominion was filling out, at first slowly and then rapidly. The greatest change came on the prairie. The land of buffaloes and Indians, as it had been for countless ages, became a country of farmers and towns, the home of a large white population. Phenomenal as this development may seem to Canadians who look back, their grandfathers were surprised that it was so slow in coming. The Dominion acquired the West to get room for growth, and straightway the government set about preparing for it. The 1871 promise of a railway to the Pacific in ten years was gladly given, not only because the road would bind British Columbia to Canada but also because it was necessary to open the prairie for settlement.

The government took great precautions to prepare the prairie regions for the arrival of the expected settlers, determined that Canada should avoid the troubles of the United States, where the pressure of settlement upon the hunting grounds of the western Indians had caused and was still causing bloodshed. In 1873 the federal government organized the North West Mounted Police to prevent the lawlessness of the American "Wild West" from spreading across the line.

The danger was serious. All the way out to the Rockies traders with whisky-laden wagons and carts were crossing the international border and corrupting the Indians of Canada. Their liquor turned the red men into madmen who fought and killed without restraint. Scalps were becoming almost as common as furs. Wherever two tribes chanced to meet, they were as like as not to fly at each other's throats. Sometimes they met at a Hudson's Bay Company post where they had gone to trade, and then the men of the company had to lock themselves in while the natives fought out their quarrel until one side drove the other away. The Indians were growing so dangerous that their cousins, the half-breed buffalo hunters of Manitoba, stout fellows as they were, did not dare go out on the western plains unless they went in large numbers, heavily armed.

Most of these whisky peddlers from the American West were desperate characters who thought little of shooting a man, red or white. A few months before the police were organized, a quarrel over stolen horses led to the Cypress Hills massacre, just north of the forty-ninth parallel, near the present boundary of Alberta and Saskatchewan, where a party of white devils fired volley after volley into a village of red men. About forty were killed, many more were wounded, and only a few escaped in the hills. It was no easy task to curb such lawlessness on the part of whites and to tame the savage passions that were being roused in the tribes roving over the plains, for these Indians numbered about thirty-six thousand, the country was huge, and the border was nearly a thousand miles long. Yet the police did it, though they were a mere handful—three hundred in all.

This is one of the miracles of Canadian history. It is explained by the fact that these were no ordinary men but a carefully picked lot. They had strong bodies and bold spirits, and they had something more. They had superior intelligence and education; they were able to think quickly and act wisely in emergencies. There was no difficulty in recruiting this little corps in Eastern Canada. The pay was small, but the call of an adventurous life in the wilds of the West was great. Most of the original force had had some military experience, and from that day to this it has not been uncommon for its officers to hold military rank. The first commander was a colonel of the British army and one of the latest was a general of the Canadian forces in the First World War. The military flavor is also suggested by the fact that the noncommissioned officers of the police are called sergeants and corporals. But the rank and file are termed constables; the ordinary commissioned officers, inspectors, with superintendents above them; and the chief is officially known as the commissioner —for the police are not a military unit but a civilian organization. Perhaps no law-enforcing body in all the world is more famous than this North West Mounted Police, later called the Royal North West Mounted Police and today the Royal Canadian Mounted Police, who "always get their man."

Filling Out

In the summer of 1874, the training of the men having been completed, the whole force set out on its greatest march—right across the prairie. First came the men on their mounts. They were in six divisions or troops, and each troop had horses of the same color. They also had several field guns and mortars. But this was only the beginning of the procession. These men were to live far away from all settlement and therefore had to take with them all the means of supporting themselves. Thus it was that the rest of the cavalcade was made up of nearly two hundred wagons and Red River carts, with all kinds of agricultural implements and a whole army of cattle.

The line of march was straight west along the border—to strike at the root of the evil, the whisky traffic, which was prohibited by law. After keeping together for three hundred miles, one division struck off to the north and made for Edmonton, where the Hudson's Bay Company had maintained an establishment since the end of the previous century. The rest of the men pushed on to the foothills of the mountains, in what is now southern Alberta. There dwelt the most warlike tribes of the West, there was the favorite haunt of the most lawless traders who came up from Fort Benton in Montana, and there three of the divisions were left under Colonel Macleod, the assistant commissioner, while the remaining two headed back for Manitoba.

Macleod and his men did not wait until they had provided shelter for themselves and their horses at Fort Macleod, which soon became the headquarters of the force and later the nucleus of the town of Macleod, before they began to run down the whisky smugglers. The police had hardly arrived when a chief named Three Bulls brought word that one of these evil men, who had got two of his horses for a couple of gallons of whisky, was fifty miles away. Thereupon an inspector and ten men rode off. Shortly afterward they returned with five traders, several wagonloads of liquor, and a great stock of buffalo robes, guns, and revolvers. The firewater was promptly poured out on the snow, the furs were confiscated as having been bought with the contraband stuff, and the men were given their choice of imprisonment or a heavy fine.

The sudden appearance of this handful of police had a magical effect over the whole country. At the close of the year Macleod could write: "I am happy to be able to report the complete stoppage of the whisky trade throughout the whole of this section of the country, and that the drunken riots, which in former years were almost a daily occurrence, are now entirely at an end; in fact, a more peaceable community than this, with a very large number of Indians camped along the river, could not be found anywhere."

The natives were quick to see that these skillful and fearless "riders of the plains," clad in scarlet, gold, and blue, had come not to make war upon them but to protect them from all wicked men, whatever their color. Less than three years after their arrival, the head chief of the proud Blackfeet Indians spoke the mind of his people when he said, "If the police had not come to this country, where would we all be now? Bad men and whisky were killing us so fast that very few of us indeed would have been left today. The Mounted Police have protected us as the feathers of the bird protect it from the frosts of winter." It was therefore easy for the police to keep the Indians in order. Whenever a red man committed murder, or stole horses, or perpetrated any other crime, the red coats went after him, and they would go through fire and water until they got him. It was not unusual for a single constable to ride into an Indian camp and arrest a wrongdoer in the midst of his armed people. The rest knew that the captive would be set free if he were really innocent or punished as he deserved if he were guilty.

Having won the confidence of the Indians, the police were able to help the Dominion government to clear the country for settlers. This was done by a number of treaties with the various tribes, who agreed to give up their rights to the land and let settlers come in. As compensation the government promised to pay twenty-five dollars a year to each chief, fifteen dollars to each "headman," and five dollars to each man, woman, and child. In addition, the tribes were allotted lands for their own use, where no white men were allowed to settle. These reserves were generous, averaging a square mile for every family of five Indians. The government also gave them farming implements, seed, cattle, and other necessary assistance to support themselves in a new way. These treaties were made just in time, for the natives' only means of livelihood was the buffalo, and the buffalo was fast disappearing. In 1875 the plains were often black with enormous herds, stretching as far as the eye could see; five years later they were almost gone, but the red men were saved from starvation.

These treaties were also made just in time to prevent the bloody Indian war then raging south of the border from spreading northward. Indians in the United States were sending braves and chiefs up to the Canadian Indians urging them to join them in the fight against the "Long Knives," and there is no telling what might have happened had not the North West Mounted Police and these treaties held the Canadian Indians back. After Sitting Bull and his Sioux warriors had caught and slain General Custer and every one of his cavalrymen, who numbered almost as many as the whole of the police in the Canadian West, in the summer of 1876, strong American forces were sent against the blood-drunk savages and several thousand of them retreated northward across the border. Their presence in Canada created a tense situation that threatened to develop serious international complications, but the "mounties" kept things well in hand. The good relations they had already established with the Canadian "treaty Indians" were a powerful restraining influence upon Sitting Bull and his followers, who had thought they could do as they liked under the Union Jack.

After much negotiation they were persuaded to go home. But old Sitting Bull was in an ugly temper when he came to the last police station near the border. He demanded food from the inspector in charge and on being refused threatened to take it by force. The officer replied that he would give him bullets instead of bread if he tried that game. "I am cast away!" cried the desolate chief. "No!" insisted the inspector. "You are not cast away. I am speaking for your own good and the good of your people and giving you good advice. You have been promised pardon and food and land if you return to your reservation in the United States. I advise you to go, and I will help you and your people to travel if you accept the terms that have been offered you." On the next day they rode across the border together, and the inspector stood at the side of Sitting Bull when the famous Indian leader surrendered to the commander of the United States Army post at Fort Buford in July 1881.

Meanwhile in Eastern Canada the newspapers and the people

themselves were almost in a panic. They demanded that whole regiments of soldiers be shipped out to deal with these terrifying intruders, though there was actually no need for them. The astonishment of Eastern Canadians was almost as great as that of Americans at the way the little body of police handled and got rid of these thousands of warlike Sioux who might have stirred up all the tribes of the Canadian West to engage in a ghastly war. The North West Mounted Police laid the first foundation for the growth of the Canadian Northwest by establishing law and order there. They made the country safe for settlers.

By 1880 Manitoba was beginning to fill out. It had a population of about 60,000, and Winnipeg had grown from a village of 200 to a city of nearly 8,000 people. In this year the province harvested over a million bushels of the finest wheat in the world, and its reputation had spread even before a bushel was exported. In 1876 Ontario had a crop failure, attributed to weak seed, and to prevent another failure the head of a large Toronto seed company went to Winnipeg to buy the best seed available. He got eight hundred and fifty bushels, the first shipment of wheat from the Canadian West. It went by water up the Red River, by rail across to Duluth, and thence by water. Two years later Manitoba was linked with the American railways and began exporting her famous wheat to Britain.

The beginnings of settlement appeared in three parts of the North West Territory. In the foothills of what is now southern Alberta, growing herds of cattle took the place of the vanishing buffalo. This ranching industry was a direct offshoot of that in Montana, whence the first cattle were driven north in 1879. The Dominion government began it as a demonstration of what might be done, and private individuals followed the example. These pioneer ranchers had rather a hard time until the railway reached the mountains in 1883, but after that the business expanded rapidly. The other two districts where small white settlements appeared in the late 1870's were along the North Saskatchewan, between Prince Albert and Battleford, and around Edmonton. People trekked in by Red River cart or prairie schooner to gain the advantage of a head start over the others who would follow when the railway came.

In the early 1880's, when the men in charge of the Canadian

FELLING A DOUGLAS FIR TREE, VANCOUVER ISLAND, BRITISH COLUMBIA.

PICTURESQUE LOG CHUTE ON THE JORDAN RIVER, VANCOUVER ISLAND.

LUMBERING IN BRITISH COLUMBIA. ABOVE, HAULING RED CEDAR LOGS
FROM THE BUSH TO SKIDWAY BY TRACTOR. BELOW, LOGGING TRAIN.

THE PAPER INDUSTRY IN MODERN CANADA. ABOVE, WET END SECTION OF
PAPER MACHINE, DALHOUSIE MILL, NEW BRUNSWICK. BELOW, WINDERS,
ANGLO-CANADIAN PULP AND PAPER MILL, PROVINCE OF QUEBEC.

Filling Out

Pacific Railway abandoned the northern route and ran the road straight west to the mountains, the stream of settlers was diverted to the south. All along the line the land was taken, and new communities sprang up almost overnight—Regina, Moose Jaw, Medicine Hat, and Calgary. The doors of the country were open at last; surveyors were busy laying it out according to the well-known checkerboard plan copied from the United States, in square townships of six miles to a side, with each square mile, or section, divided into quarter sections, or farms, of one hundred and sixty acres. It seemed that the great day had dawned and that this immense empty land was about to fill with a rush.

But there was no rush. Between the census of 1881 and that of 1891 the growth of population in Manitoba was ninety thousand, while the increase in the much larger territory beyond was only ten thousand. Settlement was still limited to a ribbon of land along the railway and to a few patches in the valley of the North Saskatchewan. What was the matter? One reason that many people give for this disappointment is that the country was blighted by a rebellion at the very moment when, after long years of preparation, it was ready for settlement.

This supposed blight was the Saskatchewan, or second Riel, Rebellion, for which the Canadian government was perhaps even more to blame than it had been for the first Riel Rebellion. Again it had forgotten the half-breeds. In establishing the Province of Manitoba, it had promised the *métis* land there as soon as the survey was completed, but the promise was slow in being fulfilled, and many *métis* moved west to join others who had left before the troubles on the Red River occurred. They settled chiefly in the region where the two branches of the Saskatchewan flow together. There they took up land after their old fashion copied from the French settlement on the St. Lawrence, in long, narrow strips running back from the water, two miles deep and an eighth of a mile wide. For some years the half-breeds paid little attention to their farms, for they lived chiefly by the hunt. When the buffalo began to disappear they saw that they would have to live by working the land. At the same time they began to see something else. According to the orders of the government away off in Ottawa, the whole country was to be laid out in square farms, which would cut across every one of their holdings. Once more it seemed that their lands were to be stolen from them—and just as land was coming to be their only means of existence.

On top of this grievance came another. The government was doing everything for their cousins, the red men, but nothing for them. The *métis* wanted security for their lands and demanded that they should be helped as much as the full-blooded Indians. Again and again they petitioned the government, and their cry for justice was supported by many white people, including the lieutenant governor and also Taché, who had become an archbishop; but the government was deaf.

The building of the Canadian Pacific Railway brought matters to a head in an unexpected way. Many *métis* had been earning money by carting goods into the country from Manitoba. By destroying this freighting business and substituting the shorter haul from the nearest station to the south, the railway did them vital injury. It also threatened to hurt them in the future by pouring in white settlers to crowd them out. In 1884 the half-breeds decided to act for themselves. With the backing of a number of white settlers they sent for the only man who they believed could secure justice for them—Louis Riel, whom they found teaching school in Montana. His coming, which was no secret, was a further warning to the government. It should either have kept him out of the country or have removed the grievances that brought him back.

The storm broke early in the spring of 1885, when Riel set up a rebel government at Batoche, a few miles down the South Saskatchewan from the present city of Saskatoon, and summoned the red men to rise and slay the whites. Fortunately most of the Indians, already settled on their reserves, refused to stir. Some police from a nearby post and a number of volunteers from Prince Albert, a few miles down the North Saskatchewan, advanced to nip the rebellion in the bud. But it nipped them, instead. They were caught in a trap that took the lives of twelve of these hundred men. The rest escaped. The startling news that the white men were defeated in battle was flashed over the country by mysterious native signals, and the rebellion spread. Some two hundred miles up the river, near the present border of Alberta, a band of Indians wiped out a little white settlement by massacre. This was the western limit of the rising. Its eastern

MR. MACPHERSON'S OPPORTUNITY

A grand chance for the minister of the interior to win
Canada's gratitude

"The North West land policy persisted in by the Canadian Government
was having the effect of driving Canadian settlers into the American territories where the regulations were more liberal. *Grip*, November 17th,
1883."

end was Prince Albert, where many settlers gathered for safety. The only other place of refuge that remained was Battleford.

The terror did not last long, thanks to the telegraph and the railway. Between four and five thousand Canadian militia soon arrived from the East. Detraining at several points, they closed in on the seat of the rebellion and crushed it by the end of May. In the autumn the captives were tried at Regina. Some were sent to prison; a few, including Riel, were condemned to death.

But to come back to the question, what delayed the development of the Canadian West? Though many have placed the blame upon this rebellion, it may have attracted as many settlers as it frightened away. Some of the militiamen who went west settled there immediately; others went home to persuade friends and relatives to join them in a peaceful conquest of the great new country.

Some people blame the Canadian Pacific's preference for the drier southern route. But if the company had followed the original plan, it might have collapsed. All the financial resources it could master were barely sufficient to complete the construction of the shorter and cheaper line. The railway has also been criticized for not building a number of branch lines until later years. By the end of 1892 it had northern arms to Prince Albert and Edmonton and southern arms to Estevan, Lethbridge, and Macleod. Had many more been built in the early years, would they not have filled the country with settlers? There is reason for doubting this, as we shall soon see.

Many have accused the government at Ottawa of holding back the development of the West by its land policy. In each township it set aside two of the thirty-six sections for the support of schools and nearly two for the Hudson's Bay Company, and it offered only half the remainder as free homesteads, keeping the other half for the railway or for sale at a later date. These reserved sections formed a much larger proportion of the whole than had the Crown and clergy reserves that retarded Upper Canada's growth. And yet after some years the long-expected flood of immigrants began, and it continued in spite of these adverse conditions, which did not disappear until after the provinces of Alberta and Saskatchewan were formed in 1905.

The chief explanation for the delay may be found in condi-

Filling Out

tions in the United States. After the Civil War, as is well known, people rushed to the free lands of the American West. The wealth they produced quickened the life of the older states in many ways, enlarging the demand for manufactures and stimulating the growth of cities. Never had the world seen such vigorous expansion. It was so powerful that it drew millions of immigrants across the Atlantic, and it drained off much of the youth of Eastern Canada. Until the American West was pretty well filled, the Canadian West could not hope to have anything more than a slow growth. In the last decade of the century the westward-flowing tide in the United States was checked by the disappearance of free homesteads that were good for farming. The price of land rose; in Iowa it reached sixty dollars an acre in 1898—nearly twice what it had been eight years before. The tide was dammed; it backed up and began to spill over into Canada.

Two hundred thousand people entered the Canadian West during the decade of the 1890's. Half of them stayed in Manitoba, raising its population to more than 250,000, while the other half increased the population of the North West Territory to a little over 180,000. This distribution may seem surprising, because the Territory was many times the size of Manitoba. But Manitoba had plenty of room, and it possessed several advantages. It was the older country; it was much nearer the outside world; and it was better served by railways, for there was considerable building there during the 1890's.

After 1900 there was almost a stampede to the Canadian prairie. Nearly 1,250,000 people entered the Canadian West before the First World War. They came from the United States, from Eastern Canada, from the British Isles, and from the continent of Europe, particularly from southeastern Europe, which now supplanted northern Europe as the chief source of the great migration from that continent. Thus the Canadian Northwest, compared with the American Northwest, received relatively few immigrants from the Scandinavian countries. Some people of Scandinavian origin were among the immigrants from the United States, but the best known Scandinavian element in Canada was planted some years before when there was quite a little migration from Iceland to Manitoba.

The continental Europeans who participated in the rush to the Canadian prairie were mostly Ruthenians and Poles from what was then the Austrian province of Galicia, Ukrainians from the neighboring region of Russia, and Doukhobors from farther east. There were fears that the influx of these strange people, who spoke only unintelligible tongues, dressed in sheepskin coats, and lived in mud shacks where pigs, chickens, and children were mixed up together, would create a sort of national indigestion. But the bulk of the population that settled in the Canadian Northwest came from the United States, Eastern Canada, and the British Isles; and time has proved that the southeastern European can be assimilated.

This was the great age of railway building in the West. The Canadian Pacific Railway thrust out lines everywhere, and two new roads appeared, the Canadian Northern and the Grand Trunk Pacific, now amalgamated in the Canadian National system. They covered the country with a network of steel and spread the human flood far and wide. Manitoba had then more than 500,000 people, and twice as many dwelt on the plains beyond. The prairie was no longer an empty land. Towns and cities grew like mushrooms in the midst of thriving communities.

The kind of life that was growing out there was in one important respect very different from that in any other part of Canada. It was very like what had already appeared on the prairie south of the border, with large flat farms so specialized in the production of wheat for the European market that they produced little else. The reason for the rise of this new type of agricultural society is fairly simple. During the latter half of the nineteenth century, the population of Europe became more and more industrialized and as a consequence more and more dependent on North America for a large part of its daily bread. At the same time the development of agricultural machinery completely changed farming methods, making it possible for a family to work much more land and to produce a large surplus, the export of which was made possible by the building of railways. As it was the cheapest place to grow wheat, the American prairie was almost wholly given over to wheat farming wherever the rainfall was sufficient; and the same conditions governed the settlement of the Canadian prairie, where, because of the climate, even better wheat could be grown.

Meanwhile, the character of the government of the Territory was completely changed. With the early growth of settlement, the appointed council was enlarged by the addition of elected members. The district around Prince Albert chose the first popular representative in 1881. Seven years later the appointed legislative councilors disappeared, and a regular assembly was set up. The Dominion, which still controlled the actual administration, or executive, then faced a strong demand for self-government. Ottawa resisted, just as London had resisted the demands of the older colonies half a century before, and, like London, Ottawa yielded in the end. The Territory was given responsible government in 1897, though not all the rights enjoyed by regular provinces under the British North America Act. This defect was remedied in 1905, in the midst of the rush onto the land, when the Dominion Parliament passed two acts creating the provinces of Alberta and Saskatchewan.

Turning from the prairie to see how the rest of the Dominion was faring, we find the next most remarkable development in British Columbia. As a province it was a year younger than Manitoba, but it had the advantage of greater population at the start—about 12,000 white people, whereas Manitoba had only 1,500. Nevertheless its growth lagged behind that of its prairie sister chiefly because of its more remote geographical position. At the end of the century, when Manitoba's population reached 250,000, British Columbia's was only 175,000. Then the latter began to catch up. During the next ten years it had an increase of 215,000, while Manitoba's was only 200,000. Thousands of miles away to the south the opening of the Panama Canal was revolutionizing the geographical position of Canada's Pacific province.

British Columbia had a very different sort of life from that seen on the prairie. There was relatively little farming except fruit growing, which, during the few years before the First World War, came to rival that of any other part of the Dominion. Much more important was the lumbering and pulp industry, and more valuable still was another product of British Columbia—the fish caught and canned on its coast. Almost every housewife in Canada, except in the Maritime Provinces, soon became familiar with British Columbia salmon. But the greatest wealth of this wealthy province was found neither in her forests nor in her sea. Her chief riches were discovered beneath her mountains, where untold quantities of gold, silver, lead, copper, and coal still lie, making British Columbia one of the most important mining areas in the world. The new geographical position of the province was now telling in her favor. Trade with the Orient, and on the Pacific generally, was growing; and through Canada's western door a great stream of commerce flowed. Vancouver was well on the way to becoming what it now is, the third city of the Dominion and one of the great seaports of the world.

The Maritime Provinces experienced no such development as that west of the Great Lakes. The population of Prince Edward Island, limited largely to agriculture, has actually shrunk since the census of 1891, while that of its two neighbors has increased relatively little. Instead of a boom, a great blow struck this part of the Dominion. It came in the ten years following 1875 when iron ships and steam engines ruined the local ship-building industry. These provinces were also disappointed in not becoming the Dominion's front door. They saw Central Canada's stream of Atlantic trade divide and flow past them on either side—over the St. Lawrence in summer and through American ports in winter. But the Maritime Provinces did not stagnate. The exhaustion of the nearer United States forests created a healthy demand for New Brunswick timber and pulp, while coal mining and steel manufacturing grew in Nova Scotia. Indeed one is struck by a certain similarity between the varied life to be found in Canada's two extremities. But in fairness to the people on the Atlantic we must remember that their country was already well developed before the resources on the Canadian Pacific Coast were scratched. Also, if the Maritime Provinces are added together, their total area is little more than one tenth the size of British Columbia, and yet in 1914 their combined population was considerably more than double that of the Pacific province.

Until nearly the end of the century the strong pull of the United States prevented Central Canada and the Maritime Provinces from developing as rapidly as they might otherwise have

Filling Out

done. Industrial New England tempted French Canadians from the land and transformed them into factory hands. Their migration was very noticeable, because they were largely concentrated in a relatively small area—the mill towns of New England—and they retained their racial identity. It was not so with the English-speaking Canadians who left the country. Though more numerous, they were more widely scattered and were indistinguishable from native-born Americans.

Despite this drain from Central and Eastern Canada to the United States the older parts of the Dominion were growing industrially. In this development Central Canada possessed certain advantages over the Maritime Provinces. It did not lie off to one side, as they did; it had a population many times larger; and it had much more capital. Therefore it tended to become the chief manufacturing section of the country and the main seat of its business. It had become such before 1900, but the growth had been slow, for in addition to the pull of the United States it was laboring under several handicaps—a lack of mineral resources, particularly coal, a need for more capital, and a limited market for the sale of its products.

Around 1900 conditions in this part of the country were improving. The Dominion as a whole was beginning to experience such an industrial and commercial growth as it had never known, and naturally this growth was greatest in Central Canada. Among the causes for this remarkable change was the discovery of rich mineral deposits in the northern rocky area, which had earlier discouraged agricultural settlement. Though no coal was found there, and coal had been regarded as absolutely essential for any great industrial development, a substitute appeared, which in some respects was better. This was hydroelectric power, produced by harnessing the Niagara and other rivers of the region. This new kind of power was cheaper than coal; it could be distributed more easily to the places where it might be used; and there it could be made to turn machinery with less trouble. This was also the time when American capitalists, having exploited the resources of the United States, turned to exploit the resources of the Dominion.

Much as Central Canada profited by the discovery of its immense mineral wealth, by the development of cheap and convenient power from its waters, and by the application of American enterprise and capital, it owed still more to the rush of people to the prairie. The needs of the West were enormous —more railways and all manner of manufactured goods—and these needs provided Central Canada with a rapidly expanding market for its industrial products. Capital as well as people poured into the West to develop it, and this capital was largely spent on goods produced east of the Great Lakes. Moreover, the West was creating new wealth on an ever greater scale. Each year it was selling millions upon millions of bushels of wheat in Europe, and the money these sales brought back to the country was spent on goods made in Central Canada.

Great industries sprang up in the wilds of the North, where forests and mines were yielding their riches. The forests provided the material for the huge pulp and paper plants that were built to supply the American public with newsprint. The mines contained untold quantities of many different ores, and gigantic smelters were built beside the mines to refine these ores and pour out silver and gold and other metals, such as copper, cobalt, and nickel, in astonishing abundance. In a few years half the world's supply of cobalt came from the district around the town of Cobalt, Ontario, and Sudbury in the same province produced nine tenths of the world's nickel supply. All this northern development, like the development of the western wheat lands, gave a great stimulus to the growth of the older parts of Central Canada. The necessary machinery and supplies were purchased in Ontario and Quebec, and there too was spent the money that came back from the sale of these northern products in foreign markets. This northern influence was a good second to the western influence in transforming the life of the older, settled parts of the Dominion.

Here and there throughout Central Canada quiet little villages and towns became bursting hives of activity, towns suddenly blossomed into cities, and cities grew almost out of all recognition as new industries were founded and old ones expanded. This section of the country rapidly became one of the more important manufacturing areas of the world, producing all kinds of machine-made articles from steamships and railway engines to clothing and buttons. So great was the growth of this industrial society that it absorbed as many immigrants as did the West. Indeed some industries that had been established to meet Canadian needs soon became so large that they too went into the export business. This was particularly true of those turning out farm implements and automobiles.

While the wheels of factories hummed and business houses could scarcely keep up with the orders that were flooding in, the farmer in this part of the country shared in the general prosperity. Though he grew less wheat, because it could be produced more cheaply on the prairie, he was able to make more profit by developing intensive agriculture. The increasing urban population provided him with an expanding market for dairy and garden produce.

Thus did the whole country fill out in a way that recalled the phenomenal growth of the United States in the nineteenth century; and many people predicted that the twentieth century would see in Canada just such a development as the previous century had seen in her great neighbor.

CHAPTER 15

Coming of Age

THE war that shook the world in 1914 burst upon Canada like a thunderclap from a blue sky. Few Canadians had believed it was possible. Most of them were chiefly interested in the material development of their own country and were looking to the West, where the mainspring of this development lay. The war drew their interest across the sea and kept it there until after the fighting ceased.

As part of the British Empire, Canada found herself automatically at war on August 4, 1914. This did not mean that the country had to take an active part in the fighting, but the people of their own free will threw themselves into the struggle. They did it out of loyalty to the mother country and out of a desire to stand shoulder to shoulder with her in the great hour of trial. They did it also out of a firm belief in the righteousness of the Allied cause and the necessity to defeat Germany, which had become a mighty militarist state threatening to enthrone its spirit in the world. These two loyalties—to Britain and to a peaceful civilization based on law and order—expressed what was more or less instinctively felt to be the interest of the country, and running together they roused an intense conviction that Canada's honor was at stake and that no sacrifice should be spared in maintaining this honor before the world.

The government at Ottawa, supported by the opposition, immediately decided to send a division of twenty-five thousand soldiers and called for recruits. Ten thousand more than the required number appeared, and on October 1 about thirty-three thousand men sailed for Britain to complete their training. While they were still on the water a second division was organized in Canada. Before the war ended nearly six hundred and twenty thousand Canadians donned khaki, and two thirds of them went overseas. These figures may seem as nothing when we remember the colossal size of the conflict, in which the combatants were numbered by the tens of millions. But Canada's contribution was surprisingly large when we compare it with her population, then barely eight million; and, though the Canadian soldiers played a relatively small part in the war, they gave a good account of themselves.

In April 1915 the first Canadian division went into action before Ypres, and on that very day these Canadian soldiers saw the first use of poison gas in the history of warfare. Like a green fog it rolled down on their immediate neighbors to the left and sent them flying in panic. The line was broken! Though in danger of being surrounded, the Canadians stood firm. Even when the deadly gas was launched against them they did not budge. Relief came on the fourth day, after some of their units had lost more than half their men. In describing the engagement the British commander in chief praised the Canadians for their "magnificent display of tenacity and courage" and credited them with having "averted a disaster."

Later in the year the second division joined the first to form an army corps that was enlarged by the arrival of two more Canadian divisions in 1916. Early in this year Sir Julian Byng, later Lord Byng and governor general of the Dominion, became commander of the Canadian corps, and as such he endeared himself to thousands of Canadians. In 1917 he was promoted to a larger command in the British army, and his place was taken by a Canadian, Sir Arthur Currie. His appointment, which he retained to the end of the war, meant much to the people of the Dominion, who felt that it was a further recognition of their autonomy.

Of the many battles in which the Canadians fought in different parts of the front, the most famous was in April 1917, when they captured Vimy Ridge, a high position from which the Germans had constantly menaced the Allied line. They also won a remarkable series of successes in the closing period of the war. Again they drew ringing praise from the head of all the British forces, and after they had taken Mons on the very last day of the war, King Albert of Belgium publicly declared them to be "unsurpassed by any corps in Europe."

The price Canada paid for participating in this war was tremendous. Out of every three of her sons who reached the front, two were wounded. The loss of Canadian life almost equaled the loss of American life in the grim struggle. Of the Canadians, 35,684 were killed in action and 12,437 died of wounds, making a total of 48,121. The corresponding American figures are 35,556 and 15,130, making a total of 50,686. Humanly speaking, the war thus ate into Canada about twelve times as much as it did into the United States. It also multiplied the Dominion debt seven times and left a correspondingly heavy burden of taxation.

Much more serious was the strain the war imposed on the national unity of the country, a strain for which there was no American counterpart. Until 1917 the Canadian forces were raised by voluntary enlistment, and it soon became apparent that the two races were not supplying recruits in equal proportion. There were several reasons for this inequality. One was that, early marriage being the custom among French Canadians, a much higher percentage of young French Canadians were married men with families, and therefore were more bound by home ties and responsibilities than other Canadians. Moreover, they were much more cut off from the outside world than were English-speaking Canadians. In 1914 the Dominion contained nearly a million people who had been born in the British Isles, and few of the native-born in English Canada were removed from the mother country by more than a generation or two. The French had no such bond with Europe. Practically every one of them had to go back nearly two and a half centuries to find an ancestor who lived on the other side of the Atlantic. Their religion also held them back because of two peculiar circumstances —one in France and the other in Ottawa.

During the previous ten years the government of France had openly turned against Roman Catholicism, closing monasteries, withholding from all the clergy the incomes that had been paid them for a hundred years, and confiscating the property of the church. Some of the priests who were driven out of France had come to Canada, and from these as well as from their own clergy the French Canadians had been hearing bitter denunciations of the persecuting French Republic. Therefore, far from being impelled to rush to France's rescue, devout French Canadians were inclined to regard Germany's attack as something like a judgment of God upon the irreligious and wicked French in Europe. At the same time it was highly unfortunate that the Canadian minister of militia, the cabinet minister responsible for raising and training the Canadian forces, was one of the leaders of the Orange Order, which was notoriously hostile to French Canada and the Roman Catholic church. He actually put a colonel's uniform on a leading Protestant clergyman of Toronto, an Englishman who had recently come to the country, and sent him to stimulate recruiting in French and Roman Catholic Quebec! But in spite of all this, French Canada supplied between twenty and thirty thousand men.

Few people in English Canada understood the situation. Most of them were inclined to think that the French were slower to enlist because they were slackers. If they had only examined their own numbers they would have observed that the Canadian-born were far behind the British-born. The latter formed three quarters of the first division, though English Canada had four times more Canadian-born than British-born people. This discrepancy was most natural because the British-born part of the population had the highest proportion of young unmarried men and the strongest ties with the mother country. But it is human nature to excuse one's self and to accuse others, and throughout English Canada there was a growing animosity toward French Canada. It came to a head in 1917. Canadians were falling in France faster than they were being recruited at home. Something desperate had to be done to keep faith with "the boys at the front" and to save the country's honor.

Sir Robert Borden discussed the problem with his Cabinet, and they decided that conscription was necessary. He was convinced, however, that a government composed of only one party should not force such an extreme measure upon the country, and he invited Laurier, the leader of the opposition, to join in forming a union government in which both parties would be equally represented. The Liberal chieftain refused because acceptance would commit him to support conscription. English Canada believed that if Laurier, the greatest French Canadian, would only take this step he would draw his people after him and unite the nation in a greater war effort. Laurier held the opposite belief, and he was in a better position to know. He was convinced that it would destroy his influence over French Canada and throw his people into the arms of Bourassa and his Nationalists, who were preaching that this war was no affair of Canada's.

When Laurier refused, his party split. Many prominent English-speaking Liberals supported Borden's proposals. Therefore the premier introduced his conscription bill and continued negotiations for a coalition government. The bill passed, although nearly every French Canadian in Parliament voted against it, and the negotiations led to the formation of a union government. It included not a single French Liberal, and its two French Conservatives were regarded by most French Canadians as traitors to their race. The general election that followed in December was perhaps the bitterest in the history of the Dominion. Conscription was the main issue, and with the exception of a few English-speaking Liberals who clung to their old leader the country was divided according to race. Not since the first half of the previous century had French and English been so opposed. Wild words were loosed and dangerous passions were aroused. The English-speaking part of the country gave the union government an overwhelming majority in Parliament—and then the French Canadians showed their good sense. Though still opposed to conscription, they submitted to it, and the Canadian army overseas was maintained to the end of the war.

As a youth suddenly grows into a man when he is thrust out into the world to fend for himself, Canada, through being plunged into the war, quickly attained national maturity. Canadians had felt little responsibility except for the internal development of their country until the shock of 1914 turned them face about. In bearing the new and mighty responsibility that they then shouldered, they discovered their strength and felt that it was the strength of maturity. They were taking their place as one of the nations of the earth. Never again could they be just a colony.

A similar awakening was occurring in the other self-governing dominions, so that the whole empire was rapidly transformed in character. From being a mother country with a number of colonies more or less dependent upon her for their protection and for representation of their interests in the world at large,

SALMON FISHING IN BRITISH COLUMBIA. ABOVE, CANNERY GILL-NET BOATS GETTING
THEIR POSITION IN THE LINE OF TOW LEAVING FOR THE FISHING GROUNDS, SKEENA
RIVER. BELOW, SALMON TRAP FISHING AT SOOKES HARBOR.

FISHING INDUSTRY IN NOVA SCOTIA. ABOVE, HOISTING ABOARD A 680-POUND TUNA FROM A SPILLER NET. BELOW, A FIELD OF DRIED FISH.

SHIPPING IN CANADA. ABOVE, THE LINER DUCHESS OF ATHOLL PASS-
ING UNDER THE QUEBEC BRIDGE, QUEBEC. BELOW, THE
C.P.R. DOCKS, VANCOUVER, BRITISH COLUMBIA.

SCENES IN NOVA SCOTIA. LEFT ABOVE, CORNWALLIS VALLEY; RIGHT,
MEMORIAL CHURCH AND STATUE OF EVANGELINE AT GRAND PRÉ.
BELOW, APPLE BLOSSOMS IN THE GASPEREAU VALLEY.

THE GREAT WHEAT FIELDS OF CANADA. ABOVE, EIGHT REAPERS CUT-
TING GRAIN IN ALBERTA. BELOW, SPEEDING THE HARVEST WITH
COMBINES (HARVESTER-THRESHERS) IN SASKATCHEWAN.

ONTARIO NICKEL. LEFT ABOVE, PORT COLBORNE SMELTING PLANT, IN-
TERNATIONAL NICKEL COMPANY; RIGHT, INSERTING A NICKEL ANODE
IN AN ELECTROLYTIC CELL. BELOW, AN ELECTROLYTIC TANK HOUSE.

GOLD MINING. ABOVE, GENERAL VIEW OF PIONEER GOLD MINES, BRITISH COLUMBIA. BELOW, AERIAL TRAM AT THE HOLLINGER MINES, TIMMINS, ONTARIO.

GOLD MINING. ABOVE, MEN COMING OFF SHIFT, HOLLINGER MINES. BE-
LOW, CAGE HOIST WITH SAFETY DEVICE, MCINTYRE MINES, ONTARIO.

GOLD MINING. LEFT ABOVE, LOADING TRAIN FROM POWER CHUTE;
RIGHT, STEEL CONSTRUCTION IN NEW SHAFT, MCINTYRE MINES.
BELOW, LUNCH HOUR AT ONE OF THE DOMES MINES, ONTARIO.

ABOVE, QUEBEC, WITH CHATEAU FRONTENAC AND DUFFERIN TERRACE IN
THE FOREGROUND AND IN RIGHT CENTER THE LOWER TOWN AND HARBOR.
BELOW, MONTREAL; LOADING OCEAN VESSELS WITH GRAIN FOR EXPORT.

ABOVE, SAULT SAINTE MARIE, ONTARIO; SPANISH RIVER PULP AND
PAPER COMPANY'S PLANT. BELOW, VERMILLION LAKE AND
MOUNT RUNDLE, BANFF NATIONAL PARK, ALBERTA.

ABOVE, VANCOUVER, BRITISH COLUMBIA; WATERFRONT AND BUSINESS
DISTRICT. BELOW, VICTORIA; THE INNER HARBOR, LEGISLATIVE
BUILDINGS, AND QUAY, WHERE VISITORS STEP ASHORE.

AERIAL TRANSPORTATION. ABOVE, LOADING A BOAT FRAME ABOARD
A PLANE, NORTH WEST TERRITORIES; BELOW, AIRPLANE BASE,
NORANDA MINES, PROVINCE OF QUEBEC.

FEDERAL PARLIAMENT BUILDINGS, OTTAWA. LEFT ABOVE, THE
PARLIAMENTARY LIBRARY; RIGHT, HALL OF HONOUR BETWEEN LOBBY
AND LIBRARY. BELOW, INTERIOR OF THE PARLIAMENTARY LIBRARY.

OTTAWA. PARLIAMENT AND GOVERNMENT ADMINISTRATIVE
BUILDINGS, WELLINGTON STREET.

THE PEACE TOWER, OTTAWA.

the British Empire became the British Commonwealth of Nations. In this transformation Canada forced the pace, for she was the senior dominion and her peculiarly close relationship with the powerful United States made it impossible for Britain to deny the Canadian demand—as in the days when responsible government was granted. In thus leading the way, Canada owes more to her wartime premier than is realized by most British people, even in Canada.

Sir Robert Borden was as different from his two great predecessors as they were from each other. Few anecdotes are related about him, for he was not the sort of man people tell stories about. He lacked Macdonald's conviviality and Laurier's silver tongue, and many thought him pompous. But he was really one of the least self-conscious and self-seeking men in public life. His speeches had a remarkable way of reading much better than they sounded, he was a capital companion on the golf course or at the dinner table, and he was a perfect host. Unlike Macdonald and Laurier, who never made any particular mark in their legal profession, Sir Robert was already a very successful lawyer when he gave himself over to politics. Before the war, and even after it began, there were doubts of his ability as a leader, but he proved to be the only Allied premier who remained in power throughout the war. After he retired he became Canada's one and only "elder statesman" until his death in 1937.

Early in the war Borden made it pretty plain to the authorities in London that it was not only unfortunate but even dangerous to imagine that Canada would continue to throw her weight into the struggle and be content with no voice in its management. Was this a war being waged by the United Kingdom alone, or by the whole empire? If the latter, why did the statesmen of the British Isles arrogate to themselves the sole right of directing the fighting forces supplied by other self-governing parts of the empire? Such questions caused considerable heart-searching on the Thames. Finally Lloyd George decided to invite the premiers of the dominions to sit as members of the war cabinet in London. Thus in 1917, through her prime minister, Canada gained a voice in the conduct of the empire's foreign affairs. Then followed a further step along the road toward full nationhood. In the summer of 1918, when the dominion members of the imperial war cabinet were admitted to sit as members of the supreme war council of the Allies, Canada and her sister dominions gained their first direct official contact with foreign governments.

When the struggle drew to a close, they were all in danger of slipping back into a subordinate position. According to the first plans for the peace conference in Paris, neither Canada nor any other British dominion was to have been invited to attend. But Sir Robert Borden insisted that the dominions had earned a right to membership in the conference, along with all the independent states that had fought in the war, and it was he who persuaded the British government to break down the opposition of foreign governments to this claim. At the close of the conference the Canadian delegates, like those of other countries represented there, signed the peace treaties. Then the government in Ottawa, in spite of British pressure to the contrary, refused to ratify the treaties until the Canadian Parliament accepted them. At the same time Canada became a distinct member of the League of Nations, again along with the other dominions, and after some international discussion in which Sir Robert Borden forced the issue, it was recognized that any dominion might be elected to membership in the council of the League, as Canada was in 1927. The position of equality with other nations, which had been temporarily gained in the Allied war council and in the peace conference, was thus confirmed in the organization of the League. Incidentally the American campaign against the League, which criticized the League for giving the British Empire several votes and the United States only one, stirred resentment in Canada as an attack upon the new international status that she had so hardly won.

This new status of the Dominion as a full-fledged member of the League needed to be broadened. If all Canadian external relations other than League business were to be carried on, as they had been, through the British government and its diplomatic service, the government in Ottawa would still be subject to the government in London. Nor was this the only way in which Canada was still a subordinate member of the empire. As the law stood, the Dominion power of legislation was limited from above. An act of the Canadian Parliament could be vetoed by the British government, though there had been only one example of this and that was in the early days of the Dominion; or it could be overridden by an act of the British Parliament; and there were some matters with which no authority in Canada could deal. The British Parliament, for example, had sole authority to regulate the merchant marine of the whole empire. Canada was no longer content with this relationship of inferiority. The change sprang from no resentment against Britain, no desire to break away from the mother country. It was caused by the war effort, which had awakened in Canada a fuller sense of nationality than her people had ever felt before.

It seemed absurd for all official transactions between the Dominion and the Washington government to be conducted through the devious channel still necessary—through the governor general's office in Ottawa to the colonial office in London, thence to the foreign office, through this to the British ambassador in Washington, who communicated with the secretary of state, and then back again through all these intermediaries. It was awkward, to say the least. It was also grossly unfair, because three quarters of the business handled by the British ambassador was purely Canadian, and Canada paid not a penny for the support of the embassy. Why should not the Dominion deal directly through its own paid diplomatic representative in the American capital? Sir Robert Borden pressed London to concede this right. His demand that Canada be allowed to handle her own external affairs, like the nineteenth-century demand for self-government in domestic matters, raised fears for the unity of the empire. How could it be held together if each dominion had its own diplomatic service and foreign policy? But in 1920 the British government yielded to the pressure of the one man who, more than any other, forced the transformation from the British Empire to the British Commonwealth of Nations. Political considerations, arising chiefly out of the readjustment of Anglo-Irish relations then taking place, and difficulties in working out the practical details of diplomatic representation abroad were responsible for the fact that it was seven years before a Canadian minister went to reside in Washington and an American minister was established in Ottawa. Then in the following year two further exchanges of ministers were arranged—with France and with Japan. Canada was being recognized by foreign powers.

At the same time the Canadian position within the empire

was rising. The imperial conference of 1926 proclaimed an important principle in the following words: "The group of self-governing communities composed of Great Britain and the Dominions . . . are autonomous communities within the Empire, equal in status, in no way subordinate one to another." This declaration, however, did not alter the law. That had to be done by the British Parliament, and as some of the necessary legal changes agreed upon took considerable time to prepare, it was not until the end of 1931 that the British Parliament passed the Statute of Westminster, which reduced the last vestiges of imperial control over the dominions.

Today the only limitations upon Canadian autonomy exist by Canadian consent. One is in the administration of justice. The courts of the Dominion do not always have the last word in deciding Canadian cases, for some of them may be appealed to the Privy Council in London. Britain does not insist on the maintenance of this old tie, however. Criminal appeals have been stopped, but civil suits may still be carried to the empire's capital. Many Canadians would have liked to stop these too, but their government has hesitated to do so. Perhaps the strongest argument that has been advanced for preserving this judicial link with the mother country has been inspired by the dual nationality of the country. If there were a final court of appeal in the Dominion this court would of course be the ultimate interpreter of the constitution. This fact created the vision of a predominantly English court twisting the constitution against the interests of the French. But French sensitiveness on this score has been declining, and in both parts of the Dominion there has been a growing feeling that the Privy Council in London has interpreted the constitution contrary to the intentions of its framers and of the desires of those who live under it. It is not improbable that Canada may soon put an end to Privy Council appeals. Here it is perhaps interesting to observe that the other dominions are divided on this question. The Privy Council still hears appeals from Australia and South Africa, but not from Eire, which stopped them while it was still the Irish Free State.

The only other limitation upon Canadian autonomy is in the method of amending the constitution. It cannot be done except by an act of the British Parliament. This may seem strange in

Coming of Age

light of the fact that other dominions can amend their constitutions without going to London, but here again we see the influence of the country's dual nationality, which is embedded in the constitution. Of late years, however, some of the best minds in the country have been wrestling with the problem of how the people of Canada might amend their own constitution, and the national spirit of the country has been pressing for a solution with such vigor that it may not be long in coming.

Finally we should notice the disappearance of another question that worried many Canadians after the last World War. They maintained that as long as the Dominion retained the British connection the country might be plunged into war by a decision of the mother country over which Canada had no control. But when Britain went to war in 1939, Eire declared her neutrality, South Africa wavered on the brink before plunging in, and Canada asserted her autonomy in this most important decision of all by making her own declaration of war. The British king is the king of Canada and he can take no action that binds Canada in any way save on the advice of his Canadian ministers, who are responsible to the Parliament in Ottawa and through it to the people of the Dominion. Canada has come of age.

CHAPTER 16

From War to War

THE First World War shook the foundations of Canadian economic life, though its full effect was not realized until the approaching shadow of the next World War began to lengthen over the land. From the beginning of the century Canada's prosperity had rested chiefly on the rapid development of the Prairie Provinces, and this in turn was based upon the willingness of industrial Europe to pay a profitable price for all the wheat that Western Canada could supply.

Here was a condition that could not last because other countries were also extending their wheat lands and the world's production of wheat was expanding more rapidly than its needs. The time was approaching when a decline in the Old World market would check the speed of Canadian development. The writing on the wall appeared in the grain exchange of Winnipeg, where the average price of No. 1 Northern rose from seventy-four and a half cents a bushel in 1900 to a dollar eight and a half cents in 1909. This was the high mark, and from then on there was a gradual recession to less than ninety cents before the war broke in 1914.

The war put off the day of reckoning and made it worse when it came. By reducing production and increasing consumption in Europe, the war boosted prices. In 1917, when the Dominion government took over the marketing of wheat for the period of the war and the Winnipeg exchange was closed, the Canadian prairie farmer got two dollars and twenty-one cents for No. 1 Northern at the head of the Lakes. For the next year's crop he got two twenty-four, and for the following one, two sixty-three. When the exchange reopened in the summer of 1920, prices advanced to two eighty-five and five eighths. Stimulated by such rewards, production in the Prairie Provinces increased enormously. Before the war Canada was the world's third largest exporter of wheat. Now in 1920 she was second only to the

From War to War

United States, and three years later her impetus carried her into first place—an unenviable prominence, as her people later discovered.

The war gave to the Canadian West a feverish prosperity, and this made things boom in the East, where the war also exerted a direct influence of the same kind by creating a new and huge demand for a great variety of manufactured goods, munitions, ships, machinery for new industrial plants, and countless other things. Central Canada and the Maritime Provinces had never known such economic activity. The Dominion rapidly became one of the leading manufacturing countries of the world; in the early 1920's it rivaled Belgium for sixth place.

Meanwhile the Dominion government was becoming worried by the railway problem. During the years before the war, when immigrants were pouring into the country and people were rushing to take up new land in the West, there was an astonishing amount of railway building. Instead of following settlement, railways pushed ahead of settlement to attract it and to spread it out, and two new transcontinental lines appeared. The Canadian Northern, begun as a local railway in Manitoba, spread through the West, reached out to the Pacific at Vancouver, and in the opposite direction carried its line down to the East, where it also spread. The old Grand Trunk, hitherto confined to the East so that its operations now seemed to be cramped, formed a subsidiary corporation, the Grand Trunk Pacific, which built a road from Winnipeg to the Pacific at the northern port of Prince Rupert, and was to have leased and operated a government-constructed road, the National Transcontinental Railway then undertaken, from Winnipeg straight across the uninhabited northern country to Quebec and thence down through New Brunswick along a shorter route than the Intercolonial's. All this building was of course based on the supposition that things would continue as they had been, that the stream of immigrants would go on swelling, and that the population of the country would be multiplied in a few years. There was no thought that this expected population might not come. Then suddenly the stream was stopped at its source by the outbreak of the war.

The war also tightened the money markets of the world by forcing governments to float huge loans, and this made it more difficult to finance the railroads. Some of them soon found their resources strained to pay interest on the money borrowed to build them, and yet they needed more money to keep going. They turned to the banks of the country, borrowing as much as they could, but still they needed more. Then the government came to their aid by giving them generous loans, with the result that they were in debt more hopelessly then ever. By 1917 the Canadian Northern was bankrupt, and as it owed fifty million dollars to one of the principal banks there was grave danger that the failure of this railroad would let loose a whirlwind through all the financial institutions of the Dominion—and this in time of war. To prevent such a disaster the federal government took over the railway and its debts.

The return of peace ushered in a new set of world conditions that, coming on top of those existing during the war, were little short of disastrous to Canada, though their full effect was not felt for some years. Hopes that the flood of immigration had been only temporarily checked by the war were now dashed, as it gradually became apparent that the age of transatlantic immigration had come to a definite close. Events outside the Dominion thus determined that its population could not grow with anything like the rapidity that had been expected. Another blow was dealt by the recovery of agricultural production in Europe. But this had been foreseen and it did not take place suddenly— so great had been the dislocation caused by the war and its attendant upheavals, including the Russian Revolution. Very shortly, however, the country discovered that the war-born urge to grow more and more wheat on the Canadian prairie had extended cultivation into areas that should never have been put under the plough. Good ranching land had been ruined to make a Dust Bowl.

Looking again at the world at large, we should notice the creeping paralysis that was coming over international trade. In prewar days trade had functioned freely, with tariffs relatively low and stable and with credit balances paid by such small shipments of gold between countries that their currencies were unaffected by them. Now all this was changed. Out of the war came new and gigantic international financial obligations, the like of which had never been seen before: reparations and inter-Allied debts that amounted to many times the value of all the gold in the world. The old automatic machinery of international finance, which had preserved the economic balance of the world's trade before 1914, was violently disrupted and made incapable of operation. National currencies got out of line with one another. Some sagged badly and a few collapsed completely, with disastrous results to the national economic structures that had rested upon them.

The exchange of goods, by which most international payments had been made, was being choked by all this financial dislocation and also by what was happening to tariffs. Each of the new countries established in Europe was eager to build up its own independent life and tried to do so by the old method of protection against producers in other lands. New customs barriers arose where none had been before, and old customs barriers were also pushed up to new heights, for the war had made most countries wish to depend more upon themselves and less upon others. Economic nationalism was running mad. The progressive strangling of international trade hurt some countries much more than others. Here we notice a great difference between the United States and Canada. The American people produced nearly everything they consumed and consumed nearly everything they produced, with only a small adjustment to be made by foreign trade. The Canadian people were not so happily situated. A very much larger proportion of what they produced had to be sold abroad in order to buy what they needed at home. Their prosperity was much more dependent upon a free international economy, which by this time had been pretty well destroyed.

The railway problem, which might have disappeared if the expected flood of immigration had come and if the world's trade had been allowed to flow with the freedom of prewar days, soon became acute, as other railways were hastened into bankruptcy for want of traffic to sustain them. In 1919 the Dominion government was obliged to take over first the Grand Trunk Pacific and then the Grand Trunk with its other subsidiaries. In addition to these the government now had on its hands the Canadian Northern, the old Intercolonial, and the National Transcontinental Railway, which the Grand Trunk Pacific had earlier refused to lease in spite of its agreement to do so. Together they constituted all the railways of the country, with the exception of the great Canadian Pacific and a few little lines; and the government organized them into one system, the publicly owned and operated Canadian National Railway, thereby giving better service at less cost than if they had been kept separate. But this arrangement did not solve the railway problem.

Instead of getting profits from the national railways, the government shouldered a debt as great as that piled up by the war. There was talk of easing the burden by bringing about a greater combination still, a union of the Canadian National and the Canadian Pacific railways, but at once serious objections appeared. The national debt was already far too great for the public to contemplate increasing it by the large amount that would be necessary for the purchase of the Canadian Pacific. The obvious alternative was also out of the question. If this privately owned railway were to buy the national system, the government would still have to shoulder its net railway debt, and the people would be at the mercy of a huge railway monopoly owned by a private company. Yet the burden was so great that something had to be attempted. If the two systems could not be united to do away with all the expense caused by their efforts to get business from each other, at least some of this might be saved by an agreement to divide what business there was. This was the course adopted by the government; it lightened the load a little, but only a little. The main problem still remains.

There has been much nonsense talked about the Canadian National Railway, particularly in the United States. Many advocates of private enterprise have cited this Canadian example as convincing proof that public ownership does not pay. But one may just as truthfully argue that it proves the failure of private enterprise, for most of the system is made up of the wrecks of private undertakings. The people of Canada and their government undertook this grandiose extension of public ownership "with no enthusiasm, and from necessity rather than from choice." *

The political scene in Canada between the end of the war and the late 1920's recalls the Granger and Populist movements of

* G. P. deT. Glazebrook, *A History of Transportation in Canada* (New Haven, 1938).

earlier days in the United States and the contemporary agrarian movement in the American West. Canadian farmers had long been more or less impatient with the political game as it was being played. They believed that their special interests were being neglected by both the Liberals and the Conservatives. This belief was particularly strong on the prairie, where agriculture was the main occupation of the people. There the farmers were so dependent upon the railroads, the elevator and grain companies, and the banks for the distant marketing of their crops that they felt at the mercy of a small number of businessmen who were making too much money out of them. As these businessmen were organized in their own way to protect their own interests, the farmers decided to organize for the same purpose. Years before the war they began to form associations of different kinds, some of which failed and others succeeded. Their cooperative societies, particularly those for the storing and selling of grain, were perhaps their greatest success. The governments of the Dominion and of the Prairie Provinces helped them from time to time in various ways, such as by a closer regulation of railway and elevator services and charges, by lending public credit to some of their enterprises, and during the war by taking the crop off their hands and selling it in Europe. Much as they had been aided by Liberal and Conservative governments, however, the farmers still felt that more should be done, and therefore at the close of the war they organized to enter politics.

Meanwhile Canadian labor was abandoning its traditional policy of keeping aloof from politics. Prices had been rising faster than wages, so that the wage earner was getting less value for his day's toil. He was being pinched into political action, for he too felt that the historic parties were not much concerned with his interests.

Both the farmers and the trade unionists hoped to get a sufficient number of seats in Parliament and in provincial legislatures to force whatever government was in power to do as they demanded; they did not expect to be able to seize power themselves. The farmers were much more successful than the labor party. Indeed they surprised themselves and the rest of the country. In the Ontario election of 1919 the United Farmers of Ontario won more seats than either of the old parties. Thereupon they entered into partnership with the small group of labor members who had been elected, and together they formed their own government. The same thing happened in Alberta in 1921 and in Manitoba in 1922. In Saskatchewan, which was almost wholly devoted to agriculture, the Liberal government was obliged to be so solicitous of the interests of the farmers that they decided to keep their provincial organization out of politics—which explains what would otherwise appear to be a strange anomaly.

In all three provinces captured by the United Farmers, the successful candidates of the new party were chosen because they were neither Liberals nor Conservatives, and the new cabinets were therefore made up of men who had little experience in politics and government. This lack of training was a serious handicap in Ontario, where a large proportion of the population lived in towns and cities and where the old parties were still strong. The result was that at the next election in this province the farmers' government disappeared. In the West, however, most of the people lived on the land, and the old parties were weaker. The United Farmers of Alberta remained in office until 1935, when yet another new party, the Social Credit party, turned the farmers out. The United Farmers of Manitoba have survived in a different way, by forming coalitions with their opponents.

From the local and provincial organizations of the farmers arose the Canadian Council of Agriculture, which concerned itself with national affairs, and from this council sprang the Progressive party, which sought to gain seats in the Dominion Parliament. Though others supported it as a protest against traditional politics, it was chiefly a farmers' movement. The party's program called for a general reduction of the tariff and for reciprocity with the United States. The second demand was in line with the Liberal effort of 1911, the failure of which had brought much disappointment to farmers in Ontario and more to those of the prairie, who were even more dependent upon outside markets. The first demand was one that the farmers believed neither a Liberal nor a Conservative government would grant without being forced to do it, for the Conservatives had introduced the policy of high protection and the Liberals had continued it. This policy seemed unjust to the farmers. It made them pay higher prices for what they bought but could not give them higher prices for what they had to sell, for they produced much more than the country consumed and they had to sell abroad. The Progressive party had no chance of forming a Dominion government because Ontario was the only part of the country outside the prairie where the new movement had any strength. Still it created considerable disturbance in federal political life, beginning with the general election of 1921, the first after the war.

Already the union government of 1917 had become Conservative by the retirement or conversion of the Liberals who had joined it, and both the old parties were under new leaders. Early in 1919 Sir Wilfrid Laurier died, and later in the year a national convention of Liberals chose William Lyon Mackenzie King, a Harvard Ph.D., to be their head. As his name suggests, he is a grandson of the famous Reform champion of a hundred years ago. He had been a great favorite with Laurier but had not taken sides when the party split over conscription. This advantage, which he owed to his withdrawal from politics to serve for a time as director of Industrial Relations of the Rockefeller Foundation, enabled him to pull the party together again. Meanwhile, as he was concentrating his efforts on this task, the Conservatives were showing signs of breaking up. They suffered a great loss in 1920, when ill-health compelled Sir Robert Borden to resign, and a member of his Cabinet, Arthur Meighen, became the new prime minister. When he appealed to the country in the following year, his government suffered a worse defeat than any government of either party had experienced in the history of the Dominion.

In the general election of 1921 the Progressives swept the Prairie Provinces and secured nearly a third of the Ontario seats, making them the second largest party in the House of Commons. Their success created a strange situation. For the first time since federation no party had a clear majority in the house. As leader of the largest group of members, Mackenzie King was called upon to form a government, and he tried to combine with the Progressives, who were even more opposed to the Conservatives than the Liberals were. But the Progressives would not sell their independence for a few seats in the Cabinet, and he was forced to organize a purely Liberal government which they would support only so long as it did what they wished. The result was that during the entire session of Parliament no one could tell from day to day whether the government would have a majority. The prime minister humorously summed up the situation by saying that if he went out to dinner his government might fall.

To end this state of uncertainty a general election was held in 1925, but it only made the situation worse. The Liberals lost some seats, and the Progressives lost still more, so that together they barely outnumbered the Conservatives, who became the largest group in the new house. By voting with the government, the Progressives kept Mackenzie King in power until the summer of 1926, when a few of them withdrew their support and left him in a minority. Then occurred the curious incident known as "the constitutional crisis." Having lost his majority, the prime minister had to resign or call a general election. He asked the governor general, Lord Byng, to dissolve Parliament; but Byng refused, Mackenzie King had to resign, and the governor general called upon Meighen as the leader of the largest party in the House of Commons to form a government. In a few days the new Conservative ministry also suffered defeat in the house, and Byng then granted Meighen what he had denied to Mackenzie King. A second general election within a year was something new in the history of the Dominion, and so was the governor general's refusal of the advice offered by a prime minister. Was this refusal constitutional, or was it not? Throughout Canada people debated the question hotly.

The election of 1926 put an end to the political deadlock. The country was weary of it. Only a fragment of the Progressive party survived, many of its members becoming undoubted Liberal supporters. Throughout the Dominion there was also a considerable feeling that the people rather than the governor general ought to decide who should be prime minister. Then Mackenzie King came back into office with a good majority. In the defeat of the Conservatives even their leader lost his seat, and for some time they had only a temporary head. In the fall of 1927 a national convention of the party selected Mr. R. B. Bennett, a native of New Brunswick and a wealthy corporation lawyer of

Calgary, who led his party back to victory in 1930. But it was really not he who defeated Mackenzie King in that year. It was the condition of the country, of which something more must now be said.

The price of wheat, which means much more to Canada than it does to the United States, reached its peak in September 1920 and then began to decline. Down and down it sank to ninety-three and a quarter cents at the end of 1923. Other commodities also fell in value but, on an average, little more than half as much—which meant that the chief weight of the postwar slump in Canada fell upon the grain growers. Though this slump was not responsible for the farmers' entering provincial and federal politics, which they did while prices were still high, it undoubtedly spurred the Progressive movement once it had started. It is also interesting to observe that the collapse of the Progressive party followed a recovery of prices that lasted until 1929. The collapse of grain prices early in the 1920's also made the farmers agitate for a revival of the wartime arrangement by which the Dominion government marketed their crop, for this would reduce the cost of handling and bring a greater return to the producers. But there were difficulties in the way, and the farmers had to fall back upon their old method of voluntary cooperation.

When their leaders decided to do this, in the summer of 1923, they imported an eloquent American lawyer, Aaron Sapiro, who had played a successful part in promoting cooperation among fruit growers in California. Though his first name was Aaron, he quickly became the Moses of the Western Canadian farmers, for he led them into the Promised Land by helping them to organize what soon came to be known as the Pool. In reality there were three pools, one in each of the Prairie Provinces, with a central selling agency. The Pool built or bought a large number of elevators throughout the West, at the head of the Great Lakes, and at the ocean ports. By 1926 it controlled more than half the crop, and for several years it was very successful. It was well managed, a remarkable thing for such a quickly formed and gigantic enterprise—one of the biggest businesses in the world. It was also fortunate in that its inception coincided with a fair recovery of grain prices and was followed by a period of market steadiness.

In Canada as in the United States and in many other countries, though not in all, the middle and late 1920's were a time of prosperity, and many people believed that the worst had passed. But it had yet to come, for this prosperity was like a house built upon the sand and supported by props that would soon fall. The conditions noted in the beginning of this chapter were the sand, and the props were further loans advanced by creditor nations, principally the United States. The crash came in 1929.

As the great depression gathered momentum, it caused political upheavals all over the world; for people grew desperate and, as few in any country pay much attention to what is happening abroad, most of them were inclined to blame their own government for the plight they were in, or at least to believe that a change of government would help them. In Canada the Conservative party charged the Liberal administration with not doing what it ought to do to dispel the encircling gloom. Bennett and his followers pointed out that the country was buying from foreigners goods that might be made at home. Higher customs duties, they argued, would stop this unnecessary trade and give work to the growing army of unemployed. They also insisted that the government should "prime the pump" by spending money in the building of public works. When a general election was called in 1930 it was a foregone conclusion that Mackenzie King would be defeated.

The new Bennett government promptly carried out the pre-election promise of a higher tariff and more generous public expenditure, but conditions continued to grow worse. The refusal to purchase from abroad made it more difficult to sell abroad, and Canada's export trade, so vital to her economy, was further curtailed. The spending of the Dominion government soared as its revenue sank, and the mounting deficit swelled the burden of the national debt.

Already the Pool was in a very bad way. To cushion the blow of the falling Liverpool market, which regulated world prices for wheat, it had bolstered the Winnipeg market. This swallowed its reserves. Then it turned to the banks and, like the railways a decade before, borrowed until the banks were afraid to lend any more. Early in 1930 the governments of the Prairie Provinces came to the rescue by guaranteeing additional loans to the Pool, but it was not long before these governments found

ROBERT BORDEN, CANADA'S PREMIER IN
THE FIRST WORLD WAR, 1911–20 (CH. 16).

RICHARD B. BENNETT, CONSERVATIVE
PRIME MINISTER, 1930–35 (CH. 16).

PRIME MINISTER W. L. MACKENZIE KING AND FRANKLIN D. ROOSEVELT
DURING THE PRESIDENT'S VISIT TO QUEBEC IN 1936 (CH. 16).

J. L. RALSTON, MINISTER OF FINANCE, GIVES DETAILS OF CANADA'S
BILLION DOLLAR WARTIME BUDGET IN THE HOUSE OF COMMONS, 1940.

SENATE CHAMBER, OTTAWA, WHEN THEIR MAJESTIES KING GEORGE VI AND
QUEEN ELIZABETH ATTENDED PARLIAMENT ON MAY 19, 1939.

THEIR MAJESTIES KING GEORGE VI AND QUEEN ELIZABETH WITH W. L.
MACKENZIE KING AT BANFF DURING THE ROYAL TOUR, 1939.

From War to War

themselves in financial difficulties because the people who supported them were suffering from the low price of grain. All over the Dominion, also, the provinces and the municipalities were staggering under the load of providing relief to the growing number of people destitute of the bare necessaries of life, and the federal government had to come to the rescue of the rescuers.

General conditions grew so bad that a number of people began to think there was something seriously wrong with the way society was organized, and two new political parties appeared, each striving for a radical change. The first adopted a cumbersome name—the Cooperative Commonwealth Federation, commonly shortened to C. C. F. This was really a socialist movement. Its supporters found difficulty in agreeing upon how much and what kind of socialism they wanted and were accused of being Russian communists. Yet they polled a large vote and won a number of seats, particularly in some western provincial elections. The other party, called the Social Credit party, was the creation of one man, William Aberhart, a schoolteacher of Calgary, who would cure the current economic ills by abolishing banks as we have known them and by turning their control of credit over to the government to be used for the general social welfare. His party defeated the United Farmers of Alberta in the provincial election of 1935 and at once began to spread outside the province. Aberhart passed legislation to inaugurate the new era, but his efforts soon ran foul of the constitution, for in Canada banking is wholly under federal jurisdiction. The fact that there were no bank failures in Canada during the depression only proved to Social Creditors that the Canadian banks were sucking the blood of the Canadian people.

Meanwhile the Dominion government was slowly getting rid of the wheat incubus of the West, and a social readjustment was taking place on the prairie. With the aid of public funds to steady the market, the federal government went into the grain business and undertook over a period of years to sell the huge surplus collected by the Pool after the onset of the depression. The readjustment of life on the prairie was a movement toward the solution of the economic problem that had overwhelmed the farmers. Unable to sell wheat at a profit so that they might buy what they needed, they were raising less wheat and more of the other things they needed and could grow on their own land. As there was little else that they could raise in the southern parts of Saskatchewan and Alberta, where lack of water restricted the keeping of stock, some of the population migrated northward, partly at government expense. By making the farmers more independent of world conditions, this shift toward mixed farming is helping to develop a more solid agricultural society in the Canadian West.

More general was the desire to escape from the depression by reversing the process that had precipitated it. Many people believed that prosperity would return if the countries of the world would make it easier to buy from one another, but they realized that most nations were too suspicious to be willing to do so. There was one group of countries, however, whose friendly relationship might make it possible for them to come together in such an agreement—the members of the British Commonwealth —and on the invitation of the Canadian government an imperial economic conference met at Ottawa in the summer of 1932. To an onlooker at this conference it seemed that each part of the empire was anxious to get more than it was willing to give. But a number of agreements were reached to lower the tariffs that had checked trade within the empire, and on the whole the result was good. Before the Hull policy of trade agreements got under way, many Americans resented this apparent British exclusiveness. But they did not know what Canadians knew instinctively, that a tight imperial *zollverein,* or customs union, was impossible because the economic life of the Dominion was too closely knit to that of the United States to be torn away from it. When the Washington government was converted, as the Ottawa government had been, to the gospel of freer international trade, the imperial agreements reached in the Canadian capital were gladly modified for the sake of closer trade relationships with the United States.

When all the banks of the United States were closed in the spring of 1933 the world at large had passed the low mark of the depression, and conditions in Canada were beginning to improve steadily. The improvement was soon noticeable throughout the Dominion, as it was in other countries. There were fewer unemployed, fewer business failures, more traffic on the railways, and more deposits in the banks. But the recovery was slow, for the world was like a man who has been very sick for a long time; and just as the growing impact of the depression contributed to turn Mackenzie King out of office in 1930, its lingering weight helped to bring him back to power in the general election of 1935.

At the same time there was an ominous racial movement in Quebec, produced by the same causes, though this was not fully understood in the rest of the country. The English-speaking minority, who had dominated business in the province ever since the conquest, possessed such economic control that they found it fairly easy to cooperate with the provincial government. Whether Liberals or Conservatives were in office in Quebec, there was little doubt that the seat of power was St. James Street in Montreal, the Wall Street of Canada. This explains why the popular discontent born of the hard times, which elsewhere expressed itself as a revolt against the ruling political party or the established economic system, was focused in a racial movement in French Canada. It triumphed in the summer of 1936, when the Liberal government that had run the province for nearly forty years was routed at the polls by the newly organized *Union Nationale,* led by Maurice Duplessis. Except by his followers, Duplessis was generally regarded as a dangerous man. His words and his actions strongly suggested that he was a fascist, and he certainly pandered to race prejudice. The forces he let loose threatened to disrupt the country. Some of the extremer elements in the movement were talking of establishing a French and Roman Catholic republic on the shores of the St. Lawrence. It was to be called Laurentia and was to include the adjoining part of New England inhabited by French Canadians. When a paper advocating this radical change in the political map of North America was published, the voice of the church destroyed it by telling the people that good Catholics would not read it.

The strain that this insurgent racial movement imposed on the national unity of the country was felt more and more as the clouds gathered on the international horizon. The isolationism of the United States did not infect French Canada. It could not, because French Canada was naturally more isolationist than the United States. But the contagion had been spreading in English

Canada where, since the return of the soldiers from France, quite a number of people had openly expressed themselves in favor of keeping aloof from Britain's future wars. The question remained largely an academic one until 1935, when the Ethiopian crisis split the country along racial lines. Led by Duplessis, French Canada sided with Fascist Italy, while English Canadian sympathies were almost solidly behind Britain. There was not the same clear-cut division over the League of Nations in this crisis. French Canadians unanimously denounced the League as a troublemaker, but though some English Canadians condemned Britain for exposing herself in its defense, the majority wished her to uphold it in the interests of international law and order.

Then occurred a significant incident. On the League committee responsible for initiating sanctions against Italy, sat a Canadian, the permanent representative of the Dominion at Geneva. He proposed to add oil sanctions, which Italy promptly announced would be an act of war necessitating reprisals. As the Dominion seemed to be taking the lead in forcing the issue and was not at all prepared to assume such a responsibility, Ottawa hastened to declare that the proposal represented the personal opinion of the man who made it and not the views of the Canadian government. This statement roused cheers in half the country and jeers in the other half. If the Ethiopian crisis of 1935–36 had exploded in a European conflict, Canada could not have entered it without facing a grave danger of civil war in which the French might have found many friends in English Canada.

The anti-British and anti-League attitude of French Canada can be only partly explained by its native isolationism and its schismatic nationalism. Much more important in the light of subsequent events was another influence. The Roman Catholic world feared and hated communism as the greatest menace of the age. Mussolini was also the sworn foe of communism. Moreover, the rise of Nazi Germany had recently frightened Moscow into reversing its international policy. For years Russia had been an enemy of the League of Nations, a so-called capitalist institution, but in 1934, a year after Hitler withdrew Germany from it, Russia joined the League and became its most vigorous champion. In Roman Catholic eyes the devil had entered into the system of collective security, and upholding the League meant playing the game of Communist Russia.

During the protracted crisis of the Spanish Civil War, which began in 1936, English Canada reflected the confused opinion in Britain, while French Canadians were vehemently pro-Franco. The disclosure of the working alliance between Mussolini and Hitler did not alarm them at all, for they saw these dictators saving Catholic Spain from the clutches of the wicked republic and of godless Communist Russia. As the international tension increased, so did the national tension in the Dominion. Visions of Canada being torn asunder as it had never been before were raised by the prospect of Britain's going to war again. The French and a considerable number of English-speaking Canadians were for staying out and perhaps leaving the empire, while others were for plunging into the war and sticking with the empire. The federal government was urged to declare its policy, and the best it could do was to say that the decision would be left to Parliament when the time came—such was the distraction of the country. The youth of the land tried to give a lead, and from Atlantic to Pacific the university students voted strongly against fighting. The Munich crisis of September 1938 divided the country more than ever, and in the spring of 1939 the overthrow of what was left of Czechoslovakia did not unite Canada as it did Britain. When summer came and Armageddon drew visibly closer, Canadian opinion was still confused.

Suddenly, late in August, came the news that Russia would not join Britain and France to stop Hitler, as many people had hoped, but was actually signing a nonaggression treaty with him. This pact, which loosed the war upon the world, released Canada from an almost intolerable internal strain. Parliament was summoned for a special session to begin on September 7, and after two days of debate a resolution supporting the Dominion's entry into the war was carried unanimously. Duplessis could not believe that Canada had gone to war as a united nation, and he quickly brought on a provincial election that was fought on the issue of Canadian participation, which he opposed. He suffered a smashing defeat at the polls on October 27.

The new-found unity of the Dominion was yet to face two important tests, the first of which was quite unforeseen. It came

A Short History of Canada

in June 1940 with the fall of France. There were whispered fears in Parliament and elsewhere throughout the country that the French of Canada might wish to follow the French of France out of the war, assisted perhaps by aspersions that English-speaking people might cast upon the humiliated nation. But the children of France in the New World reacted proudly. As part of the fighting British Empire they would help to restore the lost liberty of their fallen mother. The next test came a year later when Germany, without any warning, struck at Russia. Many Canadians had been uneasily asking themselves what would be the reaction in Quebec if Hitler and Stalin should fall out. Would the violent dissolution of the Nazi-Soviet combination undo the effect of that combination in Canada and split the nation? Would French Canada be willing to fight on the same side as Communist Russia? But French Canada did not waver; it remained resolutely steadfast. Too much water had flowed under the bridge, as one prominent French Canadian said. The mad rush of events in the preceding year had opened the eyes of his people to the fact that Berlin was much more to be feared than Moscow. Moreover, it was a great relief to have gained Russia as an ally without any compromising negotiation or treaty. Thus the country which as recently as only two years before had almost despaired of preserving its solidarity had now found in this tragic struggle an even greater unity.

When in December 1941 Japan pounced on American and British possessions in the Pacific and Eastern Asia, Canada was not so shaken as the Republic. Yet Americans should not for a moment imagine that the Canadian people feel any less deeply about the war on the Pacific. The shock was not so great for Canada; she had already taken the leap into war and was spending nearly half her national income upon it. Her formal declaration of war against Japan was actually made the evening before the American declaration. Canadians knew that, even if this conflict had burst upon us with a Europe still at peace, they could not stay out of it, for the simple reason that geography had placed their country on the firing line between Japan and the United States. For years before the European explosion of 1939, and at considerable expense, the Dominion had been quietly building up its defenses on the Pacific Coast against a

262

possible Japanese attack. Now that the war has engulfed the globe and we are fighting to preserve our civilization, Canada no less than the United States will fight on to the victorious end.

When we have won the war we will face the more difficult task of winning the peace. Whatever form of international organization we may then adopt to establish law and preserve order in the world, this form will fail unless it guarantees a continuing justice between nations in a living, and therefore an ever changing, world; and as justice cannot prevail between nations, any more than it can between individuals, so long as each insists on being its own final judge in everything, there will have to be some sacrifice of national sovereignty. Exactly how Canada and the United States will be bound together in this new world order, it is as yet impossible to say, but there can be little doubt that their relations will be much closer than they ever were before this war. Fighting for very life side by side will naturally make this greater intimacy easier for both to bear, but blood shed in a common cause is not a permanent cement, as many nations have discovered. The future solidarity between these two North American countries depends on mutual confidence born of understanding.

Selected Reading List

The French period is covered by the works of the famous New England historian of the last century, Francis Parkman: *The Pioneers of France in the New World, The Jesuits in North America, La Salle and the Discovery of the Great West, The Old Régime in Canada, Count Frontenac and New France under Louis XIV, A Half Century of Conflict,* and *Montcalm and Wolfe.* They are fascinating reading and the fruit of a lifetime's painstaking research. A shorter and more recent work, also very readable, is G. M. Wrong, *The Rise and Fall of New France.* There are several interesting volumes in The Chronicles of Canada series, some of which are episodic and some biographical, and in The Makers of Canada series, all biographies, and a number of good chapters, also by different authors, in the first two volumes of the monumental *Canada and Its Provinces,* the chief reference work on the history of the country.

For the period since the British conquest, there is no historian comparable to Parkman. However, the three sets of volumes just mentioned also cover this period fairly well. The first generation of British rule in Central Canada is the theme of A. L. Burt, *The Old Province of Quebec.* J. B. Brebner, *New England's Outpost* and *The Neutral Yankees of Nova Scotia* deal with the Maritime Provinces down to the end of the American Revolution. For American relations from 1775 to 1820 there is A. L. Burt, *The United States, Great Britain, and British North America* in the new series, The Relations of Canada and the United States, being prepared under the direction of the Carnegie Endowment for International Peace.

The best history of the Hudson's Bay Company is Douglas MacKay, *The Honourable Company,* and of the West generally, Arthur S. Morton, *A History of the Canadian West to 1870–71.* The principal authority on the fur trade is Harold A. Innis, *The Fur Trade in Canada,* and for western exploration L. J. Burpee, *The Search for the Western Sea.* A short popular history of the prairie country down to 1905 is A. L. Burt, *The Romance of the Prairie Provinces.*

The best general account of the economic history of Canada is to be found in a series of chapters, the earlier ones by Adam Shortt and the later ones by O. D. Skelton, scattered through the volumes of *Canada and Its Provinces.* The new Carnegie series contains some excellent volumes on this subject, notably D. G. Creighton, *The Commercial Empire of the St. Lawrence, 1760–1850,* G. P. deT.

Selected Reading List

Glazebrook, *A History of Transportation in Canada,* and Harold A. Innis, *The Cod Fisheries.*

Two valuable volumes on reciprocity are Donald C. Masters, *The Reciprocity Treaty of 1854* and, in the Carnegie series, L. E. Ellis, *Reciprocity, 1911.* Of wider interest is L. B. Shippee, *Canadian-American Relations, 1849–1874,* in the same series.

The main authority on constitutional history is W. P. M. Kennedy, *The Constitution of Canada.* For the British North American Revolution the most interesting and important are *Lord Durham's Report on the Affairs of British North America,* edited by Sir C. P. Lucas, and J. L. Morison, *British Supremacy and Canadian Self-Government, 1839–1854;* for the formation of the Dominion, Reginald George Trotter, *Canadian Federation;* and for later constitutional development, Sir R. L. Borden, *Canadian Constitutional Studies* and *Canada in the Commonwealth.*

For much of the political history the reader has to rely on the biographies of the leading public men, particularly Sir Joseph Pope, *Memoirs of the Right Honourable Sir John Alexander Macdonald* and O. D. Skelton, *The Life and Times of Sir Alexander Tilloch Galt* and *Life and Letters of Sir Wilfrid Laurier.* Another good biography of the great French Canadian leader is Sir J. S. Willison, *Sir Wilfrid Laurier and the Liberal Party.* John W. Dafoe, *Laurier: A Study in Canadian Politics* is a short but penetrating analysis. *Clifford Sifton in Relation to His Times,* by the same author, is also very useful. For the last forty years the stout volumes of the *Canadian Annual Review of Public Affairs* are an invaluable reference. Other good surveys of current events and problems may be found in the Canadian section of *The Round Table,* a British quarterly magazine published in England, and in the Canadian quarterlies, such as the *Queen's Quarterly* of Queen's University, *The Dalhousie Review* of Dalhousie University, *The University of Ottawa Review,* which is the leading French periodical review of opinion, and *The University of Toronto Quarterly.*

Another quarterly, *The Canadian Historical Review,* is an excellent clearinghouse of information about all the current literature of Canadian history. The most convenient bibliography is Reginald George Trotter, *Canadian History—A Syllabus and Guide to Reading.*

Index

Aberhart, William, 257
Abraham, Plains of, 56
Acadia, founded, 10; conflict between French and English, 40–42, 44, 46–47, 50, 53
Acadians, different from Canadians, 31; deportation, 53; return of many, 57; ignored in government of Nova Scotia, 58–59
Adams, John, 94; proposal for disarmament on Lakes, 108
Adams, John Quincy, in Ghent negotiations, 110–11
Agriculture, in French régime, 21–23; in first half of nineteenth century, 136–38; in the West, 230–31; in Central Canada, 235; during First World War, 246–47, 248; postwar distress and recovery, 255, 256, 257–58
Alabama claims, 207
Alaska, effect of American purchase, 180
Alberta, province formed, 228, 231; farmers' government, 252, 257
Algonkins, 13
Allan, Sir Hugh, 133, 201
Allen, Ethan, 75
"Alouette," 33
American Civil War, *see* Civil War
American Revolution (*1775–83*), and Quebec Act, 67, 72–74; attempt to win Canada, 74–79; effect of invasion of Canada on outcome, 79–81; Burgoyne's campaign, 81–82; Franco-American plans for conquest of Canada, 82; territory taken from Canada, 87–88; people given to Canada, 88–92
Anglican Church, *see* Church of England
Annexation to United States, question raised, Manifesto of *1849*, 163–64; in Red River colony, 171, 180; in Nova Scotia, 179; in British Columbia, 184; in the Dominion, 213, 217–18

Arbitration, international, inaugurated by John Jay, 97–98
Argall, Samuel, 41
Arnold, Benedict, 77–78
Aroostook War of *1839*, 160
Ashes, principal export in *1820's*, 137
Assembly, introduced into Nova Scotia, 58–59; for old Province of Quebec, 62, 63, 64, 65, 68, 93; after American Revolution, 147, 148
Astor, John Jacob, 118
Astoria, 119
Aylmer, Baron (governor *1831–35*), 153

Bank of Montreal founded, 139
Banks, no failures during depression, 257
Batoche, 226
Battleford, Saskatchewan, 224, 228
Beauséjour, 53
Bengough, J. W., cartoons, 202, 208, 210, 212, 228
Bennett, R. B., later Viscount (prime minister of Canada *1930–35*), 89, 254–55, 256
Bienville, François le Moyne, Sieur de, 46, 49
Blackfeet Indians, 222
Boer War, strain on Canadian unity, 216
Borden, Sir Robert (prime minister of Canada *1911–20*), 89, 218; and conscription, 239–40; and national status of Canada, 241–43; retirement, 253
Boundaries of Canada, based on boundary of Nova Scotia in *1763*, 58; of old Province of Quebec by proclamation of *1763*, 61–63, 66, 87; by Quebec Act of *1774*, 67–68, 72, 87; by Treaty of Paris of *1783*, 86–88; Ghent negotiations, 109, 111; forty-ninth parallel adopted by convention of *1818*, 112; effect of definition of *1783* upon fur trade, 115; by Webster-Ashburton Treaty of *1842*, 160; by Oregon Treaty of *1846*, 170

266

Index

Index

Index

Hull, General William, 104
Hurons, Jesuit missions among, 12; smashed by Iroquois, 13; around Sault Sainte Marie, 36
Hydroelectric development, 233

Iberville, *see* d'Iberville
Icelandic settlement in Manitoba, 229
Immigration, French, 15, 42; expected from old colonies, 62; post-Loyalist, into Upper Canada, 91, 92; from Britain to Upper Canada, 107; in first half of nineteenth century, 130; English, 131; Irish Catholic, 131-32; Irish Protestant, 132-33; Scottish, 132-33; to Maritime Provinces, 133; to Lower Canada, 134; to Upper Canada, 134; into Northwest, 229; stopped by First World War, 247, 248. *See also* Loyalists, various nationalities
Imperial Conference of *1926*, 244; of *1932*, 258
Impressment, 98-99
Indians, French attitude toward, 11; missionaries among, 12, 13, 35, 36, 37; contact with British in United States, 97, 99, 110, 111; treaties, 127, 222-23; brought under control by mounted police in Northwest, 219-24; in second Riel Rebellion, 226-27. *See also* Algonkins, Blackfeet, Fur trade, Hurons, Iroquois, Sioux
Industrial development, before *1914*, 233-35; stimulated by First World War, 247
Intendant, office of, 14-16, 18
Intercolonial Railway, projected, 169, 174; constructed, 199-200; merged with others to form Canadian National Railway, 249-50
Irish immigrants, 131-32
Iroquois, wars, 13-14, 18-20, 45; empire, 19, 37-38, 43, 45; Carleton's refusal to use them against Americans, 75
Isolationism, 259-61

Japanese attack on American and British possessions, 262-63
Jay, John, signer of peace treaty of

1783, 94; treaty (*1794*), 97-98, 109, 110, 111; disarmament proposal, 108
Jesuit Relations, 12
Jesuits (The Society of Jesus), missions, 12, 36, 41, 49; explorers, 36. *See also* Marquette
Jolliet, Louis, 37, 38

Kaskaskia, Illinois, 49
King, W. L. Mackenzie (prime minister *1921-26*, *1926-30*, *1935-*), 190n, 253, 254, 256, 259
King George's War (*1744-48*), 50-51
Kingston, Ontario, site of Fort Frontenac, 19; first Ontario town, 140
Kingston *Gazette*, 145
King William's War (*1689-97*), 42

Labor in Canadian politics, 251
Lachine, origin of name, 38
Lafayette, Marquis de, plan for conquest of Canada, 82
La Hontan, Baron, on the habitant, 28
Lake Champlain route, 13, 44, 47-48, 52-53, 56, 75, 76, 80-82
La Salle, Robert Cavelier de, explorer and colonizer, 37-39
Laurier, Sir Wilfrid (prime minister *1896-1911*), 214-18; in opposition, 239-40; death, 253
Laval, Bishop, father of Canadian church, 16-18; trouble over tithe, 28-29
Laval University founded, 144
La Vérendrye, Pierre Gaultier de Varennes, Sieur de, 49-50
Law, *see* French law
Law courts, judicial review, 195-96; constitution of, 196-97
Legislative council, *see* Council
Legislature, provincial, composition and powers, 192-98
Lethbridge, Alberta, founded, 228
Lewis and Clark expedition, 118
Lexington, Massachusetts, 73
Liberal party, Brown the father of, 133; in power *1873-78*, 201-3, 208-9; opposition to protection in *1879*, 211; in favor of "unrestricted reciprocity" and defeat in *1891*, 213; return to power in *1896*, 214; opposed by Roman Catholic Church, 215;

271

Index

Index

Index

THE AUTHOR

ALFRED LEROY BURT's interest in the history and the common problems of Canada, the United States, and Great Britain has been stimulated by his experiences in those three countries. He was born at Listowel, Ontario, in November 1888. At twenty-one he received an honors B.A. from Toronto University and was elected Rhodes scholar for Ontario. During the next three years he studied at Corpus Christi College, Oxford University, where he was awarded a second B.A. with honors. Here too he divided the Beit Prize with one of the leading English historians of today and was given the Robert Herbert Memorial Prize for a piece of research subsequently published as his first book.

Returning to Canada in 1913 Mr. Burt joined the staff of the University of Alberta, where he later became professor and head of the department of history. Publication of his *Imperial Architects* (Oxford, 1913) was followed by *A Short History of the League of Nations* (Edmonton, 1924), *High School Civics* (Edmonton and Toronto, 1928), and *The Romance of the Prairie Provinces* (Toronto, 1930). He edited the third volume of *The Makers of Canada* series and contributed to Volume VI of the *Cambridge History of the British Empire*.

In 1930 Mr. Burt left Canada once more, this time to become professor of history at the University of Minnesota, the position he now holds. He continues to spend his summers in Canada, however, principally in the Public Archives at Ottawa. There he has conducted intensive research that has clarified many puzzling problems in Canadian history.

Since moving to the United States Mr. Burt has published, in addition to articles in historical journals, *The Old Province of Quebec* (Minneapolis, 1933), *The Romance of Canada* (Toronto, 1937), and *The United States, Great Britain, and British North America, 1775–1820* (New Haven, 1940). This last book was written at the request of the Carnegie Endowment for International Peace.